The JOY of. Signing

Lottie L. Riekehof

SECOND EDITION
The Illustrated Guide for Mastering
Sign Language and the Manual Alphabet

GOSPEL PUBLISHING HOUSE
Springfield, Missouri 65802

02-0520

ACKNOWLEDGMENTS

Without the assistance and encouragement of many persons, this book would not have become a reality. My deepest appreciation is here expressed to the following people:

Pearl Goings, the artist who spent many hours working with me drawing new pictures and updating those that had originally been prepared by Betty Stewart for *Talk to the Deaf*

Sandy Flower, who devoted many hours to the final inking of the line drawings

Linda Martin, who patiently served as sounding board, script reader, critiquer, and who suggested the present format which makes the book readable and clear

Wayne Warner, book editor at Gospel Publishing House, for guidance along the way, and **Nancy Stevens**, for the final editing of the first edition

David Johnston, publisher, who believed in the concept of a sign book in 1963 when no book with line drawings of signs had ever been published

Bill Eastlake, present publisher, who strongly encouraged a revised edition and who made it possible

Glen Eliard, editor of the second edition, for providing overall guidance, and **Nancy Stevens**, for the final editing

My many deaf friends whose signing skills were an inspiration to me and whose knowledge of sign language, corrections of my signs, explanations, discussions of origins, and most of all acceptance of me as a hearing person brought about the original work and this revision

Copyright 1987 by the Gospel Publishing House, 1445 Boonville Avenue, Springfield, Missouri 65802

This book is a second edition of *The Joy of Signing,* published in 1978 (which was a revised and enlarged edition of *Talk to the Deaf,* published in 1963 by Gospel Publishing House). All rights reserved. No part of this book may be reproduced, stored in a retrieval system, or transmitted in any form or by any means—electronic, mechanical, photocopy, recording, or otherwise—without prior written permission of the copyright owner.

Videotape Edition

The Joy of Signing is available on videotape. Information may be obtained by writing to Joy Enterprises, Inc., P.O. Box 10376, Arlington, VA 22210-1376. Please enclose a stamped self-addressed envelope.

Puzzle Book

The Joy of Signing Puzzle Book, by Linda Lascelle Hillebrand with Lottie L. Riekehof, is available from Gospel Publishing House (order no. 02-0676).

Fourth Printing 1993

Library of Congress Cataloging in Publication Data

Riekehof, Lottie L.
   The Joy of Signing: Second Edition

   First edition published in 1978 under the title: The Joy of Signing. Published in 1963 under the title: Talk to the Deaf.
   Bibliography: p.
   Includes index.
   1. Sign language. 2. Deaf—Means of communication.
I. Title.
HV2474.R53   1987   419
86-80173
ISBN 0-88243-520-5

Printed in the United States of America

169963

BELMONT UNIVERSITY LIBRARY

HV
2474
.R53
1987

AAY-3787

Contents

Appendix

Introduction to the
Second Edition

The acceptance of *The Joy of Signing* has been and continues to be extremely gratifying. It has been used as the main vocabulary reference for sign language students in schools and colleges across the country, by parents of deaf children, by professionals, and also by deaf persons themselves.

The important new feature of the Second Edition is the Appendix, which gives the learner information about the most effective way to add signs to spoken English. The revision also includes some changes in the introductory pages; however, the same basic information remains. An updated bibliography has been prepared, listing primarily those references that will give the interested reader an understanding of the effects of deafness. Entries of some signs have been changed and updated, but page numbers have remained the same in order to match the videotape edition.*

The signs included in this manual are not inventions of the author but observations of signing by deaf persons and professional interpreters with whom the author associated not only at Gallaudet University and in the Washington, D. C., area, but also in other parts of the country. Intended as a dictionary for anyone wishing to learn a basic sign vocabulary to communicate with deaf people, this manual will also help persons interested in preparing for entry into interpreter training programs.

Sign language is a living, growing language and, as is true of spoken languages, its vocabulary will continue to increase. The adult deaf population is interested in enlarging the sign vocabulary but not in unnecessary innovations, initializations, and markers, particularly if the traditional basic sign provides sufficient clarity. The section of this manual covering word endings and word-form changes will explain this further and will point out markers that have

been in use over the years as well as those now recommended for use in some educational settings.

The Joy of Signing does not attempt to include the many new signs developed in recent years for use with children. Its purpose is to provide the learner with the basic, traditional signs used by deaf adults as well as a knowledge of the base from which new signs have been developed. This knowledge will help the signer to judge whether some of the new signs are conceptually based. This is not to say that all "new" nonconceptually based signs are unacceptable, but it is important to know the basic signs that are acceptable to the deaf adult before venturing into newer signs and systems.

Reactions to some of the new signs appearing in various texts today have been varied. The consensus among deaf adults is that conceptually based new signs have a place, particularly for deaf children who should have as much language stimulation as possible in as precise a form as possible and in as many modes as possible in order to provide them with the tools they will need for their educational development.

All the signs listed in this manual are not used by all deaf people, just as all words in a dictionary are not in the everyday vocabulary of all hearing people. The number of signs in one's vocabulary is not as important as the way the signs are used. A sign does not exist for every word in the English language, but a good signer will know how to choose the sign that most nearly expresses the desired thought.

When a sign cannot be found to portray the exact meaning, fingerspelling is perfectly acceptable. Although beginners find this a chore, experienced signers frequently fingerspell even words that do have signs. Certain short words, such as *car, bus,* and *job,* are usually fingerspelled. To find or to invent signs for such short words is not necessary since the fingerspelled configuration is read as a sign.

Signs in this manual have been grouped by chapter into natural categories, but the search for an individual sign is best made by using the index. If the word you are searching for is not listed, look for the word closest in meaning and check the usage in that entry to see whether it would be an appropriate choice. This manual contains a number of glosses for many of the signs but is by no means meant to be exhaustive. The group of words listed for an entry will give you a general idea of the words that are included in the concept being signed. Close observation of the ways deaf people use signs is the best way to improve your own skill.

Using the Manual

To learn signs accurately from this manual, study the complete entry. First, look at the picture to get a general idea of the sign (remembering that in front-view drawings the signer's right hand appears on the left). Next, read the origin of the sign so you will understand the reason for a particular sign formation, or movement. Often the relationship between a sign and its meaning is quite obvious. When the origin is understood, a sign is more easily remembered.

An attempt has been made not only to present a clear drawing but also to provide a step-by-step description of the handshapes and movements. Read each description to see whether you are making the sign properly.

The sentences included with each entry provide either a model of correct usage in context (needed for words having multiple meanings, such as *like, train, kind,* and *run*) or practice material. Such practice sentences are important since context influences sign production and a trained teacher of signing can use these or other sentences to develop correct usage as well as production skill.

Phrases and sentences have been prepared in English word order. Adding signs to this word order while speaking is called the Simultaneous Method of Communication and is considered by most deaf people a very natural form of communication between deaf and hearing persons. This type of signing is not to be confused with the manually coded English systems used in educational settings, but speech or lip movement does follow the pattern of the English language.

The order in which signs are learned is up to the signer or the teacher. It is suggested that signs having an obvious relationship to their meaning be learned first since the signer will feel more comfortable with such natural signs. Sports and foods are both categories in which natural motions are made and it is suggested that these be among the first to be studied.

Enjoy signing—it is more than a means of communication. Signing frees you to express yourself in a natural way. It is the author's pleasure to introduce you to *The Joy of Signing!*

---

*Information regarding *The Joy of Signing* videotape may be obtained from Joy Enterprises, Inc., P.O. Box 10376, Arlington, VA 22210-1376. Please enclose a stamped self-addressed envelope.

History of Sign Language and Fingerspelling

Throughout the world deaf people have developed visual language. The language used by deaf people in the United States is a blend of the signs brought from France early in the 19th century and the signs already in use in this country. With no formal sign language in existence here at that time, home, local, and French signs blended together to become the American Sign Language, now considered to be one of the most refined and complete sign systems in the world. Although American Indians used signs for intertribal communication, this does not appear to have influenced the sign system that evolved among deaf persons and which is use today.

In 1815 a group of men in Hartford, Connecticut, became interested in the establishment of a school for deaf children but lacked information on the proper means of educating them. One of these gentlemen, Dr. Mason Cogswell, was particularly interested since his own daughter, Alice, was deaf and had been taught on an experimental basis by a young minister, Dr. Thomas Hopkins Gallaudet, a graduate of Yale University. As a result, Dr. Gallaudet was sent abroad to investigate methods then being used in England.

In London, Dr. Gallaudet met the Abbe Sicard, who invited him to cross the Channel and visit his school, which had been founded in Paris in 1755 by the Abbe de l'Epee. The Abbe, who is said to be the inventor of the French Sign Language, eventually published a volume describing both his sign system and his method of educating the deaf. After Dr. Gallaudet had spent several months studying educational methods as well as signs, he was ready to return to America. Accompanying him was a young deaf instructor from the French school, Laurent Clerc, who had proven most helpful and who agreed to assist in the new American school.

The first permanent school for the deaf was established in Hartford, Connecticut, in 1817. Many years later, after Thomas Hopkins Gallaudet had seen the establishment of a number of schools for the deaf across the United States, he envisioned the establishment of a college. This dream was passed on to his son, Edward Miner Gallaudet, who was responsible for establishing Gallaudet College, the world's first and only college for deaf students, located in Washington, D.C. The charter for the college was signed in 1864 by President Abraham Lincoln.

Fingerspelling, the use of hand positions to represent the letters of the alphabet, is considered a vital and historical element of manual communication. The positions of the fingers of the hand do, to some extent, resemble the printed letters of the alphabet. Illustrations of the manual alphabet have been found to exist early in the Christian era. Latin Bibles of the 10th century show drawings of such hand positions and it is known that persons who lived in enforced silence, such as monks of the Middle Ages, used fingerspelling as a means of communication. Most European countries use a single-handed alphabet while England's alphabet requires the use of two hands. Today each country that has a manual alphabet uses its own version, which is therefore understood only by users of that particular system.

Signs usually represent ideas and not single words. Many signs are iconic, that is, they use a visual image for signing the idea. Most clearly falling into this category are animals, for example, *deer* (the antlers), *elephant* (the trunk), *donkey* (the ears), and *goat* (the beard and horns). Signs are also represented by actions, such as in the following: *milk* (milking a cow), *coffee* (grinding the coffee beans), *love* (giving a hug), *grow* (coming out of the ground). Other

7

signs are arbitrary and although the originators may have had reasons for forming or moving a sign in a particular way, these reasons are unknown today.

It is interesting to note that many of the older signs have remained as originally created even though the connection to the origin no longer exists. One example of this is the sign for *toast,* represented by placing a fork into the bread in order to hold it over the flame. Although an attempt was made to change this to represent the use of an electric toaster, deaf signers have continued to use the old form. The sign for *deaf* was originally made by pointing to the ear and mouth, probably to match the now outdated terms "deaf and dumb" or "deaf mute." Although a change has been made to point to the ear and sign *closed,* many deaf people continue to use the old sign.

The question is often asked whether sign language is universal. Although signs are used in many countries, each has developed its own system, which has been standardized to some extent within that country. In recent years an international sign language has been developed that crosses national barriers and permits communication between deaf persons of many countries. This language, sometimes called Gestuno, has been found useful for international events, such as conferences and Olympic Games for the Deaf. Persons knowing the language of signs find they can cross the language barrier more easily using signs with a deaf person than using the spoken language with a hearing person.

In educational circles the language of signs has now gained respectability and a number of colleges and universities offer credit-bearing courses. Several also accept proficiency in signs to fulfill the foreign language requirement.

Sign language is viewed by some as a new art form and is used in performances by the National Theater of the Deaf, a professional drama group, as a means of presenting deaf people and their language to a hearing world. Also being introduced is signed interpretation of music, a beautiful and expressive means of portraying the lyrics, emotions, and rhythm of songs. Both deaf and hearing people are enjoying new experiences through communication in the language of signs, making it possible for them to live together with better understanding and mutual enrichment.

Terminology

Adventitious Deafness—Deafness in persons who are born with normal hearing but in whom the sense of hearing becomes nonfunctional later through illness or accident.

American Sign Language—A visual-gestural language used by deaf persons in America.

Audiogram—A graph on which hearing test results are recorded.

Congenital Deafness—Deafness in persons who are born with nonfunctional hearing.

Dactylology—Generally refers to fingerspelling but has been used by some to include signs as well.

Deaf Persons—Those in whom the sense of hearing is nonfunctional for the ordinary purposes of life.

Expressive Skill—The ability to express oneself in the language of signs and fingerspelling.

Fingerspelling (also called the **Rochester Method** or **Visible English**)—Use of the manual alphabet to form words and sentences.

Hard-of-Hearing Persons—Those in whom the sense of hearing, although defective, is functional with or without a hearing aid.

Interpreting—A signed and fingerspelled presentation of another person's spoken communication.

Lipreading, Speechreading—The ability to understand the oral language or speech of a person through observation of his lip movement and facial expression.

Manual Alphabet—The 26 different single-hand positions representing the 26 letters of the alphabet.

Manual Communication—Communication by use of signs and fingerspelling.

Manually Coded English—The use of signs, fingerspelling, and markers to represent as specifically as possible the basic essentials of the English language. An umbrella term used to cover the various signed English systems that have been devised to parallel English exactly.

Nonmanual Behaviors—Those features of the language that are not portrayed with the hands (i.e., facial expression, head and body movement, and body posture).

Oralism, Oral Training—A method of training or educating a deaf person through speech and speechreading without employing signs or fingerspelling.

Pidgin Sign English (PSE)—A term used by some to refer to signing that combines the grammatical structure of English and the signs of the American Sign Language.

Post-Lingual Deafness—Deafness occurring after language has been acquired.

Pre-Lingual Deafness—Deafness occurring before language skills have been acquired.

Receptive Skill—The ability to understand what is expressed in both fingerspelling and in the language of signs.

Sign Language—A language that uses manual symbols to represent ideas and concepts. The term is generally used to describe the language used by deaf people in which both manual signs and fingerspelling are employed.

Sign Language Continuum—A concept presenting the range in manual communication that exists among users of signs, moving from the completely English representation used in educational settings to the non-English pattern (having its own grammatical features) used by many deaf persons, with all the variations between these extremes.

Sign-to-Voice Interpreting—An oral presentation of another person's signed and fingerspelled communication.

Simultaneous Method of Communication—The simultaneous use of manual and oral communication.

Total Communication—A philosophy of educating the deaf child which advocates the use of any and all means of communication to provide unlimited opportunity to develop language competence. Included are the following: speech, amplification (hearing aids), auditory training, speechreading, gesturing, signing, fingerspelling, pantomime, reading, writing, pictures, and any other possible means of conveying ideas, language, and vocabulary.

The Art of Signing

You, the new learner, are embarking on a journey into a community that enjoys communication. You have decided that signs are important and should be learned. Your enthusiasm is high and your first course in signs will give you skills with which to begin conversing with deaf people.

As is true with any language, the more one communicates with a native user of the language, the more fluent one becomes. If you will associate with deaf people, carry on conversations, attend their social and athletic events, you will find your communication skills improving rapidly. Formal training in sign language is strongly encouraged, but regardless of the means of acquiring fluency, one should usually count on a period of 1 or 2 years before attaining an adequate level of conversational competency.

To become a proficient interpreter for the deaf, an additional learning period of several years is required, preferably in a formal interpreter training program. The interpretation of a language is a skill learned after a basic fluency in the language has been attained. Additional study of manual communication alone does not prepare a person to interpret.

Combining Signs, Fingerspelling, and Speech

Signing and fingerspelling along with speaking or forming the English words on the lips is called the Simultaneous Method of Communication. This is not a simple matter, particularly for those who speak rapidly and would therefore

9

have difficulty maintaining a smooth flow of language while attempting to combine the two modes of communication. The sign should begin at the same time the word is spoken. This is true also of fingerspelling but is, of course, more difficult. Signs follow each other in a natural sort of progression and a pause is made at the end of a thought. The pause is equivalent to the drop in voice that usually comes at the end of a sentence.

The concept of speaking or of forming words on the lips is emphasized to a much greater extent today than it was in the early days of sign language when speech was not as much a part of the deaf child's training. Since deaf children are taught speech and lipreading (also called speechreading) very early, it is important for signers either to vocalize or to use lip movement at all times when communicating in English word order. Signers are cautioned, however, not to engage in exaggerated mouthing of words. Only the normal amount of lip movement is necessary. Those whose lip movements are difficult to read should attempt to develop the necessary clarity if they intend to work with deaf people in any extensive capacity.

Location of Signs and Visual Background

The location of the hands when signing and fingerspelling is usually in front of the chest in a comfortable manner. The clothing, particularly from the waist up, becomes the backdrop against which signs are read. It is therefore desirable when signing for a considerable length of time to wear a solid color that contrasts with the skin color of the hands. The eyes of the reader tire quickly and interpreters, teachers, and speakers should keep this in mind.

Facial Expression and Body Language

Facial expression and body language are as important as manual communication, if not more so. All of them should be coordinated to properly convey the intended meaning. Signs showing emotions, such as happiness or sadness, should show the appropriate expression on the face. When the sign "tired" is made, the whole body indicates a sag, while the sign for "strong" calls for a show of strength by throwing the shoulders back and the chest forward.

Head movement and facial expression can completely change the meaning of a sign. For instance, when the sign for "like" is accompanied by a pleasant expression it is clearly indicative of enjoyment, while exactly the same sign accompanied by a negative shaking of the head will portray dislike. Deaf persons do not focus so much on reading each other's hands as they do on reading the face and the overall body language.

Speed, Motion, and Force of Signs

A sign can be made slowly or with speed; it can be static or have motion; it can be made gently or with force. All of these elements are an important part of portraying the full meaning of your message. You may love a person by gently crossing your hands over your chest or you may indicate a stronger feeling by clasping the hands more tightly to the chest and even adding a rocking motion. The sign for "beautiful" takes on different shades of meaning when facial expression, size, strength, and feeling are added in varying degrees. The spoken equivalent of the sign will then be one of the following: "lovely," "pretty," "attractive," "beautiful," or "gorgeous."

The speed of the sign also influences its meaning. For example, the sign "hurry" is moved more rapidly when one is saying, "Hurry, we're leaving now," than when saying, "Don't hurry, we have plenty of time." When the sign for "growing up" is made (raising the downturned palm), a difference is shown in using the phrase in the following statements: "My boy is beginning to grow up now." "It seems as if my son grew up overnight!" In the latter, the sign is made with a faster and higher upward movement. The sign for "require" becomes "demand" when made more forcibly. The more forcible the sign and the stronger the facial expression, the stronger the feeling in either the positive or negative direction. Signers are cautioned not to use excessive motion but to limit the movement to that which is necessary to make the sign clear, unless some particular type of emphasis is intended.

Size of Signs

The size of your signs will be determined by the number of people for whom you are signing and the distance to be covered. On a one-to-one basis, or for very small groups, signs do not extend much beyond the body area. The larger the group and the greater the distance to be covered, the larger the sign and the less fingerspelling is advisable since enlarging the fingerspelled configuration is not possible. Although the human voice can be amplified electronically, signs can be amplified only by increasing their size. As signs increase in size they are also paced less rapidly so understanding is facilitated.

Initializing Signs

There has been a trend toward initializing signs, that is, beginning the sign with the first letter of the desired word. In this way the signer can be specific in portraying the exact word instead of making a sign that could represent any one of several glosses.

An example is the basic sign for "group," which can be initialized to form the following words: "family," "organization," "class," "department," "society," "agency," "association," "group," "workshop," "team." The basic concept remains while the letter of the alphabet used to begin the sign provides a clue to the intended word. Initializing is helpful and acceptable if it is not overdone. In other words, an initial should not be added if the sign already has a specific meaning. The sign for "happen," for instance, is read as such and does not require the initial "h" to clarify it.

Grammatical Forms

No difference is shown for the different grammatical forms of the same word. Usually the noun, adjective, and adverb are signed exactly alike. For example, "love," "loving," and "lovingly" are all signed the same way. Lip movement and context give clues to the intended form. Traditionally, a sign for the suffix "er" has been added to denote the person engaged in that activity ("law"—"lawyer"; "sing"—"singer"). Also in common use is the signed suffix for "er" or "est" forming the comparative and superlative degrees (as in "warm," "warmer," "warmest"). Some current sign systems advocate the use of additional markers or fingerspelled endings to facilitate learning in educational settings. A number of these are described in chapter 2.

Variation in Signs

For the most part, the signs presented in this manual are those in common use across America. However, variation occurs within sign language even as it does in spoken languages. An example of variation in the English language is the regional difference in words used for a carbonated drink: "soda," "pop," or "tonic," depending on the geographical area. A regional difference is commonly seen in signs for holidays, since deaf children in residential state schools tend to invent signs for Christmas, Easter, Halloween, and Thanksgiving to represent something associated with the special day. Deaf persons accept this and usually do not refer to one sign as being right and the other wrong, but simply view these as acceptable differences.

Another reason for variation in signs has to do with historical change. The sign for "help," for instance, was originally made with the right palm under the left elbow, as if politely assisting a lady by supporting her elbow. Today that sign has moved down the arm so that the right palm supports the fist instead of the elbow.

Through the years, some two-handed signs have become one-handed, such as "cow," "horse," and "devil," while some one-handed signs have become two-handed, as is the case with "hurry," "angry," and "die."

Some signs have changed through the years simply to make production easier. "Law," formerly made with the right thumb pointing forward, is now commonly made with the thumb pointing back. This is also true of "sister" and "brother," usually made with the index finger handshape one on top of the other instead of alongside each other, thus eliminating the twist of the wrist (see page 20).

Still another variation has to do with centralizing signs so they are not made as far from the center of the signing space as they formerly were. As speech began to be emphasized in the education of the deaf, focusing on the face became important. However, care should be taken that the face and lips are not obscured by signs and fingerspelling.

Signs with several parts have tended to be reduced, as in the case of the seasons. Spring, for instance, was originally signed "three-months-grow"; winter was signed "three-months-cold"; etc. Today only the last sign is used—"grow" for spring, and "cold" for winter.

Left-Handed or Right-Handed Signing

Signs are pictured in this manual for the right-handed individual; they should be made in reverse by the left-handed person. For the person who says he can sign either way, he should decide during the first lesson which will be his dominant hand. This can be done by trying some fingerspelling and signs first with one hand and then with the other; proceed with whichever hand is more comfortable. It is not good practice to make some signs with one hand and some with the other, unless this is done to show a spatial relationship or other special emphasis.

Understanding Signs

It is common for new signers to have difficulty understanding other persons signing to them. This is true of spoken languages as well. You may have learned French and felt you spoke it very well only to find you were not able to understand a word the Frenchman said to you when you arrived in Paris. To understand native users of any language requires a period of exposure. Do not be discouraged by this problem if you encounter it. Reading signs requires skill as well as a keen mind and a quick eye. Magicians say, "The hand is quicker than the eye," and this often seems to be the case when hands and fingers are moving very rapidly with sign language.

The person who is reading signs generally looks at the signer's face and not at his hands. It is possible to see signs while watching the face but it is difficult to understand lip movements while watching the hands. Deaf people will be patient with you when you do not understand them but you will have to be patient with yourself as well. Association with users of sign language is the best way to improve your receptive skill. When available, films and videotapes of signers are also helpful in improving your understanding.

Importance of Signing

Deaf people recognize the importance of signing because it is their means of daily communication within the family and the deaf community. It has been called the mother tongue of deaf people and is as valuable for their social interaction as speaking is for the hearing person. Deaf children are able to express their wants by means of simple signs long before they are able to speak.

Hearing children under a year old have been known to communicate their needs to their deaf parents by means of a few simple signs. This is earlier than children are normally able to express themselves in speech. Early use of signs will stimulate the mind and lessen the frustration that so often accompanies the communication barrier of deafness.

The usefulness of sign language extends beyond the deaf, to people with speech loss due to accidents, neurological problems, or laryngectomies, and even to divers, for underwater communication. In recent years teachers of the mentally retarded, autistic, aphasic, and speech-handicapped have found sign language useful for facilitating communication. In fact, the full extent of its usefulness has yet to be explored.

The Language Pattern of Signs— Signing on the Continuum

The American Sign Language vocabulary in this manual may be used in either the word order of the English language or in a system having its own syntax and grammatical features. The language continuum moves from a system that parallels English to one that is a complete departure from English. For the latter the sign vocabulary is almost identical but the grammatical rules differ. Signers who associate with deaf persons and become skilled both expressively and receptively in various areas of this language continuum will develop a feel for communication with deaf people and will be able to recognize the setting in which each type of usage is appropriate.

Some have taken the position that it is only when sign language departs completely from English that it may be called the American Sign Language. Others, however, prefer to use the term *American Sign Language* as an umbrella term covering the range of manual communication that uses the same basic signs, the same system of fingerspelling, and the same dependence on nonmanual features to convey meaning. Moores states, "For purposes of convenience, we shall refer to American Sign Language (ASL) as including those systems in use throughout the United States and Canada which have a high degree of mutual intelligibility, although regional and class variations may exist."

A brief explanation of manual communication at various points on the language continuum follows.

Conceptually Based Signs in English Word Order

In the middle range of the continuum and drawing from both ends is a form of communication that combines the English language with the vocabulary and nonmanual features of the American Sign Language. In this system signs are added to words spoken in English grammatical order. This blending has been referred to by some as Pidgin Sign English (PSE) and is the system most generally used by hearing persons who are learning to communicate with deaf people. It is considered a natural and very acceptable means of communication and is the way many deaf persons prefer to communicate. Signs for both definite and indefinite articles ("a," "an," and "the") are omitted and one sign is used for the verb "to be," instead of initializing as in the manually coded English systems. Speech is combined with signs in a natural flow.

In this middle range of the continuum it is up to the signer to determine the extent to which features from either end of the continuum are incorporated, that is, whether to sign more like English or less like English. The choice depends not only on the signer's skill in manual communication but also on the preference of the deaf person and on the communication setting. The Appendix contains further information on features that may be included when using signs in English word order.

Manual Communication Which Is Most Like English—Fingerspelling

At the extreme end of the continuum is a method using the manual alphabet to fingerspell all the words of the English language while speaking or using lip movement. This has also been called the Rochester Method or Visible English. Although still in use in a few educational settings, the use of fingerspelling alone is not a popular method and is tiring to the eyes of the reader.

Manually Coded English Systems

Also toward the English end of the continuum, but moving away from the complete fingerspelling system to include signs and markers, are the manually coded English systems. Those most commonly used are Signed English (Bornstein) and Signing Exact English (Gustason, Pfetzing, and Zawolko). These systems have for the most part based their signs on the American Sign Language but have formalized them into a system that provides a visual representation of all aspects of the English language.

Whereas the vocabulary of the American Sign Language may use one sign to represent several English words, using mouth movement and context as clues to the intended word, these signed English systems frequently use the first letter of the word (initialization) along with the basic movement of the sign to provide the clue to the intended word. Further, these manually coded English systems provide markers to indicate a change in the form of the word. Included are prefixes, suffixes, plural endings, tenses, and various other word-form changes. Also included are signs to designate articles and infinitives, as well as all forms of the verb "to be."

Keeping in mind the deaf child in the educational system, these authors emphasize speech along with signs and nonmanual information (facial expression, head and body movement, as well as body postures). Teachers and parents have found these systems useful when the conveying of exact English counterparts is desirable, and usually continue to use them until the child no longer needs such coding.

Although manually coded English is considered to have merit in educational settings, it is not generally accepted by deaf adults. However, a few of the initial signs as well as some endings have over the years become part of the sign system used by many adult deaf people today. Just a few examples of these are the use of "f" in family, "r" in room, "ment" in development, and "ness" in deafness.

Patterning Signs in a Non-English Format

Linguists are studying the patterns used by deaf persons when they communicate in signs in a non-English style. This communication mode is at the opposite end of the continuum from formal English. Studies show that American Sign Language used in this manner is indeed a unique and recognizable language with its own grammatical pattern. Its vocabulary is conceptually based and nonmanual behaviors are a vital part of this type of communication. Articles are not included and speech is not used, although there may be some lip movement. Fingerspelling is used primarily for names of persons and places.

Word order is being studied and some definite patterns are emerging. One of the structures used frequently is that of stating the topic first and then commenting on it. In other words, the subject of the conversation is mentioned so the receiver will know at the start what will be talked about. This is followed by whatever information the signer is giving about the subject.

Signing at this end of the continuum is usually seen among deaf persons when no hearing people are involved, although some native users are hearing, having parents whose communication preference is at the non-English end of the continuum.

Communicating Effectively

The important skill to be developed is that of signing so effectively that clear communication takes place. It is generally true that a deaf person can understand the signing and fingerspelling of a hearing person who may have only a fair amount of skill. The deaf person is able to accommodate himself to the limited skills of the new signer. However, as the new signer gains proficiency (i.e., fingerspelling well, using signs appropriately, forming them accurately, and at-taining a comfortable flow) it is also important for him to become aware of and sensitive to the type of signing preferred by the deaf person—whether to sign more like English or to move into a non-English style. The setting must also be taken into consideration, since it is sometimes more appropriate to stay close to the English language than to move toward the non-English usage.

It is important to respect differences of signing style along the continuum and to realize that one type of signing is not superior to another, only different. Sign language, with its broad range and versatility, affords the communicator unlimited possibilities in visual expression.

Fingerspelling

Fingerspelling is an important part of the communication system of deaf persons. It is simply the American alphabet produced in 26 hand positions, some of which are exact representations of the printed block letter.

Fingerspelling is used in combination with the language of signs for proper nouns, names and addresses, and for words that have no sign. Its importance cannot be overrated and it is therefore essential for the beginner to concentrate on developing both expressive and receptive skills in order to become proficient.

Alexander Graham Bell, who appeared before a Royal Commission in 1888 to give evidence on teaching the deaf, commented: "We want that method, whatever it is, that will give us the readiest and quickest means of bringing English words to the eyes of the deaf, and I know of no more expeditious means than a manual alphabet."

Hand Position

The palm of the hand should face the audience at a slight angle, with the arm held in a comfortable, natural position. Since it is important to see lip movement, the hand should not be held where it will block the view of the mouth. Neither should the hand be held so far from the mouth that the lips cannot be read simultaneously with the fingerspelling.

Flow and Rhythm

Each letter should be made clearly, distinctly, and crisply with a slight pause between words. This pause is shown by holding the last letter of a word for a moment before beginning the first letter of the next word. The hands do not drop between words. If there is movement while fingerspelling, it should be a gradual move to the right but there is no need to bounce letters or to push letters forward in an attempt to be clear.

Some letters and combinations of letters are more easily formed than others, producing a tendency to spell them more rapidly than the more difficult ones, but this is not advisable. Speed should not be a concern; it is a natural by-product of practice. However, establishing and maintaining rhythm in fingerspelling is important since it aids readability.

Vocalization

The words you fingerspell (not the individual letters) should be spoken or formed on the lips. One- and two-syllable words present no problem, but longer words are a challenge. It is possible to develop skill in simultaneous fingerspelled communication by practicing in syllabic units. (Interpreters use silent lip formation, since vocalization would interfere with the speaker's presentation.)

Double Letters

When double letters are formed the hand is opened slightly before repeating the second letter of the series. Letters such as "c" and "l" are already open and are simply moved from left to right (or to the left if you are left-handed) with a very slight bounce. In other words, the repeated letter is not merely moved over to the right, since a clear separation is needed to indicate that the letter is being made twice. The movement for the letter "z" is simply repeated. Try the following words using the principles outlined above:

Aaron	sunny	haggle	spelling
cool	chubby	padded	rolling
better	massive	apple	letter
summer	beet	hurry	dazzle
soccer	offer	swimming	fizz

Capitalized Abbreviations

To distinguish a word from an abbreviation, it is necessary to circle the individual letters clockwise very slightly when they represent names of places, organizations, etc. Try a few: U.S.A.; N.A.D. (National Association of the Deaf); R.I.D. (Registry of Interpreters for the Deaf).

Reading Fingerspelling

Fingerspelling should be read in the same way you read the words on this page, in units instead of letter by letter. As you read fingerspelling, first short words and then longer ones, do not allow your partner in conversation to slow down when you do not understand, because this will tend to get you into the habit of reading letters instead of syllables or words. If you do not understand the word being spelled, ask the person with whom you are practicing to repeat at the same rate, even if a great deal of repetition is required. This forces you to read in word units and will increase your comprehension more rapidly.

Practice Hints

It is suggested that you begin fingerspelling two- and three-letter words, gradually increasing the length of words, breaking them down into syllables, until a smooth flow is attained. Speech or lip movement should always accompany fingerspelling and signs as you practice.

It would be well to find a partner with whom to fingerspell but if this is not possible try looking into a mirror (although this will show you a left-handed signer). You will then become aware of word-unit formations, and you will also be surprised at the errors that will be clearly visible and that can be corrected before bad habits are formed.

The following are examples of one- and two-syllable words that will be helpful in developing your skill.

an	bat	ban	bane
at	cat	can	cane
it	fat	Dan	dane
he	hat	fan	lane
of	mat	man	mane
so	pat	pan	pane
as	rat	ran	wane
be	sat	tan	
up	vat	van	

date	dated	bet	bid
fate	hated	get	did
gate	fated	jet	hid
hate	mated	met	lid
late	rated	net	rid
mate		pet	
pate		set	
rate		wet	

old	older	ham	cot
bold	bolder	jam	dot
cold	colder	Pam	got
fold	folder	ram	hot
gold	holder	Sam	jot
hold	solder	tam	lot
mold			not
sold			rot
told			

For additional word lists and practice material see Guillory's manual, *Expressive and Receptive Fingerspelling for Hearing Adults* (listed in the Suggested References).

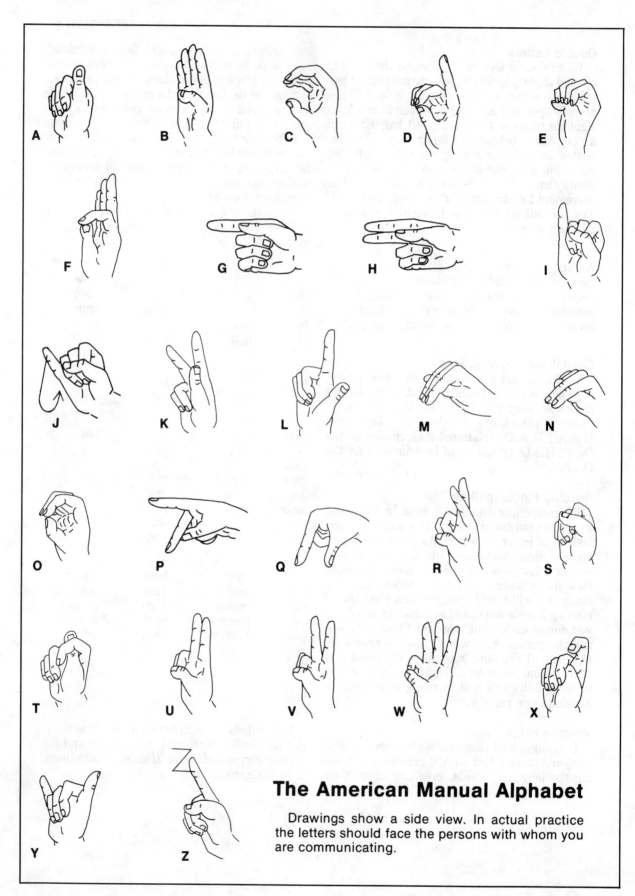

The American Manual Alphabet

Drawings show a side view. In actual practice the letters should face the persons with whom you are communicating.

1

Family Relationships

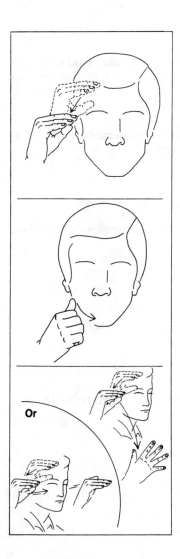

MALE

Grasp the imaginary brim of a hat with four fingers and thumb.
Origin: tipping the hat
Usage: the first *male* in the family
Note: Although this is primarily a basic sign intended as a prefix, it is often used alone to indicate any male.

FEMALE

Move the inside of the thumb of the right "A" down along the right cheek toward the chin.
Origin: represents the old-fashioned bonnet string
Usage: male and *female* applicants
Note: Although this is primarily a basic sign intended as a prefix, it is often used alone to indicate any female.

MAN, GENTLEMAN

Sign "MALE"; then make the sign for "FINE" (tip of "FIVE" hand at the chest). Or sign "MALE"; then bring the flat hand, palm down, away from the head at the level of the hat.
Origin: first description—a ruffled shirt
second description—indicates the height of the male
Usage: *man* of the house
a real *gentleman*

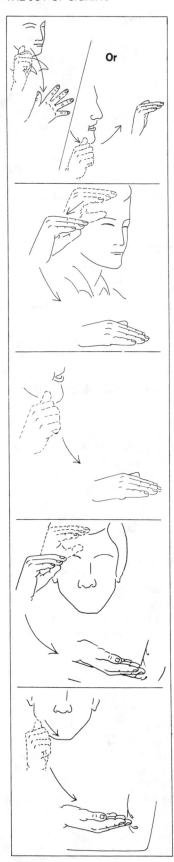

WOMAN, LADY

Sign "FEMALE"; then make the sign for "FINE" (tip of "FIVE" hand at the chest). Or sign "FEMALE"; then bring the flat hand, palm down, away from the face at the level of the cheek.
Origin: first description—a ruffled blouse
second description—indicates the height of the woman
Usage: a young *woman*
       ladies and gentlemen

BOY

Sign "MALE"; then bring the right open hand down to about waist level, palm down. Frequently only the sign for "MALE" is used and the indication of height is omitted.
Origin: a male of small stature
Usage: an active *boy;* a 3-year-old *boy*
Note: The hand would be brought considerably lower for a 3-year-old child than for a 12-year-old.

GIRL

Sign "FEMALE"; then bring the right open hand down to about waist level, palm down. Frequently only the sign for "FEMALE" is used and the indication of height is omitted.
Origin: a female of short stature
Usage: a pretty *girl*
Note: The hand would be brought considerably lower for a 3-year-old child than for a 12-year-old.

SON

Sign "MALE"; then place right hand, palm up, in the crook of the left arm.
Origin: a male baby
Usage: our only *son*

DAUGHTER

Sign "FEMALE"; then place the right hand, palm up, in the crook of the left arm.
Origin: a female baby
Usage: my successful *daughter*

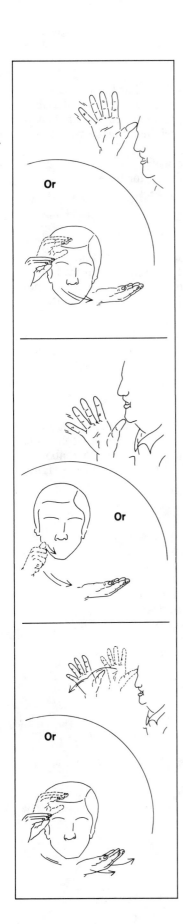

FATHER

Using the "FIVE" hand, place the thumb tip against the forehead twice. Or sign "MALE"; then open the right hand and move it toward the left, palm up.
Origin: man holding a baby (represented by the second description above)
Usage: *Father's* Day
Our Heavenly *Father* (use second description)

MOTHER

Using the "FIVE" hand, place the thumb tip against the chin twice. Or sign "FEMALE"; then open the right hand and move it toward the left, palm up.
Origin: woman holding a baby (represented by the second description)
Usage: a new *mother;* a wonderful *mom*

GRANDFATHER

Place the thumbtip of the "FIVE" hand at the forehead and swing it away in a double movement. Or sign "MALE"; then swing the right open hand, palm up, to the left just below chin level. (This sign was originally made with two hands.)
Origin: a father one generation back
Usage: our old *grandfather* clock

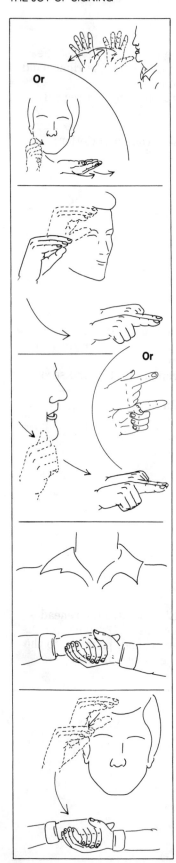

GRANDMOTHER

Place the thumbtip of the "FIVE" hand at the chin and swing it away in a double movement. Or sign "FEMALE"; then swing the right open hand, palm up, to the left just below chin level. (This sign was originally made with two hands.)
Origin: a mother one generation back
Usage: *Grandmother* was babysitting for us.

BROTHER

Sign "MALE" and "SAME" (place both index fingers side by side, pointing to the front). This sign is often made by placing the hands, in index finger positions, one above the other, right hand facing left and left hand facing right.
Origin: male in the same family
Usage: older *brother*

SISTER

Sign "FEMALE" and "SAME" (place both index fingers side by side, pointing to the front). This sign is often made by placing the hands, in index finger positions, one above the other, right hand facing left and left hand facing right.
Origin: female in the same family
Usage: youngest *sister*

MARRY

Clasp the hands, with right hand on top.
Origin: clasping the hands in marriage
Usage: happily *married* for 10 years

HUSBAND

Sign "MALE"; then clasp hands, right hand on top, as in "MARRIAGE."
Origin: a male who is married
Usage: a good *husband*

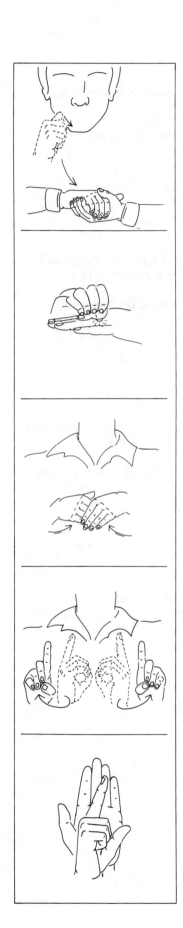

WIFE

Sign "FEMALE"; then clasp hands as in "MARRIAGE."
Origin: a female who is married
Usage: my *wife's* parents

ENGAGEMENT (To be married)

Place the right "E" on the fourth finger of the left hand.
Origin: The engagement ring is placed on the finger.
Usage: Beth is *engaged* to Don.

WEDDING

With palms facing the body and fingers pointing forward,
bring the right hand into the left between the thumb and
index finger; left hand grasps right.
Origin: hands placed together in the wedding ceremony
Usage: Eddie and Barbara had a beautiful *wedding*.

DIVORCE

Place the "D" hands before you, palms slightly inward, and
give them a quick twist outward and away from each other
ending with palm side out
Origin: initial hands moved away from each other
indicating a separation
Usage: The *divorce* rate is high in America.

IN-LAW

Place the right "L" against the palm of the left hand
(thumb pointing either away from self as pictured or
toward self).
Origin: The left hand represents a book and the right hand
the law that is in the book.
Usage: Rosemary is my sister-*in-law*.

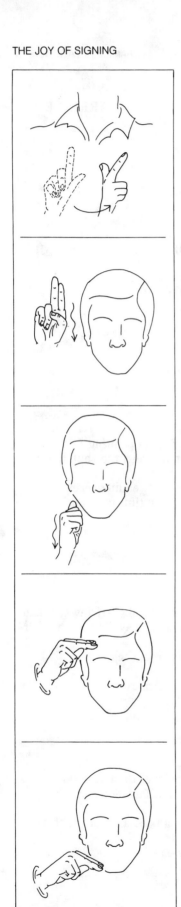

STEPMOTHER, STEPFATHER, etc.

Place the "L" before you, twist it slightly inward; add the sign for "mother," "father," etc.
Origin: second mother or second father
Usage: an understanding *stepmother* and *stepfather*

UNCLE

Place the right "U" at the side of the temple and move it downward in a wavy motion. Or move the "U" in a counterclockwise circular motion.
Origin: an initial sign at the location of the "male" sign
Usage: The kids like *Uncle* Hank.

AUNT

Place the right "A" at the side of the right cheek and move it downward in a wavy motion. Or move the "A" in a counterclockwise circular motion.
Origin: an initial sign at the location of the "female" sign
Usage: *Aunt* Ruth is good to the children.

NEPHEW

Shake the letter "N" at the side of the temple.
Origin: an initial sign at the location of the "male" sign
Usage: six *nephews*

NIECE

Shake the letter "N" at the side of the chin.
Origin: an initial sign at the location of the "female" sign
Usage: three *nieces*

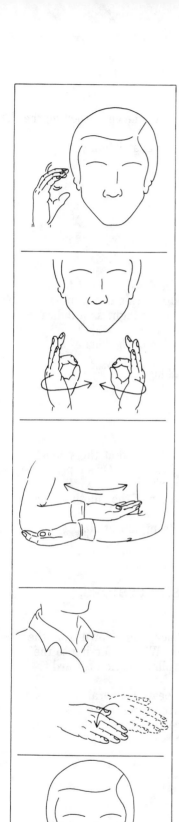

COUSIN

Shake the letter "C" at the side of the cheek.
Origin: an initial sign made between the locations of the "male" and the "female" signs
Usage: eight *cousins*

FAMILY

Place the "F" hands in front of you, palms facing forward; draw hands apart and away from you; turn until the little fingers touch.
Origin: an initial sign for a group
Usage: Your *family* tree can be traced.

BABY, INFANT, CHILD

Place the right hand in the crook of the left arm and the left upturned hand under the right arm; then rock.
Origin: rocking the baby
Usage: *baby* girl
       mother and *infant*
       a month-old *child*

CHILD, CHILDREN

Pat the head of an imaginary child. For the plural, repeat the motion several times.
Usage: an only *child*
       nine *children* in the family

KID (informal)

Extend the little finger and index finger (other fingers and thumb closed); place the hand, palm-side down, just above the upper lip and wiggle the hand slightly.
Origin: wiping the nose, as children often do
Usage: "I started as an average *kid*, I finished as a thinkin' man" (Rudyard Kipling).

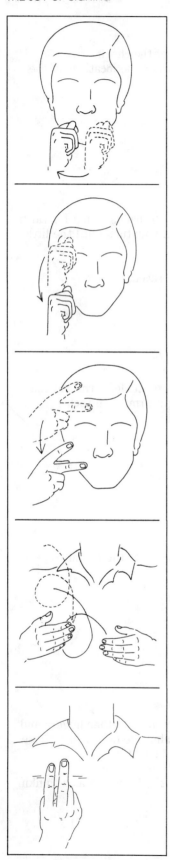

TWINS

Place the right "T" on the left side of the chin, then on the right.
Usage: pretty *twin* girls named Janna and Jenny

ADULTS

Place the "A" at the side of the forehead, then at the side of the chin. Or place the bent palm, facing down, next to the forehead and bounce it over to the right as if indicating the height of more than one adult.
Origin: an initial sign at the location of the "male" and "female" signs
Usage: The *adults* sat around talking.

PARENTS

Place the middle fingertip of the "P" hand at the side of the forehead, then on the side of the chin. Or simply make the signs for "mother" and "father."
Origin: an initial sign at the location of the "mother" and "father" signs
Usage: We all belong to a *parents'* organization.

GENERATION, DESCENDANTS, ANCESTORS, POSTERITY

Both open hands, palms facing back, come down from the right shoulder in a rolling motion. When referring to the past, as in *ancestors,* make the rolling motion toward the back.
Origin: The sign for "born" is repeated several times as it moves from past to present (or from present to past).
Usage: the next *generation; ancestors* from Ireland; many *descendants;* leave it for *posterity*

COUPLE

Sign "TWO" with palm toward self.
Usage: a beautiful *couple*

2

Pronouns, Question Words, & Endings

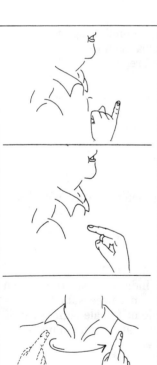

I

The "I" hand is placed at the chest.
Origin: using the initial letter while indicating self
Usage: *I* will go with you.

ME

Point the right index finger at yourself.
Origin: indicating self
Usage: Speak to *me*.
Note: This sign is also used for the personal pronoun "I."

WE, US

Place the index finger at the right shoulder and circle it forward and around until it touches the left shoulder. The initial "W" or "U" is used by some.
Origin: pointing to self, then to others and back to self
Usage: *we,* the people; come and help *us*
Note: When "we" refers to you and one other person, use the "TWO" hand, shaking it back and forth between you and the other person (palm facing up).

YOU

Point the index finger out. For the plural, point the index finger out and move from left to right.
Origin: natural sign
Usage: *You* have one vote.
        All of *you* are improving.

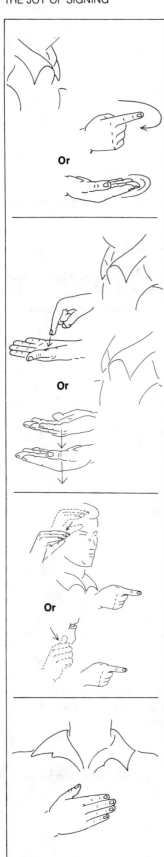

THEY, THEM, THOSE, THESE

Point the index finger toward the object and move it toward the right. Or direct the upturned hand forward and right.
Origin: indicating the object
Usage: *They* agree.
　　　　Hear *them* sing.
　　　　those chairs
　　　　these papers

THIS

1. Place the tip of the right index finger into the left open palm.
Origin: pointing to a specific object
Usage: *This* is my book.

2. When indicating time and area, the following sign is used: Drop the hands before you, palms up.
Usage: Give us *this* day our daily bread.
　　　　This farm is for sale.

HE, HIM, SHE, HER

Sign "MALE" or "FEMALE" and point forward with the index finger.
Usage: *He* is young.
　　　　Give the letter to *him*.
　　　　She sings well.
　　　　We offered *her* a job.
Note: If the sentence has already indicated that the person spoken of is a male or a female it is not necessary to precede this pronoun with the male or female sign. Also, it should be noted that these pronouns are often simply fingerspelled.

MY, MINE

Place the open palm on the chest.
Origin: showing possession by holding an object against the chest
Usage: This is *my* country.
　　　　These children are all *mine*.

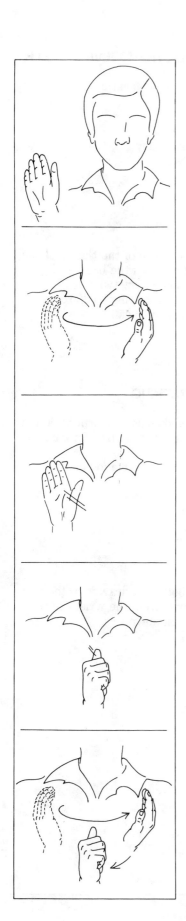

HIS, HER, HERS, THEIR, THEIRS

Face the palm out, directing it toward the individuals.
(Sometimes the sign for "MALE" or "FEMALE" precedes
the sign for clarity.)
Origin: The open palm, indicating possession, is directed
toward the person.
Usage: *his* choice
　　　　her dog
　　　　their home

OUR

Place the right hand, slightly cupped, at the right shoulder
with thumb side against the body; circle it around until the
little-finger side touches the left shoulder.
Origin: open palm indicating the possessive, as concerning
self and others
Usage: We are thankful for *our* freedom.

YOUR, YOUR OWN

Face the palm out, directing it forward.
Origin: The open palm indicating the possessive is directed
toward the person to whom you are speaking.
Usage: *Your* idea is good. (For the plural form, move the
　　　　palm forward and then toward the right.)
Note: To add "own" simply repeat the sign, as in *your
own, her own, his own.*

SELF, MYSELF

Strike the "A" hand, palm side facing left, against the
chest several times.
Usage: We all need more *self*-control.
　　　　I hurt *myself* yesterday.

OURSELVES

Sign "OUR" and "SELF."
Usage: seeing *ourselves* as others see us

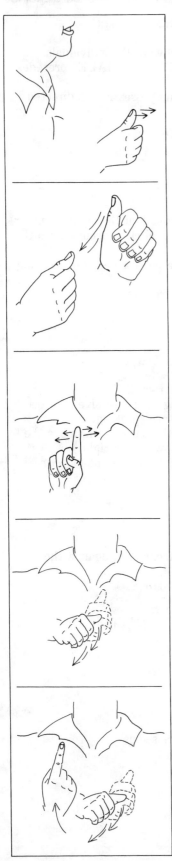

YOURSELF, HIMSELF, HERSELF, THEMSELVES, ITSELF

Direct the "A" hand away from you in several short quick movements.
Usage: You drew that *yourself?*
He painted the house *himself!*
She does not seem *herself* today.
They worried *themselves* sick.
The vase fell by *itself.*

EACH, EVERY

Hold up the left "A" and use the inside of the thumb of the right "A" to make downward strokes on the back of the left thumb. (*Each* is done once, and *every* twice.)
Usage: *Each* person here has an interesting background.
Exercising *every* day keeps us healthy.

SOMEONE, SOMEBODY, SOMETHING

Hold up the right index finger and shake the arm back and forth slightly, left to right. Palm side may face forward or self.
Origin: The index finger represents the person or thing.
Usage: *Someone* is coming.
Is *somebody* laughing?
I hear *something* upstairs.

ANY

Place the "A" hand before the body and draw it to the right while moving it up and down from the wrists so that the thumb points first up and then down.
Usage: *Any* child knows that.

ANYONE, ANYBODY

Sign "ANY" and "ONE."
Usage: *Anyone* may come.
Anybody home?

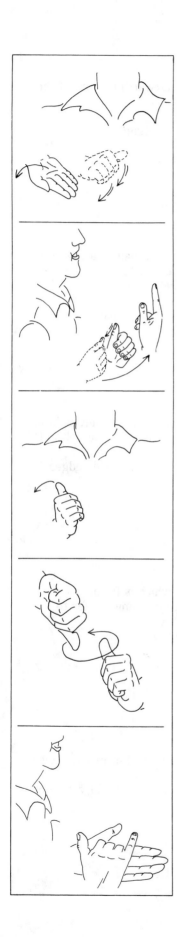

ANYTHING

Sign "ANY" and "THING" (drop the slightly curved open right hand before you, palm facing up; move it to the right and drop it again).
Usage: *Anything* can happen here.

EVERYBODY, EVERYONE

Sign "EACH" and "ONE."
Usage: *Everybody* is welcome.
The invitation is for *everyone*.

OTHER, ANOTHER

Move the "A" hand slightly up and to the right, turning the thumb up and over toward the right.
Origin: The thumb is pointing in the direction of another person.
Usage: *Other* nurses helped us.
They came from *another* hospital.

EACH OTHER, ONE ANOTHER, ASSOCIATE, SOCIALIZE, FELLOWSHIP, INTERACT

Circle the right "A" which is pointing down in a counterclockwise motion around the thumb of the left "A" which is pointing up and moving in a counterclockwise motion.
Usage: they like *each other;* have concern for *one another;* *associate* with good people; *socialize* at the party; *fellowship* with my friends; *interact* with people who use sign language

THAT

Place the right "Y" on the left palm.
Usage: Who is *that* girl? *That's* right! It costs *that* much?
Note: As a conjunctive, "that" should not be signed, as in the sentence, "I know *that* you are right." In such cases either omit the word or spell it.

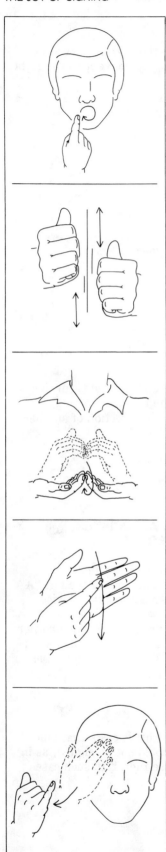

WHO

The index finger draws a circle (leftward) in front of the lips.
Origin: refers to the lip formation
Usage: *Who* is coming for dinner tonight?

WHICH, WHETHER

Place both "A" hands before you with palms facing each other and raise and lower them alternately.
Origin: Is it this hand or that one?
Usage: *Which* is your coat?
 I can't decide *whether* to work or play.

HOW

Place the curved hands back to back with fingers pointing down; turn hands away from, then toward, yourself in this position until fingers point up.
Origin: as if turning seams up to see the inside edges
Usage: *How* did you sew that?
 How is your family?

WHAT

Draw the tip of the right index (which is facing self) downward across the left open palm. Some prefer to simply fingerspell "what."
Usage: *What* kind of work do you do?

WHY

Touch the fingertips to the forehead and draw them away, forming a "Y" (palm facing self).
Usage: *Why* can't you travel around the world with me?

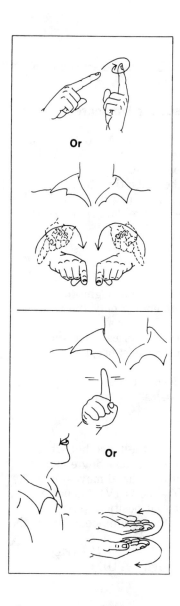

WHEN

Left index is held up facing you; right index faces out and draws a circle in front of the left index and comes to rest on the tip of the left index.

Or point the index fingers forward with palms up; bring them to the center, ending with index fingers side by side (palms down). This sign is similar to "happen" and is usually used to ask when something happened.

Usage: *When* shall we meet?

When did you get the news?

WHERE

Hold up the right index finger and shake the hand back and forth quickly from left to right.

Usage: *Where* are you going?

Or both open hands, palms up, circle outward (right hand clockwise and left hand counterclockwise).

Usage: Dr. Roberts visited the place *where* he was born.

Note: Raising the eyebrows with this sign, as with any of the "wh" question words, helps to show that a question is being asked.

WHATEVER, WHOEVER, etc.

Make the sign for the desired pronoun and add "ANY." Sometimes the question word (what, who, etc.) is used alone without the ending. Another alternative is to use the sign for "no matter."

Usage: Do *whatever* you can to help.

Whoever is interested may go.

Come *whenever* you can.

ARTICLES (Used only in Manually Coded English Systems)

A, AN, THE—As a rule, articles are omitted in the language of signs as used by deaf adults. However, in manual English systems, they are included for educational purposes. In these cases, they are made as follows: A—Move the right "A" slightly to the right; AN—fingerspell; THE—Turn the "T" from a palm-left to a palm-forward position.

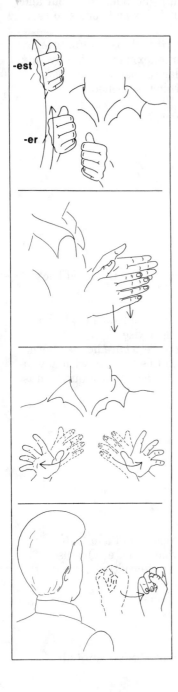

COMMONLY USED ENDINGS

The following endings are those that have been commonly used in the traditional sign system.

-ER, -EST (Comparative and superlative degree)

Raise the right "A" up and past the left "A," both thumbs pointing up. For the superlative degree the right "A" is raised higher than for the comparative.
Origin: One is shown to be higher than the other.
Usage: short, short*er*, short*est;* long, long*er*, long*est;* sweet, sweet*er*, sweet*est;* large, larg*er*, larg*est;* rich, rich*er*, rich*est*

"PERSON" ENDING

Both open hands facing each other are brought down in front of the body. This sign is an ending only and is used following verbs, occupations, and locations.
Usage: teach—teacher; America—American; act—actor; law—lawyer; south—southerner; prophesy—prophet
Note: When the word ending designates a specific person, use that sign, as: salesman = "sales" + "man."

PAST TENSE

Ordinarily the context will indicate the tense but when past tense must be shown, one of the following endings may be used: PAST—The right open hand moves back over the shoulder. FINISHED—The "FIVE" hands are turned from a palm-in to a palm-out position (pictured).
Usage: Yesterday I drove. (No tense sign needed since the word "yesterday" indicates the past.)
I *went* to town. (Sign "GO" + "FINISHED.")
I *studied* that subject. (Sign "STUDY" + "FINISHED.")

'S or S' (Possessives)

Twist the right "S" inward. This ending may be used both after signs and after fingerspelled words.
Usage: president*'s* men; Sandy*'s* children; women*'s* club; brother*'s* house; Mike*'s* pipe; people*'s* choice

PLURALS

The most common way of indicating the plural form is to repeat the sign several times. Often the context will show that a word is plural and no change or addition is needed.
Usage: three mice = "THREE" + "MOUSE"
churches on every corner (Repeat the sign for "church," i.e., strike the "C" on the wrist twice.)

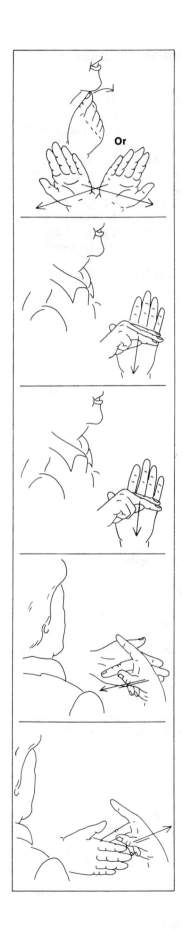

NEGATIVE PREFIXES—UN, IM, IN, DIS

Use the formal sign for "NOT" preceding the intended word.

Usage: *un*important—not important; *im*polite—not polite; *im*possible—not possible; *in*capable—not capable; *dis*interested—not interested

THE FOLLOWING ENDINGS HAVE BECOME COMMON IN RECENT YEARS AND ARE NOW USED TO SOME EXTENT BY DEAF ADULTS

-MENT

Place the side of the right "M" against the left palm (which has fingertips pointing up); move "M" downward.

Usage: develop*ment* of the system

-NESS

Place the side of the right "N" against the left palm (which has fingertips pointing up; move the "N" downward.

Usage: Deaf*ness* is increasing.

PRE-

Place the back of the right "P" against the left palm and move the "P" away from the palm toward self.

Origin: based on the sign for "before"

Usage: Renee's deafness is *pre*lingual.

The meeting was *pre*arranged.

POST-

Place the palm side of the right "P" against the back of the left hand and move the "P" away from the hand.

Origin: based on the sign for "after"

Usage: The patient needs *post*-operative care.

WORD ENDINGS USED WITH DEAF CHILDREN IN EDUCATIONAL SETTINGS

Following are some of the word endings advocated by educators for classroom use to improve the deaf child's vocabulary and to make him more proficient in the correct use of the English language. These endings are not ordinarily used by deaf adults. An alternative to adding word endings is fingerspelling the complete word. Among deaf adults, a word in its various forms is usually represented by one sign. For instance, the same sign denotes any of these words: expect, expects, expecting, expectant, expectation. Speechreading and context are called upon to identify the particular form of the word.

-ING—Move the right "I" from a palm-left to a palm-forward position for the suffix "ING."

Usage: think*ing;* walk*ing;* lov*ing;* seek*ing*

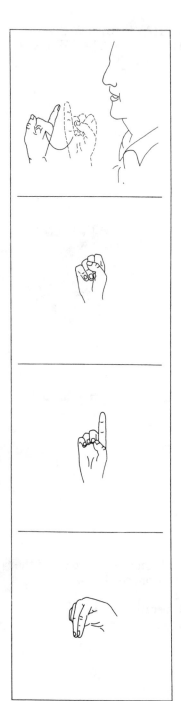

S (Plural)—Add an "S" for either the plural or the third person singular.

Usage: chair*s;* walk*s*

D (Past)—Add a "D" to the sign to indicate the past.

Usage: help*ed;* excit*ed;* learn*ed*

For the irregular form add the sign "FINISH."

Usage: taught—sign "TEACH" + "FINISH" (This form is used by deaf adults.)

N (Participle)—Add an "N" to the sign to make it a participle.

Usage: spok*en;* brok*en*

-LY (Adverbs)—Form a combination of "L" and "Y" (thumb, index, and little finger up) and move the hand downward. Or fingerspell "LY."

Usage: nice*ly;* slow*ly*

Y (Adjectives)—Add a "Y" to the sign to make it an adjective.

Usage: sleep*y;* rain*y*

-FUL—Fingerspell at the end of the sign.

Usage: use*ful;* meaning*ful*
Note: Some prefer to make the sign for "full."

3

Time

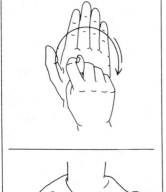

TIME

Crook the index finger and tap the back of the left hand several times.
Origin: pointing to the watch on the arm
Usage: What *time* do you have?

TIME

Make a clockwise circle with the right "T" in the left palm. This sign is used in the abstract sense.
Origin: indicating the movement of the clock
Usage: in medieval *times*

SUNRISE, DAWN, SUNSET

The left arm is held in front of the body pointing right with the palm down. The right "O" starts below and moves upward (or downward) behind the left forearm.
Origin: the sun appearing or disappearing beyond the horizon
Usage: *Sunrise* will be at five.
We arose at *dawn.*
a golden *sunset*

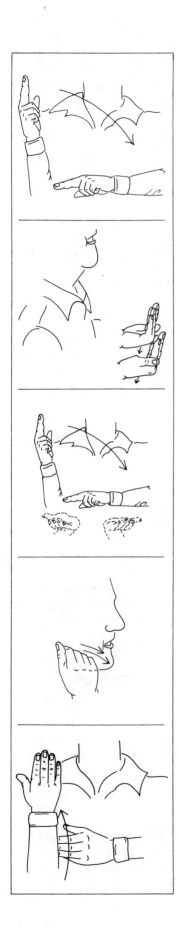

DAY

The right arm, in the index-finger position, is moved in a short arc from right to left (or from left to right) while the left index touches the inside of the right elbow. "ALL DAY" is signed with a complete arc, usually with the palm open instead of in the index-finger position.
Origin: indicates the course of the sun
Usage: a long, hard *day;* the first *day* of the week

NOW, CURRENTLY

Place both bent hands before you at waist level, palms up. Drop the hands slightly. Sometimes made with the "Y" hands instead of the bent hands as pictured.
Origin: indicates time that is immediately before you
Usage: *Now* is the time to act.
        currently performing at the Kennedy Center

TODAY

Sign "NOW" and "DAY." (The order may be reversed.)
Usage: What are you doing *today?*

DAILY, EVERY DAY

Place the side of the "A" hand on the cheek and rub it toward the chin several times.
Origin: indicating several tomorrows
Usage: *daily* bread
        drive to work *every day*

MORNING

The fingertips of the left hand are placed in the crook of the right arm; the right arm moves upward (palm up).
Origin: shows the sun coming up
Usage: Good *morning!*
        See you in the *morning.*

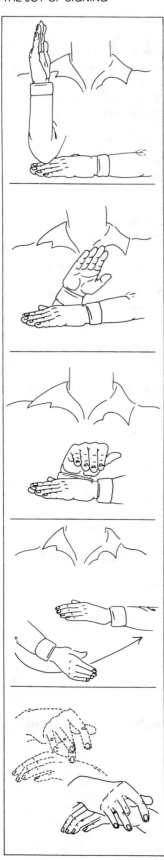

NOON

The fingertips of the left hand, palm down, support the right arm which is held straight up with open palm facing left. (Or sign "TWELVE" while the right hand is up.)
Origin: indicates that the sun is overhead
Usage: The luncheon starts at *noon*.

AFTERNOON

The left arm is in front of you, palm down, pointing to the right. The right forearm, palm facing down, rests on the back of the left hand so that the arm and hand point slightly upward.
Origin: indicates that the sun is halfway down
Usage: this *afternoon* at four

NIGHT, TONIGHT, EVERY NIGHT, LAST NIGHT

The wrist of the right bent hand rests on the back of the left open hand. Frequently "every night" is signed by moving the hands in this position to the right.
Origin: The sun has gone down over the horizon.
Usage: went to a meeting every *night*
Note: TONIGHT—Sign "NOW" + "NIGHT."
LAST NIGHT—Sign "YESTERDAY" + "NIGHT."

ALL NIGHT, OVERNIGHT

The left hand is held in front of the body, palm down and pointing right, fingertips touching the crook of the right arm. The right arm, palm open, swings down and then toward the left.
Origin: The sun moves in its course beneath the horizon.
Usage: slept well *all night*
      stayed at my friend's home *overnight*

EARLY

Place the middle fingertip of the right hand (with other fingers extended) on the back of the left open hand and tilt the right hand forward.
Usage: Please come *early*.

EARLY (In the morning)

The left hand is held in front of the body pointing right. The right arm, palm facing up, moves upward slightly.
Origin: The sun is just peeking over the horizon.
Usage: Do you like to get up *early?*

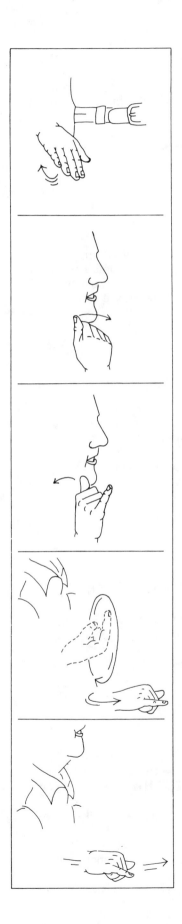

LATE, NOT YET

Place the right hand near the hip with fingers pointing down and palm facing back. Hand is moved back and forth several times.
Origin: You are behind those who have already arrived.
Usage: always *late*
　　　not yet here

TOMORROW

Touch right side of the chin with thumb of "A" and direct it slightly up and forward in a semicircle.
Origin: indicates the time that is before you
Usage: "One today is worth two *tomorrows*" (Benjamin Franklin).

YESTERDAY

Touch right side of the chin with thumb of the "Y" hand and describe a semicircle up and back toward the ear. (This sign can be made with the "A" hand.)
Origin: initial sign moved back to represent time behind you
Usage: *Yesterday* is gone.

FOREVER, EVERLASTING, ETERNAL

Sign "ALWAYS" (a circle in front of you) and "STILL" (as described below).
Usage: now and *forever*
　　　everlasting peace
　　　eternal hope

STILL, YET

Move the right "Y" hand forward, palm facing down. This sign is used only in a continuing sense.
Usage: That word is *still* used.
　　　The book is read *even yet*.
　　　He is experienced, *yet* slow.
Note: When "not yet" is used, sign "LATE."

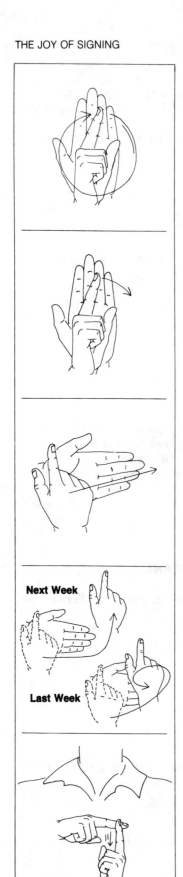

HOUR

The left hand is held in front of you pointing up, palm facing right. The right index finger and thumb rest against the left hand and describe a circle in the left palm, twisting the wrist as the circle is made.
Origin: representing the minute hand of the clock
Usage: 3 *hours* ago

MINUTE, SECOND

The left hand is held in front of you pointing up, palm facing right. The right index finger and thumb rest against the left hand and the right index moves forward slightly.
Origin: The minute hand moves forward the space of a minute.
Usage: 15 *minutes* late
Wait a *second.*

WEEK, WEEKLY

Right index hand, palm forward, is passed across the left palm which is pointing to the right. For "WEEKLY" repeat several times.
Origin: indicates one row of dates on the calendar
Usage: 52 *weeks* in a year
weekly meetings

NEXT WEEK, LAST WEEK

Sign "WEEK" and continue the movement of the right hand in an up-left-forward direction. For "LAST WEEK" sign "WEEK" and continue the movement of the right hand in an up-and-back direction.
Usage: See you *next week.*
What happened *last week?*
Two weeks ago.

MONTH, MONTHLY

The left index finger is held up, palm facing to the right. The right index is moved from the tip of the left finger down to the last joint. (For "MONTHLY" repeat several times.)
Origin: The tip and three joints indicate 4 weeks on the calendar.
Usage: twice a *month;* bills arrive *monthly*
Note: Months of the year are usually fingerspelled and abbreviated, as Jan., Feb., etc.

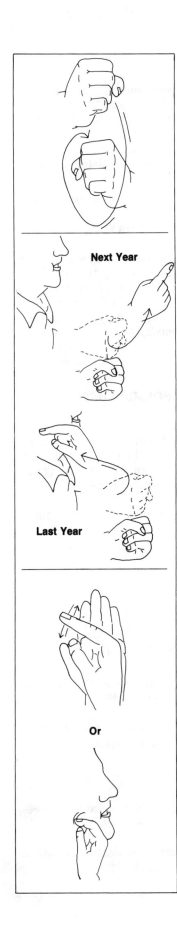

Next Year

Last Year

Or

YEAR

With palms facing in, the right "S" revolves forward and around the "S," coming to a halt resting on the left "S."
Origin: the earth revolving around the sun
Usage: during a school *year*

NEXT YEAR, LAST YEAR, ANNUAL

NEXT YEAR—Place the right fist on the thumb side of the left fist; then move the right hand up and forward into a "ONE" position.

LAST YEAR—Place the right fist on the thumb side of the left fist; then move the "ONE" hand back.
Note: These signs can be made in such fashion with any number, usually up to five.
Usage: a new job *next year*
     a vacation in Hawaii *last year*
     met her 3 *years ago*
     See you at the convention *in 2 years.*

ANNUAL—Sign "NEXT YEAR" several times.
Usage: our *annual* business meeting

RECENTLY, A LITTLE WHILE AGO, JUST, LATELY

The left hand is held in front of you, pointing up with palm facing right. Place the little finger side of the right "ONE" hand against the left palm and move the right index up and down.
Origin: backwards on the clock

Or place the right curved "ONE" hand at the right cheek, palm facing back, and move it back and forth slightly.
Origin: time that is behind you
Usage: Something happened to me *recently.*
     Paul ate *a little while ago.*
     Peggy *just* arrived.
     not feeling well *lately*

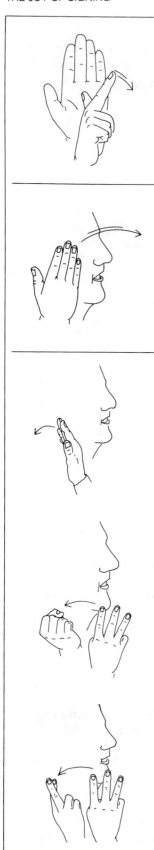

AFTER A WHILE, LATER

The left hand is held in front of you, pointing up with the palm facing right. The thumbtip of the right "L" touches the center of the left palm, acting as a pivot, and moves forward.
Origin: indicates the passing of time on a clock
Usage: I'll come back *after a while.* See you *later.*

FUTURE, BY AND BY, LATER, SOMEDAY

Raised arm, palm facing left, moves forward in a large semicircle. Note: The larger and more slowly the sign is made, the greater the distance in the future is meant.
Origin: indicating time before you and into the future
Usage: a good *future;* see progress *by and by; later* in the year; become wealthy *someday*

PAST, AGO, LAST, PREVIOUS, FORMER, USED TO, WAS, WERE

The open hand facing back moves backward over the right shoulder. The larger and more slowly the sign is made, the greater the distance in the past is meant. When the sign is moved back and forth slightly and quickly it means "recently" or "lately."
Origin: Movement back over the shoulder represents time behind you.
Usage: *past* president
　　　　long time *ago*
　　　　last month
　　　　previous occupation
　　　　former home
　　　　He *used to* drive.
　　　　Laura *was* here in May.
　　　　We *were* traveling all summer.

WAS—The right "W" is held up, palm toward the cheek; then the hand moves back, changing to an "S."

Note: This initial sign is not preferred by deaf adults but is used in educational settings with deaf children.

WERE—The right "W" is held up, palm toward the cheek then the hand moves back, changing to an "R."

Note: This initial sign is not preferred by deaf adults but is used in educational settings with deaf children.

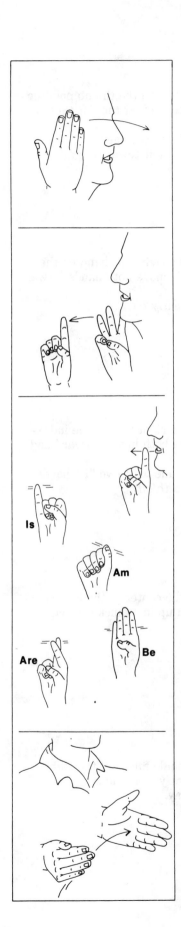

WILL, SHALL

Raised right arm with open palm toward cheek, moves forward. (This sign is used only as a verb.)
Origin: moving ahead toward the future
Usage: I *will* succeed.

WOULD

Place the right "W" near the side of the face, palm toward cheek; move the hand forward into a "D" position.
Origin: The sign for "will" becomes "would" when initials are used.
Usage: *Would* you flirt?

IS, AM, ARE, BE

Place the tip of the index finger at the mouth; move it forward, still upright.
Origin: This sign represents the verb "to be" and indicates that breath is still there.
Note: The initial signs described for *is, am, are, be, would, were,* and *was* are used to show clear distinctions between the words but are not usually used by deaf adults.
Usage: This *is* the way.
      Yes, I *am* angry.
      We *are* improving every day.
      How wonderful *to be* home again.
      She *was* in Mexico for a month.
      We *were* in St. Petersburg for a week.

AGAIN, REPEAT, OFTEN

The right curved hand faces up, then turns and moves to the left so that the fingertips touch the left palm which is pointing forward with the palm facing right. For "OFTEN" repeat the sign for "AGAIN" several times.
Usage: Say that *again.*
      Repeat that, please.
      I'd like to see Kathy more *often.*

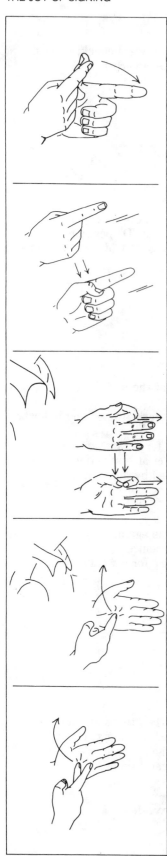

THEN

Place the left "L" in front of you with the thumb pointing up; then using the right index touch first the left thumb, then the left index finger.
Origin: first the thumb, then the next finger
Usage: First we packed, *then* we left town.

REGULAR

Place the little-finger edge of the right "G" hand on the index-finger edge of the left "G"; move both hands forward and strike together again.
Usage: went to the doctor *regularly*

FAITHFULLY

Place the little-finger edge of the right "F" on the index-finger edge of the left "F"; move both hands forward and strike them together again.
Origin: the sign for "regular" made with two "F" hands
Usage: Lowell attends church *faithfully.*

ONCE

Tip of the right index touches the center of the left palm and comes toward the body and up in a quick circular movement.
Usage: It happened *once.*

TWICE, DOUBLE

Touch the left palm with the middle finger of the right "TWO" hand and bring it toward you and up.
Usage: Take the pills *twice* a day.
　　　　 Double your money.

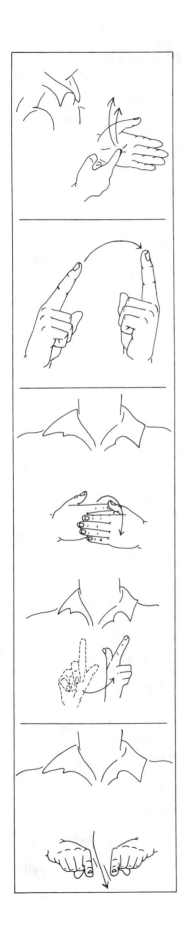

SOMETIMES, OCCASIONALLY, ONCE IN A WHILE

The sign for "ONCE" is repeated several times.
Usage: *Sometimes* we go swimming in the ocean.
The girls go biking *occasionally*.
We jog *once in a while* but not regularly.

UNTIL

Direct the right index finger in a forward arc and touch the left index which is pointing up.
Usage: It was hard to wait *until* summer for our vacation.

NEXT

The left open hand faces the body; the right open hand is placed between the left hand and the body and then passes over the left.
Origin: over and on the other side of the object
Usage: the *next* train

YOUR TURN, TAKE TURNS

When "next" is used to indicate that it is someone's turn, the following sign is usually used: Place the "L" before you palm out; make a quick turn to a palm-in position, the thumb of the "L" hand pointing toward the person whose turn it is.
Usage: *my turn; your turn; take turns* (For the latter, turn the palm back and forth several times.)

DURING, WHILE

Both index fingers, palms down and pointing forward, separated slightly, are pushed slightly down and then forward.
Origin: Hands moving forward show time moving on.
Usage: *during* the war
while we worked

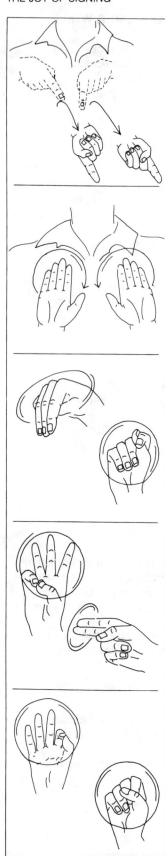

SINCE, ALL ALONG, EVER SINCE, HAS BEEN, FROM

Right index finger at right shoulder, left index finger in front of it; both index fingers are circled under-back-up-forward, ending with both index fingers facing up.
Origin: from the past to the present
Usage: *since* Wednesday; doing it *all along; ever since* childhood; deaf *from* birth; how long *has it been?*

SUNDAY

Both hands are held in front of the body, fingers pointing up and palms out. Both hands are moved in opposite circular motions.
Origin: represents the large open doors of the church
Usage: a quiet *Sunday* afternoon

MONDAY

The right "M" describes a small clockwise circle.
Usage: blue *Monday*

TUESDAY

The right "T" describes a small clockwise circle.
Usage: The program is planned for *Tuesday.*

WEDNESDAY

The right "W" describes a small clockwise circle.
Usage: a *Wednesday* afternoon appointment

THURSDAY

Form a "T" and an "H" and describe small clockwise circles. (Often made with the "H" only.)
Usage: You can ride with me on *Thursday.*

FRIDAY

The right "F" describes a small clockwise circle.
Usage: left for the weekend on *Friday*

SATURDAY

The right "S" describes a small clockwise circle.
Usage: a busy *Saturday*
Note: When referring to a regular day of the week such as "every Monday," "on Thursdays," etc., form the initial letter and draw the hand straight down (as if indicating all the Mondays in a row on the calendar).

4

Mental Action

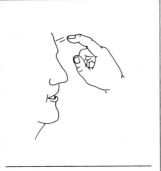

MIND, MENTAL, BRAIN

Tap the forehead with the curved index finger.
Origin: indicating the location of the mind
Usage: What's on your *mind?*
Good *mental* health is important.
The *brain* is very complex.

KNOW, KNOWLEDGE

Pat the forehead with fingertips.
Origin: a natural sign indicating knowledge
Usage: *Know* thyself!
A little *knowledge* can be dangerous.

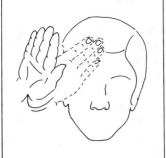

DON'T KNOW, DIDN'T KNOW

Sign "KNOW" and then turn the palm out away from the head.
Origin: "KNOW" + "NOT"
Usage: We really *don't know* everything.
He *didn't know* the answer.

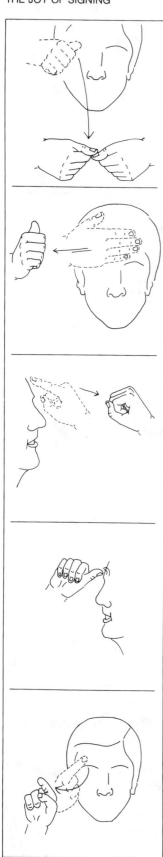

REMEMBER

Place the thumbnail of the right "A" on the forehead and then on the thumbnail of the left "A." (Originally the first part of the sign was "KNOWLEDGE" but later became the "A.")
Origin: knowledge that stays
Usage: *Remembering* names is not easy.

FORGET

Wipe across the forehead with the open hand, ending in the "A" position.
Origin: knowledge that has been wiped off the mind
Usage: Don't *forget* to call me next week.
   Forgetfulness can be a sign of age.

MEMORIZE

Touch the forehead with the index finger; then draw away into an "S."
Origin: The thought is firmly grasped.
Usage: Association helps you to *memorize* signs.

REMIND

Place the thumb of the "A" hand at the forehead and twist it. Or tap the right shoulder with the right hand.
Usage: *Remind* me about the appointment.

FOR

Point toward the right side of the forehead with the index finger; then circle downward and forward ending with the index finger pointing forward at eye level. When the sign is repeated quickly several times with a questioning look, it means, "What for?"
Usage: I have a gift *for* you!

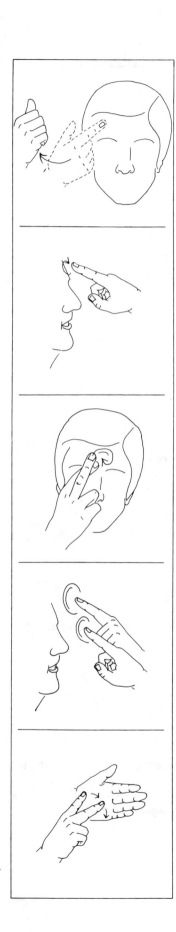

BECAUSE (SINCE, FOR)

Touch the forehead with the index finger; then draw it
slightly up and to the right forming an "A." (This sign is
sometimes begun with the open hand.) Note: When "for"
and "since" are used to mean "because," the sign for
"BECAUSE" should be used as in the examples below.
Usage: *Because* of her illness we could not respond. *Since*
we didn't know what to do we left. We can't go, *for*
it is raining.

THINK, THOUGHTS, MEDITATE, CONSIDER

The index finger faces the forehead and makes a small
circle. Two hands are sometimes used to show deep
thought.
Origin: Something is going around in the mind.
Usage: *think* deeply; kind *thoughts; meditate* often;
consider the problem

REASON

The "R" hand revolves in front of the forehead.
Origin: making the "THINK" sign with an "R"
Usage: My *reason* for coming here is obvious.

WONDER, CONCERN

Point one or both fingers toward the forehead and revolve
them slowly as in "THINK." The face should show a
concerned expression. (The right "W" is sometimes used.)
Origin: slow and deliberate thinking
Usage: Do you sometimes *wonder* about the future?
I have a deep *concern.*

MEAN, INTEND, PURPOSE

The fingertips of the right "V" are placed against the left
open hand, the "V" facing out; the "V" is turned and again
placed into the palm, the "V" facing in. Frequently the
right index touches the forehead before signing "INTENT"
or "PURPOSE."
Usage: What do you *mean?*
My nurse had good *intentions.*
What's the *purpose* behind all this activity?

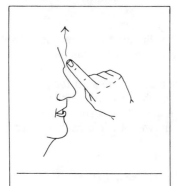

CLEVER, BRILLIANT, SMART, INTELLIGENT, BRIGHT

Index or middle finger touches the forehead and moves upward with a shaking motion.
Origin: The mind has brilliance.
Usage: *clever* idea
     brilliant scientist
     smart child
     intelligent speaker
     bright girl

IGNORANT

Place the back of the "V" on the forehead.
Usage: Lack of schooling left him *ignorant.*

STUPID, DUMB (Informal)

Strike the "A" hand against the forehead several times, palm facing in.
Origin: thick skull, hard to penetrate
Usage: For some reason he gave the impression he was *stupid,* but he was really smart.
     That was a *dumb* thing to do.

WISE, WISDOM

Crook the right index finger and move it up and down in front of the forehead, palm facing down.
Origin: indicating the depth of knowledge in the mind
Usage: a *wise* counselor
     the *wisdom* of Solomon

PHILOSOPHY

Place the right "P" in front of the forehead and move it up and down.
Origin: The sign for "wise" is initialized with a "P."
Usage: Have you studied the *philosophy* of Plato?

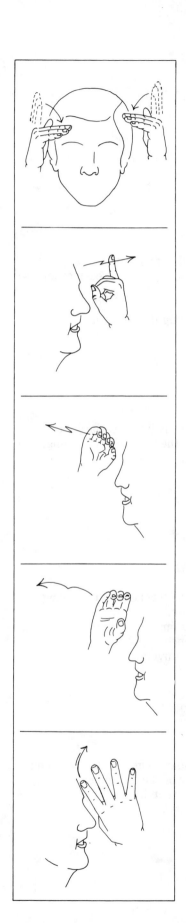

HOPE, EXPECT

Touch the forehead with the index finger; then raise the open palms so they face each other, the right hand near the right forehead and the left hand at the left. Both hands bend to a right angle and unbend simultaneously.
Origin: thinking and beckoning for something to come
Usage: *hope* for the best; *expect* changes

IDEA, SUPPOSE

Touch the forehead with the tip of the "I," palm facing in; move it forward, palm still facing in.
Origin: A little thought comes forward.
Usage: Explain your *idea*.
Suppose you received a million dollars. How would you spend it?

OPINION

Place the "O" in front of the forehead; move it forward.
Origin: The sign for "idea" is made with an "O."
Usage: Your *opinion* is valuable.

CONCEPT

Place the "C" in front of the forehead; move it forward.
Origin: The sign for "idea" is made with a "C."
Usage: the *concept* of equality

INVENT, DEVISE, MAKE UP, CREATE

The "FOUR" hand, index finger touching the center of the forehead, pushes upward the full length of the forefinger.
Origin: a thought coming out of the mind
Usage: Bell *invented* the telephone.
We *devised* a new method.
The child *made up* that story.
We saw the artist's latest *creation*.
Note: This sign is not used for the creation of the heavens and the earth.

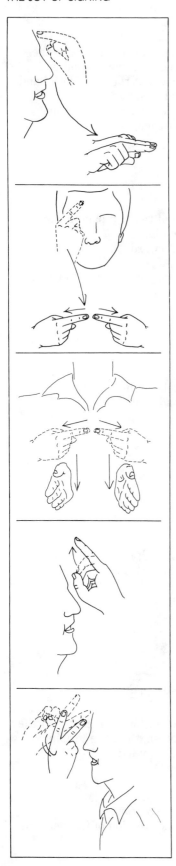

AGREE, CORRESPOND

Touch the forehead and then sign "SAME."
Origin: thinking the same
Usage: I *agree* with you.
      The stories of the two witnesses did not
      correspond.

DISAGREE

Touch the forehead with the index finger; then sign
"OPPOSITE" (index fingers pointing toward each other
pulled apart).
Origin: thinking opposite
Usage: *Disagree* without becoming disagreeable!

ENEMY, FOE, OPPONENT

Sign "OPPOSITE" (index fingers pointing toward each
other are pulled apart) and add the "PERSON" ending.
Usage: He made many *enemies.*
      There's my *opponent.*
      Are you friend or *foe?*

UNDERSTAND, COMPREHEND

Place the "S" hand in front of the forehead, palm facing
self, and snap the index finger up.
Origin: Suddenly the light goes on.
Usage: Do you *understand* French?
      I can't *comprehend* the universe.

MISUNDERSTAND

Touch the forehead with the index finger of the "V" hand
and then with the middle finger of the "V" hand.
Origin: The thought is turned around.
Usage: I'm sorry I *misunderstood.*

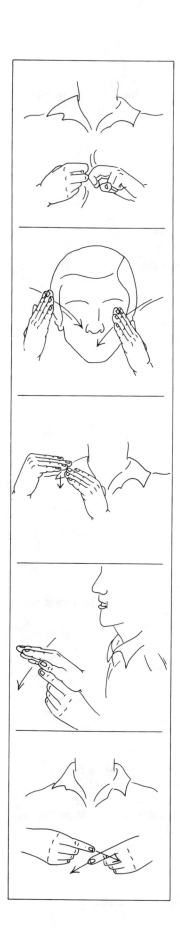

PROBLEM

Place the knuckles of the bent "V" hands together and twist them back and forth from the wrist.
Usage: a personal *problem*

WORRY, TROUBLE, CARE, ANXIOUS

Right open hand, palm facing left, passes in front of the face and down toward the left shoulder. Same motion is made alternately with the left hand several times.
Origin: Everything is coming at you.
Usage: *Worry* can cause illness.
   What's the *trouble?*
   Few people are free from *care.*
   When Joel didn't come home Roz became *anxious.*

BURDEN, BEAR, FAULT, OBLIGATED, RESPONSIBILITY

Place both hands on the right shoulder. "Responsibility" is often signed using the "R" hands in this position.
Origin: carrying a load on the shoulder
Usage: a heavy *burden;* difficult to *bear;* my *fault;* an
   obligation to my family; feeling *responsible*

PRESSURE

Hold up the left index finger, palm side to the right; place the palm of the right open hand against the left index and push forward.
Origin: bringing pressure to bear on someone
Usage: The students *pressured* their principal.
   He was working under *pressure.*

CONFLICT, CROSS-PURPOSES, CLASH

Hold the left index in front of you, palm facing right; move the right index (palm left) across it.
Origin: Instead of the index fingers being together as in "agree" they cross to show conflict.
Usage: They had *conflicting* opinions.
   We were at *cross-purposes.*
   Our ideas *clashed.*

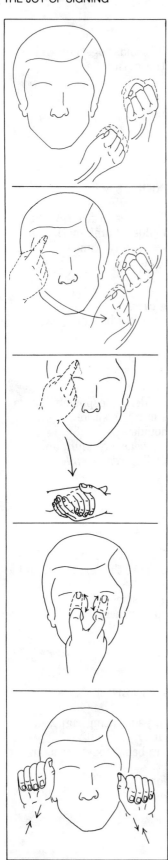

TRUST, CONFIDENCE

Bring both hands slightly to the left, closing them to "S" positions, the right one slightly below the left.
Origin: holding on to something
Usage: Jamie *trusts* his parents.
Have *confidence* in yourself.

FAITH

Touch the forehead with the index finger; raise both hands slightly to the left closing them into "S" positions with the left "S" above the right.
Origin: grasping the thought
Usage: very strong *faith*

BELIEVE

Touch the forehead with the index finger and clasp the hands.
Origin: holding on to the thought
Usage: I *believe* you're telling the truth.

DON'T BELIEVE, SKEPTICAL

Place the bent "V" in front of the eyes, palm in; crook and uncrook the "V" several times.
Usage: I *don't believe* that tale.
I'm *skeptical!*

DOUBT

Place the "A" hands in front of the face, palms facing forward, and move them up and down alternately. (Note: The above sign for "don't believe" is also used for "doubt.")
Origin: The up-and-down movement suggests uncertainty.
Usage: I have some *doubts* about that.

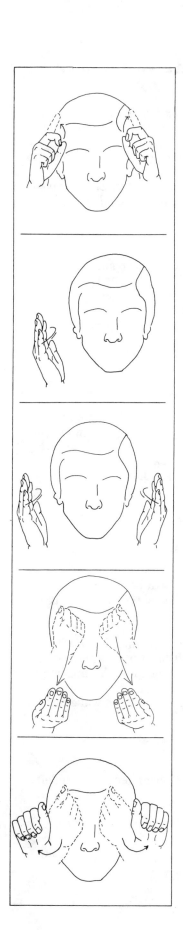

SURPRISE, ASTONISHED, AMAZED

Snap both index fingers up from the thumbs (other fingers closed) at the sides of the eyes.
Origin: eyes opened wide in surprise
Usage: a *surprise* party
astonishing news
amazed at the child's progress

SEEM, APPEAR, LOOK, APPARENTLY

Place the right curved hand, pointing up, at the side of the head and give it a quick turn so that the palm faces you. ("Look" may be signed by tracing a circle around the face.)
Origin: suddenly the palm appears
Usage: room *seems* warm; he *appears* confused; weather *looks* good; *apparently* went the wrong way

COMPARE

Make the sign for "APPEAR" with both hands and look at the palms as if comparing them.
Origin: comparing the palms
Usage: We *compared* our handwriting.

OBEY, OBEDIENCE

Both "A" hands, with palms facing the body, are dropped from eye level, opening into bent positions, facing up.
Origin: hands coming down in obedience
Usage: Why not *obey* the law?
My dog is *obedient.*

DISOBEY

Both "A" hands are in front of the face at eye level and then make a quick turn so that they face forward. (Sometimes made with only one hand.)
Origin: hands refusing to come down in obedience
Usage: Several soldiers *disobeyed* the order.

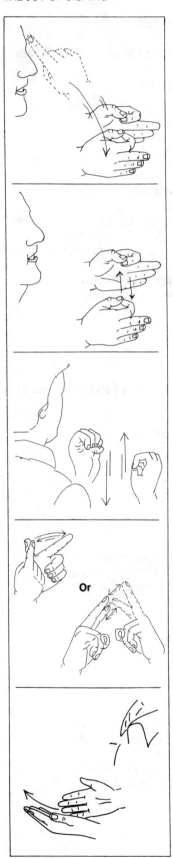

DECIDE, DETERMINE, RESOLVE, MAKE UP YOUR MIND

Touch the forehead with the index finger; then drop both hands in front of you into "F" positions, palms facing each other.

Origin: You have weighed the thoughts and have come to a decision.

Usage: The jury *decided.* I am *determined.* She *resolved* to do better. Julian *made up his mind.*

IF

Place the "F" hands in front of you, tips pointing forward and palms facing each other; raise and lower them alternately in short motions.

Origin: The thought is weighed.

Usage: Don't be frightened *if* you hear a noise.

EVALUATE

Place both the "E" hands in front of you; raise and lower them alternately.

Origin: Something is being weighed.

Usage: An expert will *evaluate* the plan.

OR, EITHER, NEITHER

Swing the right index back and forth between the thumb and index fingers of the left "L" hand. Or sign "WHICH." Or fingerspell.

Origin: Is it the thumb or the index finger?

Usage: one *or* the other; *either* book will be all right

EITHER (Alternate sign)—Left hand in "V" position; tips of right index and middle finger touch left "V" fingertips alternately.

NEITHER—Shake the head back and forth while making the sign.

ALL RIGHT, RIGHT

Place the right open hand (palm facing left) into the left open hand and move it forward.

Usage: That's *all right.*

You have a *right* to make your own decision.

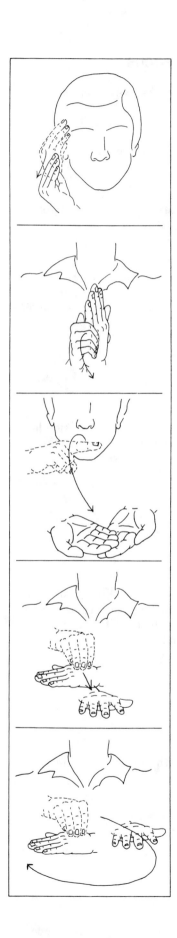

EXPERIENCE

Place the tips of the open "AND" hand at the right temple (at approximately eye level) and close to an "AND" position as you draw the hand slightly down and away from the head.
Origin: The hair at the temples is turning white (a person with experience is an older person).
Usage: Many years of *experience* made him an expert.

EXPERT, SKILLFUL, PROFICIENT, COMPETENT, EXPERIENCED

Grasp the lower edge of the left open hand with the right fingertips, which are closed against the palm, and pull away.
Usage: *expert* typist; *skilled* mechanic; *proficient* signer; *competent* physician; *experienced* teacher

PROVE, PROOF, EVIDENCE

Touch the mouth with the index finger; then place the back of the right open hand in the left palm.
Origin: Place it where one can see it.
Usage: *Prove* your point!
The judge wants *proof.*
Here's the *evidence.*

ADVISE, ADVICE, COUNSEL, AFFECT, INFLUENCE

Place the tips of the right "AND" hand on the back of the left open hand (palms down) and open the right as it is moved forward.
Usage: You cannot *advise* a fool. Wise men accept *advice.* Lawyers give *counsel.* Your mood *affects* me. We found a good marriage *counselor.* (Add "PERSON" ending.)
Note: This sign may be directed toward the signer to show that he is the recipient of the action.

INFLUENCE (Over more than one)

Place the fingertips of the right "AND" hand on the back of the left open hand (as in "ADVISE"); then circle left-forward-right.
Usage: The power of *influence* in a group is easily seen.

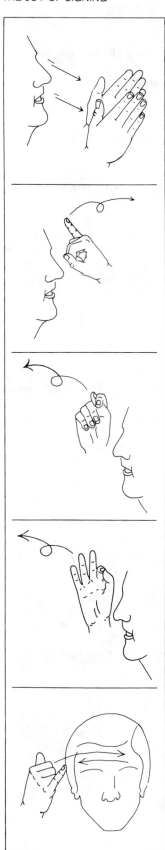

ATTENTION, CONCENTRATE, FOCUS

Place open hands at either side of the eyes; then move both hands forward. (Note: This sign is used for such phrases as "pay attention," "put your mind on it," "apply yourself.")
Origin: like blinders on a horse preventing one from looking to the right or the left
Usage: Please *pay attention.*
     I'm trying to *concentrate.*
FOCUS—The hands move forward and end with fingertips angling toward each other.

IMAGINATION

Place the "I" hand so that it faces the forehead; then circle it upward and away from the head two or three times. (This sign is frequently made with two hands, both hands making the sign alternately.)
Origin: thoughts floating around
Usage: Children have a wonderful *imagination.*

THEORY

Place the "T" hand in front of the forehead, palm side left; circle it upward and away from the head several times.
Origin: the sign for "imagination" made with a "T"
Usage: It's only a *theory* and not yet a fact.

FICTION, FANTASY

Place the "F" hand in front of the forehead, palm side left; circle it upward and away from the head several times.
Origin: the sign for "imagination" made with an "F"
Usage: Good *fiction* is educational.
     a childhood *fantasy*

FOOLISH, SILLY, ABSURD, RIDICULOUS

Shake the "Y" hand back and forth in front of the forehead several times, palm facing left.
Usage: *foolish* error
     silly girls
     absurd belief
     ridiculous action

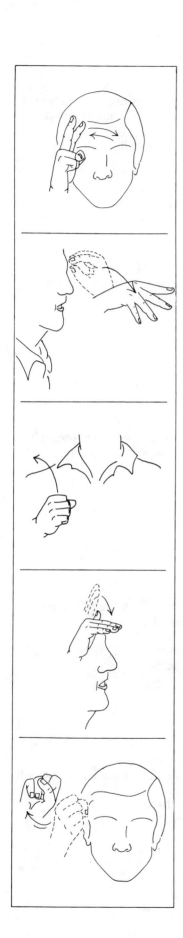

CARELESS

Pass the "V" hand back and forth in front of the forehead, palm facing to the left.
Usage: The fire started because of *careless* smoking.

DON'T CARE

Place the tips of the right "AND" hand on the forehead and open it as you turn it and throw it forward. Informally this sign is sometimes made from the nose with either the index finger or the tips of the "AND" hand.
Usage: I *don't care,* I'm going anyway.

REFUSE, WON'T

Hold up the right "S" hand, palm facing left, and draw it back forcefully toward the right shoulder. At the same time, the head turns slightly to the left.
Usage: He *refused* to cooperate.
      I *won't!*

STUBBORN, OBSTINATE

Place the thumb of the right open hand against the side of the head, palm facing forward, and bend the hand forward.
Origin: like a mule
Usage: That's a *stubborn* animal.
      He was *obstinate* and refused to listen.

REBEL, STRIKE

Hold up the right "S" and give it an outward twist.
Origin: represents the head turning suddenly away
Usage: *rebel* against authority
      workers went on *strike*

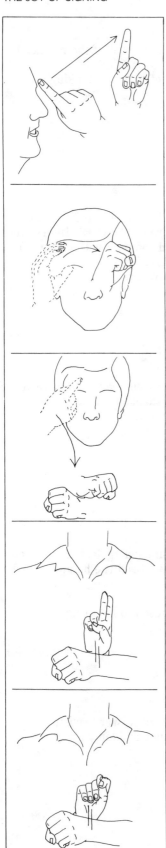

GOAL, AIM, OBJECTIVE

Touch the forehead with the right index finger and move it toward the left index which is held higher and is pointing up.
Origin: The left hand is the goal; the right hand works toward it.
Usage: What is your *goal* in life?
   Aim for perfection.
   Can you explain your *objective?*

GUESS

Place the right "C" hand near the right side of the forehead and pass the hand before the face, ending with the "S" position.
Origin: Catch it in the air.
Usage: *Guess* what happened.

HABIT, CUSTOM, ACCUSTOMED

Place the right index at the forehead, then place the right "A" (palm down) on the wrist of the left "S" (palm leftward); push downward.
Origin: Your mind is bound to an action.
Usage: a reading *habit*
   It was his *custom* to rise early.
   accustomed to the good life

USUALLY, USED TO

Place the inside wrist of the right "U" on the left wrist (left hand closed); push down slightly.
Origin: an initial sign based on "habit"
Usage: It *usually* snows in January.
   I'm not *used to* all that noise.

TRADITION

Place the inside wrist of the right "T" on the left wrist (left hand closed); push down slightly.
Origin: an initial sign based on "habit"
Usage: Some *traditions* are very strong.

BUT, HOWEVER

Cross the index fingers, palms facing out, and draw them apart.
Origin: based on the sign for "different"; *but* suggests a difference
Usage: The car is old *but* looks new.
We don't have money; *however,* we will borrow.

JOIN, UNITE, OF

Hook the right index and thumb into the left index and thumb (other three fingers separated). "OF" is usually fingerspelled.
Origin: showing a connection
Usage: Mr. Morgan *joined* the organization.
He *united* with the church.
The land *of* the free.

CONNECTION, COMBINE, BELONG TO, RELATIONSHIP, ASSOCIATION, LINK, APPLY (Relate to)

Sign "JOIN" and move the hands in this position away from yourself and back several times.
Usage: I don't see any *connection.* We *combined* our efforts. She *belongs* to a health club. We have a good *relationship.* We *associate* daffodils with spring. His name is *linked* to the project. The rule *applies* to us.

COOPERATION, UNITED

Sign "JOIN" and move the hands in this position right-forward-left in a circular motion.
Usage: We all *cooperated* in the project.
We *united* as a group.

DISCONNECT, RELEASE, LET GO

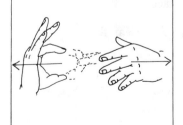

The hands in the "JOIN" position are disconnected.
Origin: releasing your connection
Usage: Our phone was *disconnected* yesterday.
I'm glad to be *released* from the obligation.
He refused to *let go* of his responsibilities.

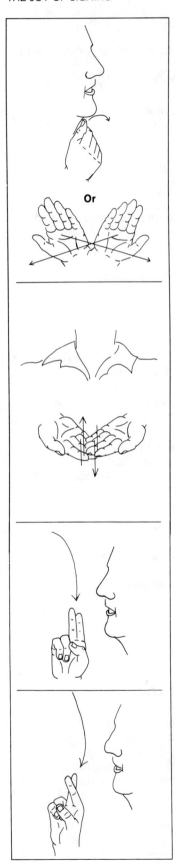

Or

NOT, DON'T, DOESN'T, DIDN'T

Place the thumb of the right "A" hand under the chin and direct it forward.
Or more formally: Cross the open hands before you, palms down, and draw them apart.
Origin: natural sign for the negative
Usage: I'm *not* planning any trips soon.
  Don't wait for me because I have to work late.
  Bill *doesn't* smoke anymore.
  He *didn't* think it was good for him.

NO MATTER, NEVERTHELESS, ANYHOW, IN SPITE OF, REGARDLESS, EVEN THOUGH, THOUGH, ALTHOUGH, DOESN'T MATTER, ANYWAY

Brush the tips of both hands up and down several times, palms facing up.
Usage: It *doesn't matter* about your age.
  She had a headache; *nevertheless,* she worked.
  I'm going *anyhow* (or *anyway.*)
  He came *in spite of* his negative feelings.
  I'll buy the TV *regardless* of cost.
  He came *even though* he had a bad cold.
  Though (or *although*) it rained, they went camping.
  Any color is all right; it *doesn't matter.*

HONOR

Bring the "H" hand toward the face and down, ending with the "H" fingers pointing up.
Usage: He brought *honor* to his school.

RESPECT

Bring the "R" hand toward the face and down, ending with the "R" fingers pointing up.
Usage: We show *respect* for the American flag.

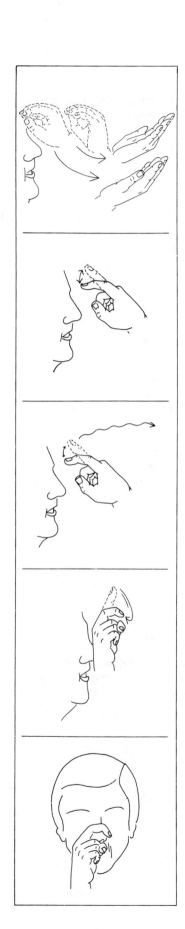

INFORM, INFORMATION, NEWS, NOTIFY

Place the "AND" hands at the forehead; move them down
and away from you, ending with open palms up.
Origin: Knowledge is passed on to others.
Usage: Be sure to *inform* your lawyer.
   The *information* came through the newspaper.
   Did you receive any *news?*
   We *notified* all members.

SUSPECT, SUSPICION, SUSPICIOUS

Crook and uncrook the index finger in front of the forehead
several times (palm facing self).
Origin: question in the mind
Usage: The police *suspected* the man.
   My *suspicions* were true.
   His actions made me *suspicious.*

DREAM

Touch the forehead with the index finger and draw it
away, crooking and uncrooking the finger several times,
palm facing you.
Origin: the mind going off into fantasies
Usage: *Dreams* sometimes come true.

PUZZLED

Draw the back of the index finger toward the forehead and
crook it.
Origin: a question in the mind
Usage: That *puzzles* me!

FOOL

Place the crooked right index against the nose and move
the head down slightly as if the finger is pulling the head
down.
Usage: Don't try to *fool* me.

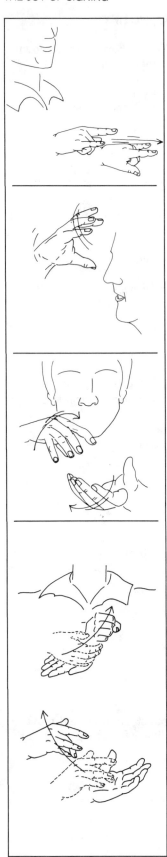

DECEIVE, BETRAY, TRICK

Place the right "Y" hand (with the index finger extended) on the back of the left hand, which is in a similar position, and slide it forward lengthwise across the back of the left.
Usage: I suspect that she *deceived* us.
The spy *betrayed* his country.
The children *tricked* us at Halloween.

CRAZY

Place the curved "FIVE" hand at the side of the forehead and give the hand a quick twist in and out several times. Or point the right index finger toward the forehead and circle several times.
Origin: brains are twisted
Usage: People accused the Wright brothers of being *crazy*.

FOULED UP, BUNGLED, TOPSY-TURVY, CONFUSED

Place the curved "FIVE" hands before you, one palm-up the other palm-down. Twist them into reversed positions.
Usage: That really *fouled up* our plans. The electrician *bungled* the job. The house was *topsy-turvy* after the children left. Her mind is *confused*.
Note: This sign preceded by "mind" refers to mental confusion.

TAKE ADVANTAGE OF

The right curved hand (palm left) sweeps across the left palm, ending in an "S" position.
Usage: Why not *take advantage of* this opportunity?
Note: In a negative sense a different sign is made. Touch the left palm with the right middle finger (other fingers extended); draw the right hand toward yourself and then up quickly. Example: She *took advantage of* my ignorance.

NOTES

a strong *will*—"MIND"
willpower—"MIND" + "POWER" or "DETERMINATION"
realize—"KNOW" or "UNDERSTAND"
resemble—"APPEAR" + "SAME"

5

Emotion and Feeling

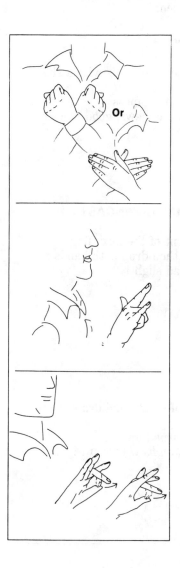

LOVE, DEAR

The "S" hands are crossed at the wrist and pressed to the heart. (Or use the open hands.)
Origin: pressing to one's heart
Usage: my first *love*
our *dear* friend

I LOVE YOU

Form a combination of "I," "L," and "Y" (thumb, index, and little finger extended) and direct the palm forward or toward the intended person.
Usage: I saw the little girl say, *"I love you."*

HATE, DETEST, DESPISE

Snap the middle fingers of both hands as the hands are pushed away from you.
Origin: pushing away
Usage: I *hate* to clean house.
He *detests* arrogance.
Honest people *despise* lying.

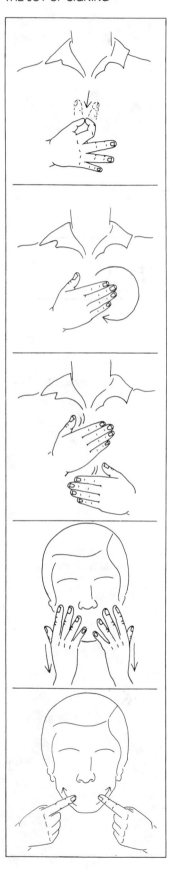

LIKE

Place the thumb and forefinger against the chest (other fingers separated) and draw them away from the body, closing the two fingers. Or use the sign for "PLEASE" described below.

Origin: The heart is drawn toward an object.
Usage: Who *likes* ice cream?
Note: To indicate that you do not like, simply shake the head negatively while signing "like."

PLEASE, PLEASURE, ENJOY, LIKE

Rub the chest with the open hand in a circular motion. When indicating great pleasure, two hands are frequently used, each one circling toward the center.

Origin: rubbing the heart to indicate pleasure
Usage: *Please* come for a visit.

It's a *pleasure* to see you.
They *enjoyed* their swim.
I *like* spaghetti very much.

HAPPY, GLAD, REJOICE, JOY

The open hands pat the chest several times with a slight upward motion.

Origin: patting the chest shows happiness
Usage: feel *happy; glad* to hear the news; good news made people *rejoice;* full of *joy*

SAD, DEJECTED, SORROWFUL, DOWNCAST

Hold both "FIVE" hands in front of the face, fingers slightly apart and pointing up; then drop both hands a short distance and bend the head slightly.

Origin: long-faced and gloomy
Usage: a *sad* face

dejected because he left
a *sorrowful* event
She looked *downcast.*

LAUGH

Place index fingers at corners of mouth and draw them upward several times.

Origin: corners of the mouth turned up
Usage: "*Laugh* and the world *laughs* with you . . . ."

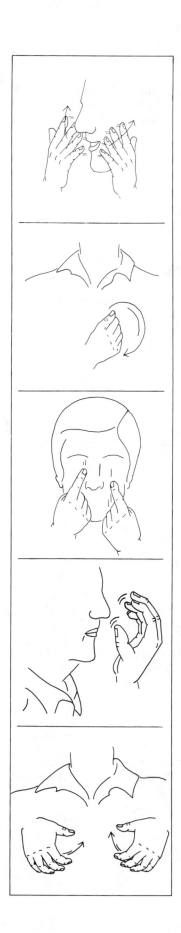

SMILE, CHEERFUL, PLEASANT, FRIENDLY

Place the "FIVE" hands near the sides of the mouth; wiggle the fingers as the hands are moved outward and upward toward the ear.
Origin: smiling from ear to ear
Usage: beautiful *smile*
   cheerful bus driver
   pleasant people
   friendly teacher

SORRY, REGRET, APOLOGIZE

Rub the "A" hand in a circular motion over the heart.
Origin: indicating pressure on the heart
Usage: I'm *sorry.*
   I *regret* my words.
   Did you *apologize?*

CRY, WEEP, TEARS

Draw the index fingers down the cheeks from the eyes several times.
Origin: tears coursing down the cheeks
Usage: Please don't *cry!*
   Beth *wept* for joy.
   no more *tears*

CROSS, GROUCHY

The curved hand, with fingers slightly separated, is bent and unbent several times in front of the face, palm in.
Origin: The face is twisted.
Usage: The teacher was *cross.*
   grouchy every morning

ANGER, WRATH

Place the curved "FIVE" hands against the waist and draw up against the sides of the body.
Origin: tearing the clothes in anger
Usage: He spoke with *anger.*
   He was full of *wrath.*

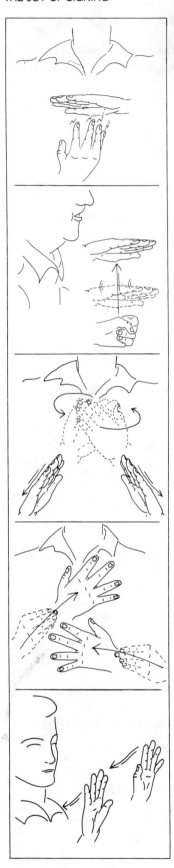

BOILING, BURNING (in anger)

Wiggle the curved right "FIVE" hand under the downturned left palm which is held close to the body.
Origin: simulates the action of boiling water
Usage: I watched his face and he was really *boiling*.

BLOWUP, BLOWING ONE'S TOP

Place the right palm on the left "S" (which is in a palm-right position); lift the palm off in a shaking motion.
Origin: The lid blew off.
Usage: We had a *blowup* in the office yesterday.
          The boss *blew his top!*

PEACE

The right palm is placed on the left palm and then turned so the left palm is on top; both hands, palms down, move down and toward the sides.
Origin: a handshake of peace
Usage: People want *peace,* not war.
          The forest looked so *peaceful.*

AFRAID, SCARED, FRIGHTENED, TERRIFY

Hold both "AND" hands in front of the chest, fingers pointing toward each other; then open both hands and move the right hand toward the left and the left hand toward the right, palms facing self.
Usage: *afraid* to swim; *scared* to death; *frightened* by the
          noise; earthquakes *terrify* people

FEAR, DREAD

Both "FIVE" hands are held up at the left side, palms facing out, right hand behind left. Draw both hands toward self with a slight shaking motion from the wrist.
Origin: hands held up to ward off danger
Usage: Do you *fear* snakes?
          My cat *dreads* water.

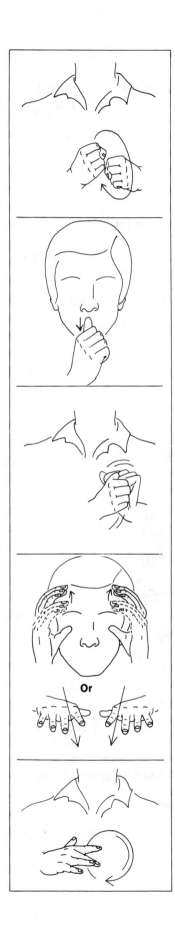

SUFFERING, AGONY

The right "S" revolves forward and around the left "S," both palms facing self. The sign is made with feeling.
Origin: inner turmoil
Usage: His *suffering* was almost more than he could bear.
    The patient seemed to be in great *agony*.
Note: In a variation of this sign the thumbtip of the "A" hand is placed at the chin and twisted back and forth.

PATIENT, ENDURE, BEAR, SUFFER, PUT UP WITH, STAND

Place the thumbnail of the right "A" against the lips and draw downward.
Origin: closing the mouth and suffering in silence
Usage: Mothers need *patience*.
    can't *endure* anymore
    How can you *bear* the noise?
    suffered with a toothache
    Can you *put up with* those neighbors?
    I can't *stand* it.

GRIEF, CRUSHED

Place the "A" hands together, palm to palm, and twist them near the heart.
Origin: The heart is crushed.
Usage: My heart was *grieved*.
    He was *crushed* when he heard the sad news.

SHOCKED, DUMBFOUNDED

Place the "C" hands at the sides of the eyes; open the "C"s to become larger.
Origin: The eyes open wide suddenly.
Or both open "FIVE" hands, palms facing down, are pushed slightly forward while the body suddenly straightens.
Origin: The body stiffens.
Usage: His language *shocked* his mother.
    The announcement *shocked* everyone.
    I was *dumbfounded*.

APPRECIATE

With the right hand in a "FIVE" position, use the middle finger to draw a circle over the heart (left-down-right-up).
Origin: touching the heart to show appreciation
Usage: We *appreciate* your assistance.

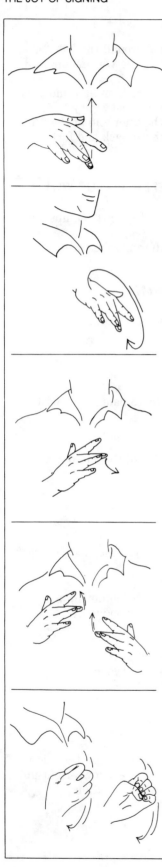

FEEL, SENSATION

Place the tip of the middle finger against the chest with the other fingers extended; draw it up a short distance.
Origin: The finger feels the heart.
Usage: What do you *feel*?
      That's an odd *sensation*.

MERCY, PITY, COMPASSION, SYMPATHY

Sign "FEEL" and, still using the middle finger, stroke an imaginary person in front of you (with one or two hands).
Origin: Feeling is extended toward an object.
Usage: show *mercy; pity* the dog; have *compassion;* letter
      of *sympathy*
Note: Use also for "poor you" or "poor thing."

FEEL HURT

Touch the heart with the middle finger of the right "FIVE" hand; give the hand a quick twist outward.
Usage: Did you *feel hurt* when he left you?

EXCITED, THRILLED, STIMULATED

Alternately brush the middle fingertips of the "FIVE" hands upward on the chest several times.
Origin: The feelings are stirred.
Usage: very *excited* about the trip
      thrilled with the award
      Work *stimulates* him.

EMOTION

The sign for "FEEL" is used in the "E" position, alternating the right and the left hand in upward circular motions.
Origin: feelings from the heart, using the initial letter
Usage: Ann has strong *emotions*.

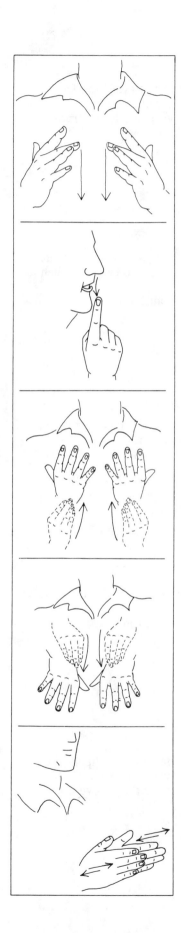

DISCOURAGED, DISAPPOINTED

Both middle fingers move down the chest side by side.
Origin: feelings sink
Usage: felt lonely and *discouraged*
The loser was *disappointed.*
Note: "Disappointed" may be signed by placing the tip of the index finger on the chin. (See p. 145, "miss.")

LONELY, LONESOME

Draw the index finger down across the lips, palm facing left.
Origin: silent and alone
Usage: *lonely* and without a friend
lonesome and alone in the city

INSPIRED

Place the closed "AND" hands against the front of the body at the waist (pointing upward, palm side in); move both hands up, gradually opening to a "FIVE" position at the chest.
Origin: Life and feelings rise to the surface.
Usage: Music can *inspire!*

DEPRESSED

Place the closed "AND" hands on the chest (pointing downward with palm side toward chest); move both hands down, opening to a "FIVE" position.
Origin: Inner feelings move down and inward.
Usage: Losing a job can be very *depressing.*

ENTHUSIASTIC, EAGER, ZEALOUS, INDUSTRIOUS, ANXIOUS

Flat hands, palm to palm, are rubbed together.
Origin: a natural motion indicating enthusiasm
Usage: full of *enthusiasm*
always *eager* to please
show *zeal* for your program
working *industriously*
anxious to learn new signs

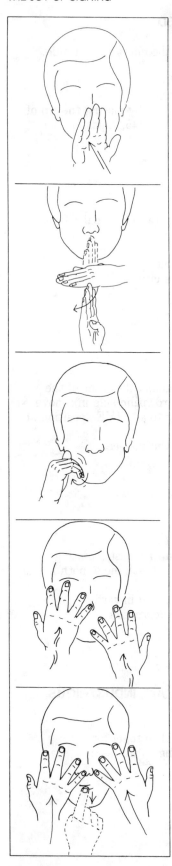

FRUSTRATED

The back of the hand moves abruptly toward the face.
Origin: coming up against a stone wall
Usage: He couldn't finish the paper and felt *frustrated.*

HUMBLE, MEEK

The right "B" is placed against the lips, palm facing left,
and is then passed down and under the left hand, which is
open with palm facing down.
Origin: One is willing to be under authority.
Usage: a *humble* log cabin
     meek, not boastful

ASHAMED, SHAME

The back of the curved hand is placed against the cheek,
palm down, and is then turned until the palm faces back.
Origin: hiding the face behind the hand
Usage: *ashamed* of himself
     felt *shame* and anger
Note: When saying, "Shame on you," start as above but
continue away from your face.

EMBARRASS, BASHFUL, SHY

Hands move upward alternately in front of the face (palms
in).
Origin: wanting to hide the face with the hands to cover
confusion
Usage: easily *embarrassed*
     young and *bashful*
     shy, not bold

BLUSH

Sign "RED" (brush index finger down across lips); then
place the "AND" hands, palms toward the face, at the
sides of the cheeks and open hands as they move up.
Origin: face becoming red
Usage: Darlene *blushes* easily.

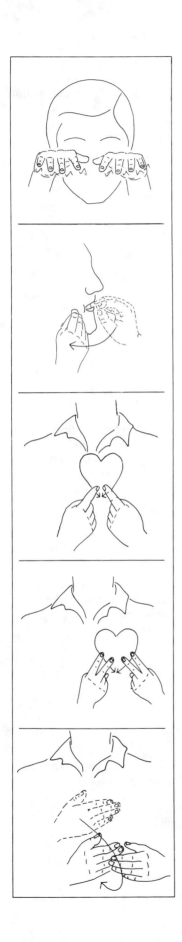

FLIRT

Place the thumbs of the "FIVE" hands together, palms facing down in front of the face (or just below it); wiggle the fingers.
Origin: the fluttering eyelashes
Usage: He *flirted* and she blushed.

KISS

Place the fingertips at the mouth and then on the cheek.
Origin: a kiss on the mouth and cheek
Usage: He *kissed* her good-bye.

HEART

Trace a heart on the chest with index fingers. (The middle fingers may be used instead.)
Origin: natural sign
Usage: from the bottom of my *heart*

VALENTINE

Use the "V" hands to trace a heart on the chest.
Origin: initializing the "heart" sign
Usage: Trixie received a pretty *valentine*.

KIND, GRACIOUS

The open hand is placed on the body over the heart and is then moved up-out-in-up around the left open hand which faces the body pointing to the right.
Origin: as if winding a bandage around the arm
Usage: a *kind* father
a *gracious* lady

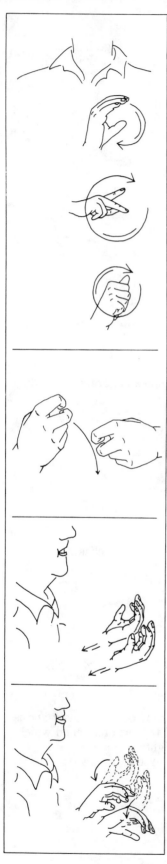

CHARACTER

Make a circle over the heart with the right "C" hand, palm facing left.
Origin: the initial letter over the heart
Usage: a man of good and strong *character*

PERSONALITY

Make a circle over the heart with the right "P" hand.
Usage: a pleasant *personality*

ATTITUDE

Make a circle over the heart with the right "A."
Usage: an *attitude* toward women

MEANNESS

The knuckles of the bent right middle and index fingers strike the knuckles of the left bent middle and index fingers in a sharp downward stroke (palms facing self).
Origin: a quick striking motion
Usage: *mean* little boys

WANT, DESIRE, LONGING

Place both curved "FIVE" hands in front of you, palms up, and draw them toward you several times.
Origin: drawing an object toward oneself
Usage: *want* a new car
    desire your advice
    a *longing* for home

DON'T WANT

Place both curved "FIVE" hands in front of you, palms up; turn them over quickly to a palms-down position.
Origin: Wants are turned down.
Usage: I *don't want* to leave.
    Tom *doesn't want* to work.

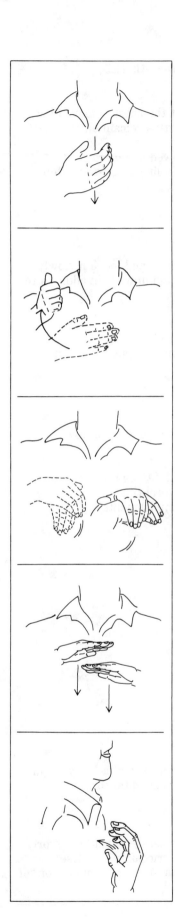

WISH

Place the "C" hand just below the throat, palm facing in, and draw it down.
Origin: This is the sign for "hunger."
Usage: I *wish* I could travel around the world.

RATHER, PREFER

Place the open hand on the chest; move the hand away toward the right and up into an "A" position. (An alternate sign for "prefer" is to touch the chin with the middle finger.)
Origin: a combination of the signs for "like" and "better"
Usage: I'd *rather* fly than drive.
　　　　prefer dark meat

COMFORTABLE, COMFORT

Using curved hands, stroke forward first on the back of the left and then on the back of the right hand.
Origin: stroking the hands as if warming them
Usage: *comfortable* in front of the fireplace
　　　　needing *comfort* at this time

SATISFY, CONTENT, RELIEVED

Both open hands, palms down, are placed against the chest, right above the left, and pushed down.
Origin: Inner feelings are quieted.
Usage: *Satisfy* your desire.
　　　　content with your decision
　　　　heard the news and felt *relieved*

COMPLAIN, OBJECT, PROTEST, GRIEVANCE, GRIPE, MIND

The curved "FIVE" hand is placed against the chest in a quick movement.
Usage: *complained* about the service in the restaurant
　　　　I *object* to that.
　　　　a written *protest*
　　　　Discuss your *grievance*.
　　　　always *griping*
　　　　I hope you don't *mind*.

DISCONTENT, DISSATISFIED, DISGUSTED, AGGRAVATED

The curved "FIVE" hand against the chest is moved back and forth slightly while the fingertips remain on the chest.
Origin: Inner feelings are stirred.
Usage: Her facial expression showed her *discontent.*
constant *dissatisfaction;* feeling *disgusted;* often *aggravated*

PRIDE, PROUD, ARROGANT

Place the "A" hand against the chest and move it slowly upward. For "arrogant" tilt the chin upward in addition to using the "A" hand.
Origin: inner feelings rise
Usage: *pride* in your success
proud parents
Arrogance makes a person unpopular.

BOAST, BRAG

Place the "A" hand against the chest and push upward in several short, quick movements.
Origin: self pushed forward
Or place the thumbtip of the right "A" against the side of the body just above the waist several times.
Usage: *boasting* about your accomplishments
Bragging again?

VAIN, VANITY

Place the "V" hands in front of you, palms facing you, and move the "V" fingers up and down simultaneously.
Origin: all eyes looking at me
Usage: beautiful but *vain*
Vanity tends to alienate.
Note: This sign is not used in the sense of fruitless effort, futility, or uselessness, as in "He tried *in vain.*" Use substitute words such as, "without success," "failed," or "of no use."

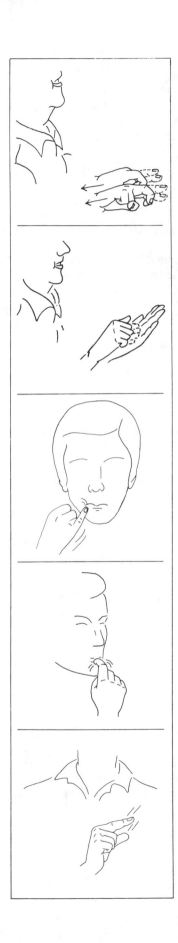

SELFISH

Point the "V" hands forward (palms down) and draw them back toward you, crooking the fingers.
Origin: drawing everything toward oneself
Usage: He was *selfish* and refused to share.

STINGY, MISERLY

Use the right hand in a clawed position and scrape the center of the left palm. (Although made by some as scraping downward on the chin, the sign pictured is preferred.)
Usage: He was careful with his money, not *stingy*.
  Mr. Scrooge, a *miserly* old man

JEALOUS

Place the "J" finger in the corner of the mouth and twist it.
Origin: The corner of the mouth is turned down.
Usage: Timmy is *jealous* of his new baby brother.
Note: This sign may be interchanged with the following one.

ENVY

Bite the end of the index finger.
Origin: biting the finger in envy
Usage: His skill made me *envious*.
Note: This sign and the one above may be interchanged.

CONSCIENCE, GUILTY

Place the side of the right "G" against the heart and strike several times.
Origin: indicates the beating of the heart, feeling guilty
Usage: His *conscience* is bothering him.
  Do you feel *guilty* about doing that?

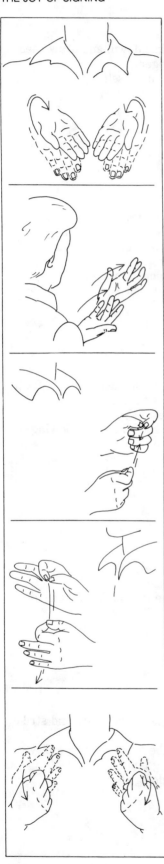

CONFESS, ADMIT

With fingertips pointing downward, place both hands against the body, draw them up and forward, ending with open hands facing up.
Origin: That which is within is brought out into the open.
Usage: an honest *confession*
I *admit* my ignorance.

TEND, TENDENCY, INCLINED TOWARD

Hands open, middle fingers extended slightly, palms facing up; right middle finger touches heart, then moves upward and away from the body. The left hand moves in exactly the same way, but is farther away from the body.
Origin: feelings are extended
Usage: *tend* to gain weight
inclined toward outdoor activities

REVENGE, GET EVEN

Strike the fingertips of the modified "A" together several times (palms facing in).
Origin: picking at each other
Usage: I will *get even* (take revenge).

UNFAIR

The fingertips of the right "F" (palm facing left) move downward in a quick motion, touching and passing the left "F" (palm right).
Origin: as if striking something
Usage: That's *not fair*.
a grievance about *unfair* treatment

COURAGEOUS, BRAVE

Place the tips of the "FIVE" hands high on the chest near the shoulders and bring them forward into "S" positions.
Usage: He had the *courage* to stand up for his beliefs.
the land of the free, and the home of the *brave*

6

People, Occupations, and Money

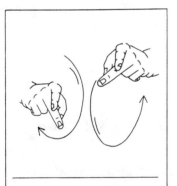

PEOPLE

Using both "P" hands, circle them alternately toward the center.
Usage: The U.S. government is responsible to the American *people.*

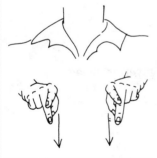

PERSON, PERSONAL

With both hands in the "P" position bring the hands down in front of the body, a short distance apart.
Usage: a fine *person*
her *personal* business

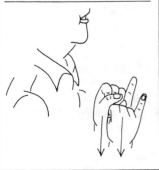

INDIVIDUAL

Both "I" hands facing each other are brought down in front of the body, a short distance apart. For the plural, repeat, moving the sign slightly to the right. (Some prefer to use the open hand, palms pointing forward.)
Usage: We worked as *individuals,* each one responsible for part of the project.

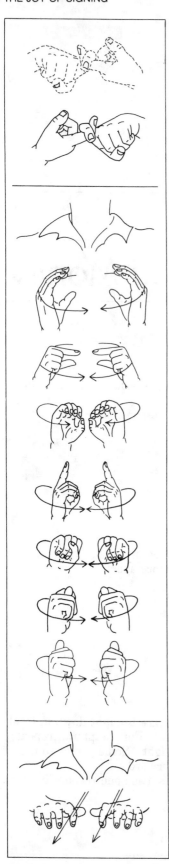

FRIEND

Hook the right index over the left which is palm-up and repeat in reverse.
Origin: representing a close-knit association
Usage: my best *friend*

GROUP, CLASS, COMMUNITY, ORGANIZATION, DEPARTMENT, SOCIETY, TEAM

Place the "C" hands in front of you; draw them apart to the sides and around to the front until the little fingers touch.
Note: Use of the "C" hands encompasses any group. Distinctions may be made by initializing as follows:

C—CLASS, COMMUNITY
Usage: a *class* in school; a *community* of nuns

G—GROUP
Usage: a *group* of doctors

O—ORGANIZATION
Usage: a women's *organization*

D—DEPARTMENT
Usage: *Department* of Health, Education, and Welfare

S—SOCIETY
Usage: the Ladies' Aid *Society;* interested in *social* work

T—TEAM
Usage: We're proud of our college *team.*

A—ASSOCIATION, AGENCY
Usage: a scientific *association;* a government *agency*

W + S—WORKSHOP
See illustration on page 201.

AUDIENCE

Place the curved "FIVE" hands in front of you, palms down, and move them forward.
Origin: rows of people in front of you
Usage: We were surprised to see such a large *audience.*

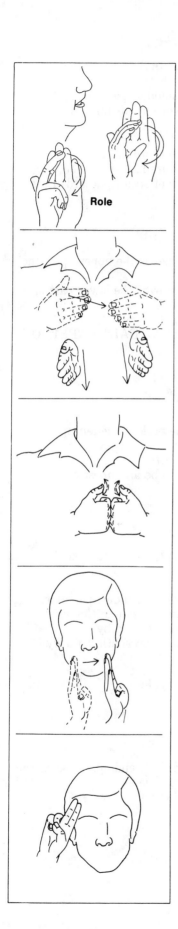

Role

CHARACTER, ROLE

Place the right "C" against the left palm and move it forward in a complete circle. For "ROLE" use the right "R" as above.
Usage: a *character* in the play
What is your *role?*

NEIGHBOR

Sign "NEAR" (the back of the right bent hand approaches the inside of the left bent hand, both palms facing the body); add the "PERSON" ending.
Origin: a person who lives nearby
Usage: a good *neighbor*

NEIGHBORHOOD—Sign "NEAR"; then make a sweeping counterclockwise movement with the right downturned "FIVE" hand.

SWEETHEART

Place both "A" hands together, palms facing the body; bend and unbend the thumbs.
Origin: two people nodding to each other
Usage: *sweethearts* since childhood

BACHELOR

Place the right "B" first at the right side of the chin, then at the left.
Usage: a popular *bachelor*

SCOUTS

Place the index tip of the right "U" at the forehead (or use a three-finger salute).
Origin: the scout salute
Usage: the Boy *Scouts* of America

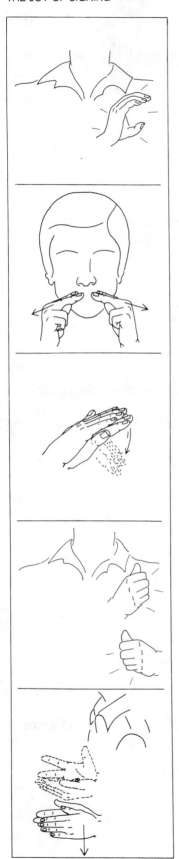

POLICE, COP, SECURITY (see note)

Place the right "C" at the left shoulder, palm facing left.
Origin: the policeman's badge worn on his uniform
Usage: The *police* protected us.
　　Call the *cops!*
Note: When "security" is used to represent law enforcement officers, this sign is used. A suggested usage would be the following: Members of *security* guarded the president.

THIEF, ROBBER

Use both "N" hands and stroke across the upper lip to the sides.
Origin: indicating the mask worn over the lower part of the face
Usage: The *thief* stole a bicycle.
Note: "Robber" may be signed as "STEAL" + "PERSON" ending.

HYPOCRITE, IMPOSTOR

Place the right open hand on the back of the left open hand; bend both hands together.
Usage: They felt he was a *hypocrite*.
　　His actions showed him to be an *impostor*.

SOLDIER, ARMY

Place the right "A" against the left shoulder, palm facing the body, and the left "A" on the left side of the waist. (The sign for "ARMY" should be followed by the "GROUP" sign made with a "C," representing a body of soldiers.)
Origin: soldier presenting arms
Usage: tomb of the unknown *soldier*
　　a large *army*

SAILOR

Sign "SHIP" and add the "PERSON" ending. Or show the bell-bottom trousers with the open hands.
Usage: Our *sailors* arrived in Hong Kong.

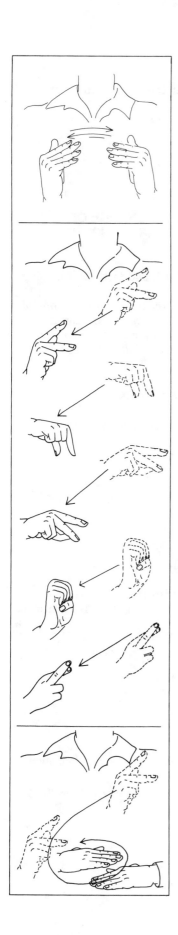

WAR, BATTLE

Place the bent "FOUR" hands in front of the body, fingertips pointing toward each other, palms down; move the hands first to the right, then to the left in front of you.
Origin: the armies forcing each other back, first one and then the other
Usage: marching to *war*
         The *battle* is over.

KING

Place the right "K" against the left shoulder, then against the right waist.
Origin: the initial letter combined with the stole worn by royalty
Usage: the *king* of England

QUEEN

Sign as in "KING" using a "Q."
Usage: *queen* for a day

PRINCE, PRINCESS

Sign as in "KING" using a "P."
Usage: the student *prince*
Note: For *princess,* precede this sign with "GIRL."

EMPEROR

Sign as in "KING" using an "E."
Usage: the *emperor* of Japan

ROYAL

Sign as in "KING" using an "R."
Usage: the *royal* throne

KINGDOM

Sign "KING" and then make a counterclockwise circle with the right open hand over the left open hand, both palms down.
Origin: a combination of the sign for "KING" and "OVER" showing his authority over the land
Usage: ruler of a great *kingdom*

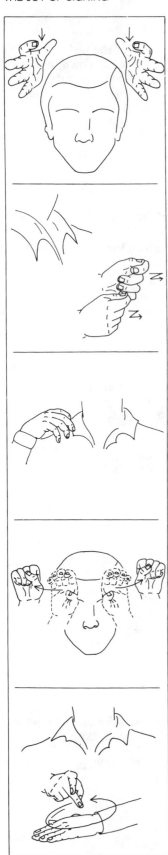

CROWN, DIADEM

Bring both "C" hands down over the head (with other fingers extended).
Origin: placing a crown on the head
Usage: a golden *crown*
a royal *diadem*

REIGN, RULE, CONTROL, RUN, IN CHARGE OF, CONDUCT, MANAGE, GOVERN, DIRECTING, DISCIPLINE, REINS

Move both modified "A" hands back and forth as if holding reins.
Usage: a king *reigns;* he *rules* his country; parents *control* children; *running* (or *conducting*) a meeting; *in charge of* the work; *managing* a group; *governing* the land; *directing* a play; *discipline* yourself; taking hold of the *reins*

CAPTAIN, CHAIRMAN, OFFICER, BOSS

Place the fingertips of the right curved "FIVE" hand on the right shoulder.
Origin: authority rests on the shoulder
Usage: a *captain* in the army
chairman of the meeting
a naval *officer*
my new *boss*

PRESIDENT, SUPERINTENDENT

Place both "C" hands in front of the forehead, palms forward; draw them to the sides, closing into "S" positions.
Origin: horns of authority
Usage: *president* of the United States
superintendent of a school for the deaf

PRINCIPAL

Circle the right "P" (counterclockwise) over the left open hand which is palm-down.
Origin: making the sign for "over" with a "P," indicating the principal is over others
Usage: *principal* of the high school

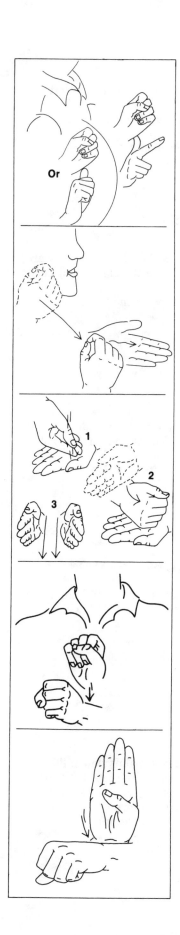

ASSISTANT, AIDE

Place the thumbtip of the right "L" against the left fist. (Sometimes made with the right "A.")
Usage: Mr. Martin is *assistant* to the president.
Rebecca is the teacher's *aide*.

SECRETARY

Take an imaginary pencil from the ear, write into the left hand and make the "PERSON" ending.
Origin: a person who takes notes
Usage: Teri is my good *secretary*.

TREASURER

Sign "MONEY" and "COLLECTION"; add the "PERSON" ending.
Origin: a person who collects money
Usage: *treasurer* of the organization

WORK, LABOR

The right "S" facing down is struck several times on the wrist of the left "S."
Origin: activity of the hands
Usage: "All *work* and no play makes Jack a dull boy" (Ben Franklin).
a skilled *laborer*

BUSINESS

Place the right "B" hand, pointing up, at the left wrist and strike several times.
Origin: the sign for "work," made with a "B"
Usage: We set up our *business* last year.

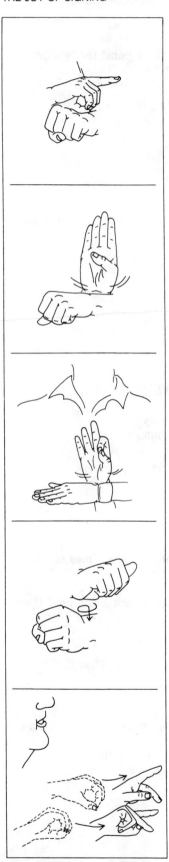

DUTY

Place the right "D" on the back of the wrist of the left closed hand.
Origin: the sign for "work," made with a "D"
Usage: Every one of us had a *duty* to perform.
Note: This sign is often used for "should."

BUSY

Place the wrist of the right "B" hand (palm facing forward) on the side of the left wrist and move the right hand back and forth slightly.
Origin: the sign for "work," made with the "B" hand
Usage: We all lead a *busy* life.

FUNCTION

Place the right "F" hand, pointing up, on the side of the left wrist and move the right hand back and forth slightly.
Origin: the sign for "work," made with an "F"
Usage: Every part of the body has its *function*.

ENGAGEMENT, APPOINTMENT, RESERVATION

Make a small clockwise circle with the right "A" hand and then place the wrist on the wrist of the left "S" which is facing right.
Origin: indicating one is bound
Usage: a dinner *engagement* tonight
a 4 o'clock *appointment*
a plane *reservation*

OPPORTUNITY

Place both "O" hands in front of you, palms down; lift both hands slightly from the wrist, forming the letter "P." Or raise both hands as in the sign for "offer."
Origin: an opportunity is something offered
Usage: a good *opportunity* to learn something

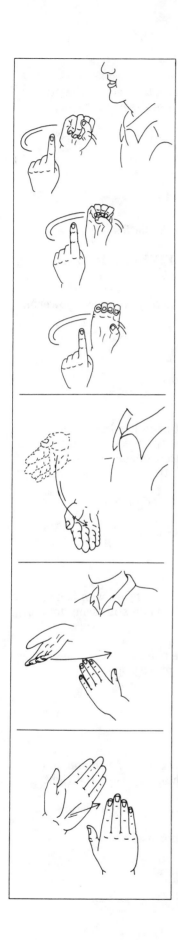

SITUATION

Hold up the left index finger; circle it with the right "S" from left to right.
Origin: being in the middle of something
Usage: finding yourself in a difficult *situation*

ENVIRONMENT

Sign as above, using the "E" hand.
Usage: living in a good *environment*

CIRCUMSTANCE

Sign as above, using the "C" hand.
Usage: I would like to explain the *circumstances* of the case.

HIRE

Bring the right open hand toward the body, palm facing up.
Usage: *Hire* the handicapped.

FIRED

Hold up the left open hand, fingertips up and palm in; pass the upturned right hand toward you across the top of the fingertips, toward the left.
Origin: as if the head were cut off
Usage: The boss had reasons for *firing* the men.

DISMISSED, LAID OFF

Move the tips of the right fingers across the lower edge of the left hand in a quick motion.
Origin: wiped off
Usage: Class is *dismissed.*
　　　laid off for a month

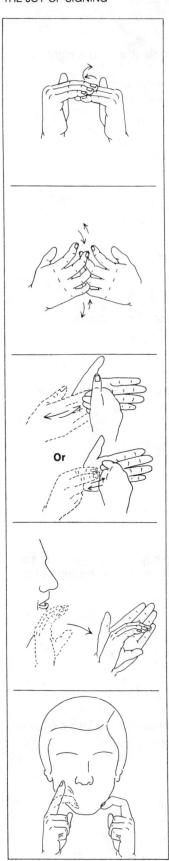

BUILD

Place the palm of one bent hand on the back of the other bent hand; alternate hands and repeat several times, moving upward.
Origin: placing one brick upon another
Usage: This house is *built* well.

MACHINE, FACTORY, MOTOR, ENGINE

Lock the fingers of the curved "FIVE" hands, palms facing you, and shake them up and down.
Origin: gears in motion
Usage: a large new *machine;* a *factory* worker; a powerful *motor;* an old *engine*

PAINT

Using the fingertips of the right open hand as a brush, draw them back and forth across the left palm. Or use two fingers if indicating painting with a smaller brush.
Origin: the actual motion of painting
Usage: He *painted* the house white.
The nurse *painted* Mercurochrome on the cut.

PICTURE, PHOTOGRAPH

Place the right "C" at the side of the face, palm facing forward; then place the "C," with palm still facing forward, against the left open palm.
Origin: The face is put on a card.
Usage: I never saw that *picture* before.
I thought it was a good *photograph*.

CAMERA, TAKE A PICTURE

Make a "C" with each hand, using only the thumb and index fingers, palms facing each other; move the right index up and down.
Origin: holding a small camera and taking a picture
Usage: Where's your *camera?*
Will you *take a picture* for me?

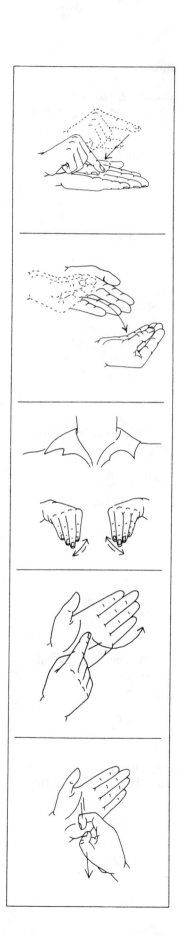

PRINT, PUBLISH, NEWSPAPER

The right "G," palm down, picks the imaginary type and places it in the left palm.
Origin: natural motion of old-style typesetting
Usage: This book was first *published* (or *printed*) in 1978.
Did you read the morning *paper?*

BUY, SHOPPING, PURCHASE

Place the back of the "AND" hand into the left palm and lift it out to the right, still in the "AND" position. (For "SHOPPING" repeat the sign several times.)
Origin: putting out money
Usage: Money cannot *buy* everything.
We were out *shopping* all afternoon.
Russia *purchased* wheat from the U.S.A.

SELL, STORE, SALE

Both "AND" hands, pointing down, are held in front of you, moving back and forth from the wrist.
Origin: holding up an item for sale
Usage: We *sold* the house.
our best *sales*man (add "MAN" sign)
The grocery *store* is near our home.
Some women like garage *sales*.

PAY, PAYMENT

Place the tip of the right index finger in the left palm and move the index finger out to the right.
Origin: pointing to the money which is paid out
Usage: Buy now, *pay* later.
high monthly *payments*

COST, PRICE, CHARGE, FINE, TAX

Place the left palm in front of you, facing right; strike the right crooked index finger against the left palm and down, palm facing you.
Origin: indicating that a part of the money is taken
Usage: the high *cost* of living
price of meat
Painters *charge* by the hour.
paid a $10 *fine*
Sales *tax* is 4%.

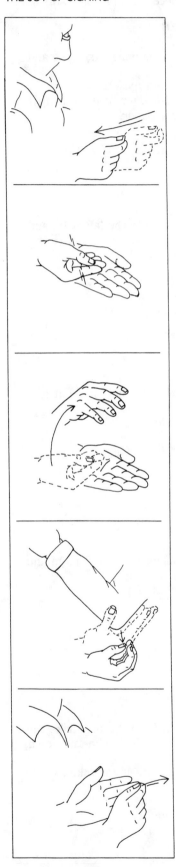

SUBSCRIBE, DRAW (Compensation)

Draw the right, modified, slightly open "A" toward
yourself, closing the "A" as it approaches the body; repeat
several times.
Origin: pulling it in
Usage: We *subscribe* to several magazines.
He *draws* social security.

MONEY, FUNDS

Strike the left palm with the back of the right "AND" hand
several times.
Origin: counting coins into the palm
Usage: The love of *money* is the root of evil.
Our *funds* are low.

RICH, WEALTHY

Place the back of the right "AND" hand in the left palm
and then lift it out, right palm facing down.
Origin: showing money in a heap
Usage: A *rich* uncle left her some money.
We are a *wealthy* nation.

POOR

The open fingers of the right hand are placed at the left
elbow and pulled downward several times.
Origin: indicating the ragged sleeve
Usage: a *poor* family
Note: This sign is not to be used in the sense of sympathy,
as in "poor Suzie." For this usage see "sympathy."

DOLLARS

Grasp the tips of the left open hand with the right thumb
and four fingers; pull the right away. Repeat several times.
Origin: counting out the bills
Usage: 100 *dollars*

CENTS (Used with a number)

Touch the forehead and follow by making the desired number.
Usage: Do you have a *nickel* or a *dime?* (Nickel—
"CENT" + "FIVE"; Dime—"CENT" + "TEN.")

COINS

Draw a small circle in the left palm with the right index.
Origin: tracing the shape of the coin in the hand
Usage: a *coin* collector
Alternate Sign: Use the thumb and forefinger to form a circle (other fingers extended); place on left palm.

CHANGE (Money)

Place the little-finger edge of the right open hand on the index edge of the left open hand and move the right slightly from side to side.
Origin: as if dividing it up
Usage: Do you have *change* for a dollar?

CHECK

Place the tips of the right "C" against the left open palm and draw the right hand toward the tip of the left hand.
Origin: indicating the size and shape of the check
Usage: If I pay by *check* I have a good record.

DEPOSIT

Place the "A" hands in front of you and then move them away from each other to the sides as the wrists turn slightly.
Usage: You will have to leave a *deposit* of $25.

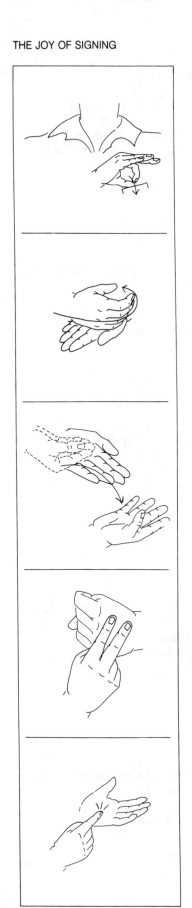

PROFIT, BENEFIT, ADVANTAGE

Place the thumb and index tips of the right "F" in an imaginary breast pocket.
Origin: placing money in the pocket
Usage: Make a *profit*.
That's to your *benefit* (or *advantage*).
Note: This sign is not to be used in the negative sense of taking advantage of a person or a situation. For this usage see page 64.

EARN, INCOME

Draw the right curved hand across the left palm starting at the fingertips.
Origin: as if gathering money together in the palm
Usage: Your money can *earn* interest.
A doctor's annual *income* is higher than a teacher's.

SPEND, WASTE

Place the back of the right "AND" hand in the left palm and open it as you slide off the fingertips. The sign for "WASTE" is made with greater emphasis.
Origin: Money slides off the palm.
Usage: Don't *spend* it all!
That's a *waste* of both time and money.

SAVE (As saving money)

Place the inside of the right "V" against the back of the left wrist.
Usage: "A penny *saved* is a penny earned."
Save a seat for me.

OWE, DEBT, DUE, AFFORD

The tip of the right index finger touches the center of the left palm several times.
Origin: pointing to where the money belongs
Usage: I *owe* you $5.
Our national *debt* is high.
Payment is *due* next week.
Can you *afford* that car?

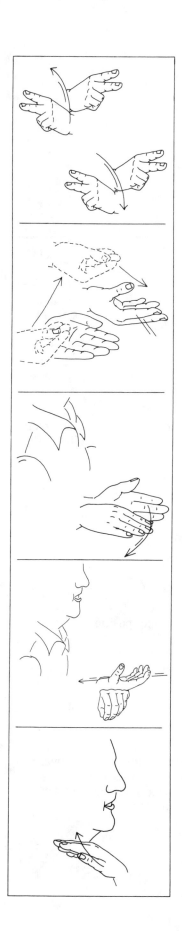

BORROW, LEND, LOAN

Make the sign for "KEEP" (the right "V" on top of the left "V" crossing at the wrist); draw it either toward or away from the body as the case may be.

Usage: People *borrow* money to buy cars (toward body).

Banks will *lend* you money (away from body).

I made application for a *loan* (toward body).

EXPENSIVE

Place the back of the right "AND" hand into the left palm; lift the right hand out and draw it away, opening it somewhat and then giving it a slight quick twist to the right.

Usage: very *expensive* clothes

CHEAP

Place the index-finger side of the right open palm against the left palm and brush downward.

Usage: I think my shoes look *cheap*.

That store has *cheap* clothes.

BEG

Place the back of the right curved "FIVE" hand on the back of the left hand; draw it back several times.

Origin: hand extended in a begging position

Usage: They *begged* for money and for help.

BROKE

Strike the little-finger side of the downturned hand against the right side of the neck.

Usage: I spent all my money and now I'm *broke!*

7

Physical Movement and Travel

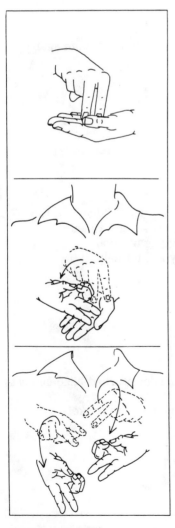

STAND

Place the right "V" in a standing position on the left palm.
Origin: The two fingers represent the legs standing.
Usage: Melba will *stand* to interpret.

FALL

Place the "V" in a standing position on the left palm; let the "V" fall, palm up, in the left hand.
Origin: from a standing to a reclining position
Usage: Don't run, you may *fall*.

FALLING (Tumbling)

Both hands in "V" positions rotate and move downward, palms out, then in, and ending with palms out.
Origin: an object tumbling downward through the air
Usage: The leaves are *falling* from the trees.

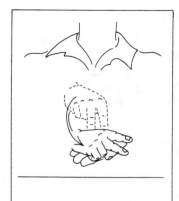

SLIDE, SLIP

Sign "STAND" and slide the "V" forward on the left palm.
Origin: moving from a standing position to a slide
Usage: It's icy, you may *slide* (or *slip.*)

LIE, RECLINE

Place the back of the right "V" in the left palm and slide it back.
Origin: Fingers represent a reclining position.
Usage: *Lie* on the grass.
      reclining on the couch
GETTING UNDER THE COVERS—Slide the right "V" (palm up) under the left palm, which is in a palm-down position.

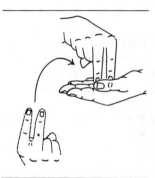

GET UP, ARISE

The right "V" with fingers pointing up and facing you is raised and then placed in a standing position on the left palm.
Origin: rising to a standing position
Usage: It's time to *get up.*
      They all *arose* and sang.

DANCE

Place the right "V" in a standing position on the left palm and swing the "V" back and forth.
Origin: the motion of the body in dancing
Usage: Barbara was known for her graceful *dancing.*

JUMP

Place the right "V" in a standing position on the left palm; lift the "V," bending the knuckles, and return to a standing position.
Origin: bending the knees in jumping
Usage: Children *jump* and play.

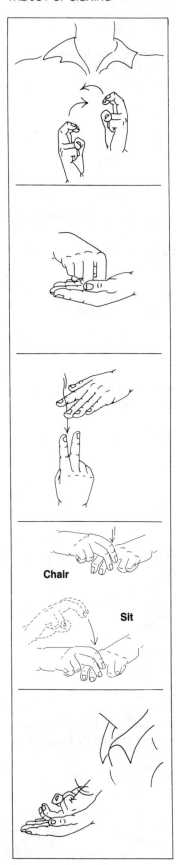

CLIMB

Place the curved "V" hands before you, facing each other; move them upward alternately in stages. (To climb a rope form "S" positions, hand over hand, as in actual climbing.)
Usage: Mountain *climbing* can be dangerous.
      He *climbed up the rope* to the window.

KNEEL

Bend the knuckles of the right "V" and place in the left palm.
Origin: Fingers are in the kneeling position.
Usage: The visitor *knelt* before the queen of England.

DROWN, SINK

Place the right "V" (palm toward you) between the index and middle fingers of the left open hand, which is facing down, and slide it down with a slightly wavy motion.
Origin: Left hand represents the water level and right hand is sinking.
Usage: No one knew the cause of her *drowning*.
      It's a *sink* or swim situation.

SIT, CHAIR

The right curved index and middle fingers are placed crosswise on the left curved index and middle fingers, both palms down. Note that one movement represents the verb *sit* and a double movement represents the noun *chair*.
Origin: Fingers represent the seated person and the chair.
Usage: I *sat down* for a few minutes.
      We will need about 50 *chairs* for the meeting.

RESTLESS, TOSS AND TURN

The back of the curved "V" is placed in the left palm and is twisted from side to side slightly, with a motion from the wrist.
Origin: as if squirming in a seat or lying restlessly in bed
Usage: feeling *restless* while waiting
      feel *restless* and can't sleep
      I *tossed and turned* all night.

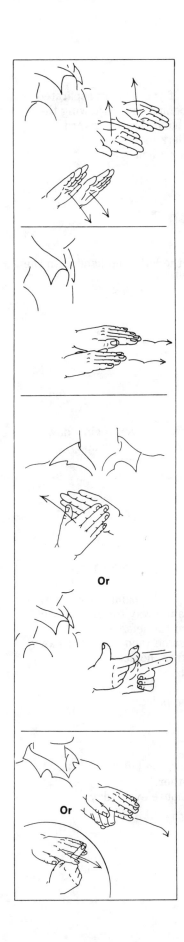

RISE, BE SEATED

Both open hands move up with palms up, or move down with palms down.
Origin: the natural motion of asking people to rise or to be seated
Usage: Will the audience please *rise?*
Everyone *be seated,* please.

WALK

Open hands, palms down, are moved in a forward-downward motion alternately.
Origin: representing feet walking
Usage: Brisk *walking* is good exercise.

RUN

The right open palm, facing up, brushes outward to the right from under the left open palm.

Or hook the index of the right "L" under the thumb of the left "L" and move hands forward in a quick motion.
Usage: Daily *running* helps keep you well.

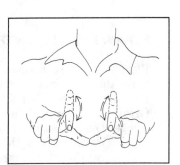

Or touch tips of thumbs, extend index fingers, crooking and uncrooking them (other fingers closed), while hands move forward.

ESCAPE, RUN AWAY

Place the right index under the left open hand which is facing down, and move it forward and out toward the right.

Or place the right index pointing up between the index and middle fingers of the left open hand (palm down); move the right index away in a quick motion.
Usage: *escaped* during the night
often *ran away* from home

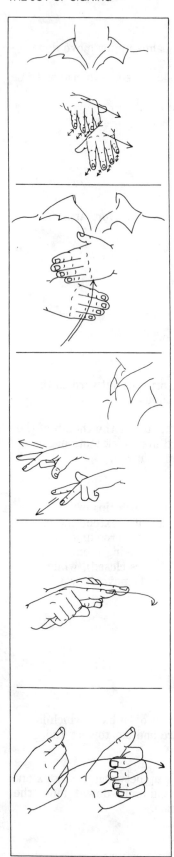

MARCH

Place both bent hands in front of you, fingers separated and palms facing down, right behind the left; swing the fingers back and forth as both hands move forward.
Origin: indicating rows of soldiers marching
Usage: The soldiers *marched* for 3 hours.

KICK

Strike the little-finger edge of the left open hand with the index-finger edge of the right "B" hand.
Origin: the motion of kicking
Usage: *kicked* by a horse

AWKWARD, CLUMSY

Place the "THREE" hands in front of you (palms down) and move them forward and backward alternately.
Origin: as if walking in a clumsy fashion
Usage: feel *awkward* on skates
a *clumsy* beginner

STRAY, DEVIATE, DIVERT, OFF THE POINT

Place both index fingers side by side (palms facing down); move the right index forward and away toward the right. Or move the right index toward the left.
Origin: Fingers begin as for "same" and one moves away.
Usage: Our cat *strayed away* from home.
deviated from the truth
cars were *diverted*
Our discussion is *off the point*.

PASS

Move the right "A" forward past the left "A."
Origin: One hand passes the other.
Usage: Many people *pass* our house every day.
A new law was *passed*.

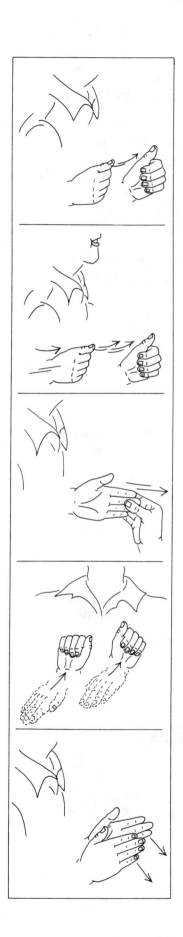

FOLLOW, FOLLOWER, DISCIPLE

Place the right "A" behind the left "A" and move them both forward. (Add the "PERSON" ending for the noun.)
Origin: One hand follows the other.
Usage: *follow* the leader
Some people are *followers.*
12 *disciples* (Some signers use a "D" with both hands instead of the "A.")

CHASE

Sign "FOLLOW" vigorously, wiggling the right wrist as it moves to catch up with the left.
Origin: one hand following the other rapidly
Usage: The police *chased* the thief and caught him.

LEAD, GUIDE

Grasp the tip of the left open hand with the right fingertips and thumb and pull forward.
Origin: right hand leading the left
Usage: *Lead* the horse to water.
our Indian *guide*

DEPART, LEAVE, WITHDRAW

Place the open hands in front of you toward the right, palms down, with fingertips pointing forward; draw the hands back and up into "A" positions.
Origin: hands moving away as if one is withdrawing
Usage: The train *departs* at 10:30.
What time are you *leaving?*
She *withdrew* from the room.

LEAVE, NEGLECT, ABANDON

Place open hands in front of you, palm facing palm, tips to the right; give them a downward twist from the wrist.
Origin: Downward movement suggests leaving something.
Usage: *Leave* your books here.
We didn't need our coats so we *left* them in the car.
Don't *neglect* your practice.
The parents *abandoned* their children.

BELMONT UNIVERSITY LIBRARY

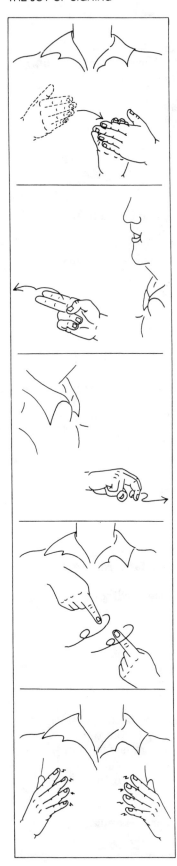

ARRIVE, REACH, GET TO

The right slightly bent hand moves forward and is placed in the left open palm.
Origin: The hand "arrives" at its destination.
Usage: When will the plane *arrive* in New York?
     We *reached* Chicago by noon.
     What time did you *get* there?

HURRY

Move the right "H" forward with a quick up-and-down movement. Or use both "H" hands in this fashion.
Origin: moving forward rapidly
Usage: *Hurry,* it looks like rain.
     Hurry up, it's late.

TRAVEL, TRIP, JOURNEY

Move the right curved "V" hand forward in a zigzag movement, palm facing down.
Usage: *travel* to another country
     trip to northern Italy
     a long *journey*

TRAVEL AROUND

The right index points down and the left index points up; they circle around each other in counterclockwise movements.
Note: This sign represents traveling *within* a specified area rather than *to* an area.
Usage: We *traveled around* in Europe for a month.
     We *went around* in the shopping center for a while.

VACATION, IDLE, HOLIDAY, RETIRE

Place the thumbs of the "FIVE" hands at the armpits and wiggle the four fingers. For "RETIRE" either sign as described or use "R" hands with thumbs under armpits.
Origin: a man standing with thumbs under his suspenders
Usage: a *vacation* in Bermuda
     never working, always *idle*
     July 4th is a national *holiday.*

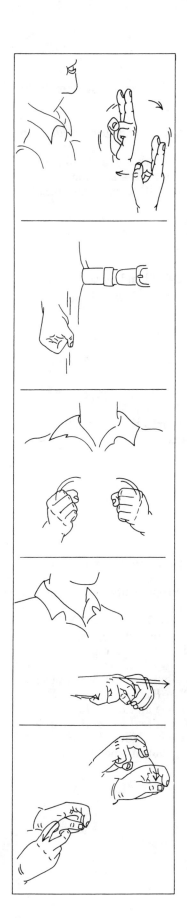

VISIT

The "V" hands, pointing up and facing you, are rotated up-out-down-in-around each other.
Origin: represents people in circulation
Usage: Why not *visit* the Smithsonian Institute?

SUITCASE

Using an "S" hand, lift an imaginary suitcase by the handle.
Usage: Linda took two red *suitcases* on her trip.
Note: To indicate that the suitcase is heavy, tilt the body forward and drop the hand a bit; to show it is light, use a bouncy motion.

AUTOMOBILE, CAR, DRIVE

Place the "S" hands in front of you, palms facing each other, and move them up and down alternately as if driving a car.
Note: When indicating that one is driving to a destination, the "S" hands are moved forward.
Usage: a beautiful, new *car*

drove around sightseeing
He *drove* right to the hospital (second description above).

RIDE

Place the right curved "V" in the slightly opened left "O," and move them forward.
Origin: placing yourself in the vehicle
Usage: May I *ride* with you?

GET IN, GET OUT, REMOVE ONESELF

Place the bent "V" in the left "O" or remove the right "V," as the case may be.
Usage: Hurry and *get in,* we have to leave.
Two people *got out of* the car.
I *stepped out of* my role.
I *removed myself from* the situation.

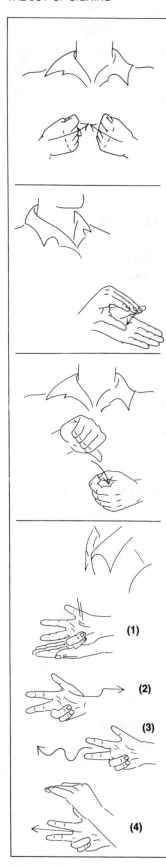

COLLISION, ACCIDENT

Bring the knuckles of the "S" hands forcibly together (palm side toward the body).
Origin: two vehicles colliding
Usage: Two large ships *collided.* We saw a bad *accident* on the highway.
Note: When speaking of an accident that does not involve a collision (an unintentional happening), the sign for "happen" is frequently used along with appropriate facial expression.
Example: The cup broke—it was an *accident.*

FLAT TIRE

Place the thumb of the open "AND" hand on the left palm and bring the right to a closed "AND" position.
Origin: showing the tire deflating
Usage: arrived late because of a *flat tire*

GASOLINE

Move the thumb of the right "A" into the left "O."
Origin: pouring gas into the tank
Usage: will need *gas* soon

PARKING (and location or movement of a vehicle)

The right "THREE" handshape represents vehicles and boats. It is used to show location or movement of a vehicle that has previously been identified. For "PARKING," simply place the "THREE" hand (palm facing left) on the left palm. Move the hand as pictured for the practice sentences given here.
Usage: (1) We drove and drove but couldn't find a place to *park.* The signs said, "No *Parking."*
(2) We saw a *parking* place and *backed in.*
(3) The car was *weaving in and out of* the traffic.
(4) I *pulled into the garage.* (Move the right "THREE" under the left downturned palm.)

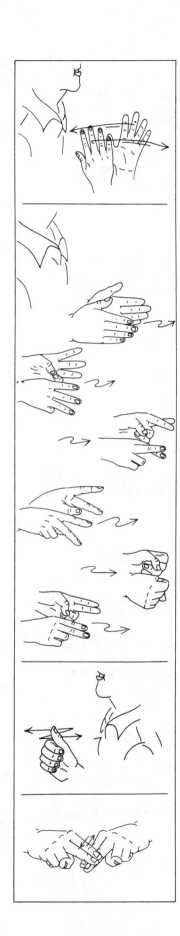

TRAFFIC

The open "FIVE" hands, facing each other pointing up, move slightly back and forth alternately.
Origin: indicating the flow of traffic in two directions
Usage: *Traffic* is heavy on Friday afternoons.

WAY, ROAD, PATH, STREET, HIGHWAY

Place both open hands in front of you, fingers pointing forward and palms facing each other; move both hands forward with a slight zigzag motion.
Origin: showing the pathway

Note: Initials are sometimes used in educational settings for the following:

W—WAY
Usage: the *way* to Los Angeles

R—ROAD
Usage: The *road* is very narrow.

P—PATH
Usage: a *path* through the woods

S—STREET
Usage: a busy *street*

H—HIGHWAY
Usage: a new, improved *highway*

BACK AND FORTH, COMMUTE

Move the "A" hand forward and backward several times.
Usage: *back and forth* to work every day
   She was impatient and walked *back and forth* constantly.
   We *commute* every day.

TRAIN, RAILROAD

Rub the right "H" back and forth on the back of the left "H," both palms down.
Origin: movement on the tracks
Usage: The *train* arrives in Philadelphia at 5 P.M.
   Railroad travel can be very comfortable.

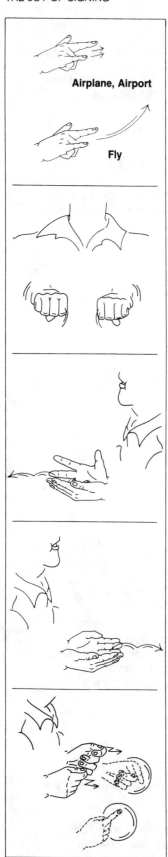

Airplane, Airport

Fly

AIRPLANE, AIRPORT, FLY

Extend the thumb, index, and little finger of the right hand and move the hand forward and up, palm facing down, to indicate the verb "FLY." For the noun "PLANE" make a short double movement.
Origin: Showing wings of the plane and takeoff.
Usage: The first *airplane* is on display in Washington.
      We *fly* to London tomorrow.

MOTORCYCLE

Place the "S" hands in front of you as if grasping the handlebars of a motorcycle; twist the hands slightly.
Usage: *Motorcycles* are fun but sometimes dangerous.

SHIP

Place the right "THREE" hand into the left palm and move the hands together in this position, indicating the motion of the waves.
Origin: represents the masts of the ship and the waves
Usage: *Ships* carry thousands of passengers every year.

BOAT

Place the little-finger edge of the open hands together to form a boat and move the hands to show the motion of waves.
Origin: Hands are in the shape of a boat; movement is natural.
Usage: People enjoy their *boats* on a beautiful day.

WAGON, CARRIAGE, CHARIOT, BUGGY

Point both index fingers toward each other and circle them forward; then hold imaginary reins with both modified "A" hands.
Origin: indicating the large wheels and also holding the reins of the horse
Usage: traveled in covered *wagons*; a *carriage* and four horses; swing low, sweet *chariot*; a ride in a *buggy*

8

Opposites

ASK, REQUEST

Place the open hands palm to palm and draw them toward the body.
Origin: Hands held as in prayer.
Usage: *Ask* for help.
What is your *request?*

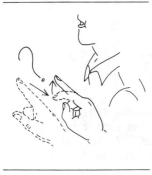

QUESTION

Draw a question mark in the air with the index finger; draw it back and direct it foward as if placing the dot below the question mark.
Usage: That *question* is hard to answer.
Note: If asking a group of people a question, crook and uncrook the index finger while moving the hand from left to right (or reverse).

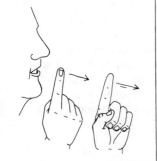

ANSWER, REPLY, RESPOND

Place the tip of the right index, palm facing left, at the lips; place the left index, pointing up, in front of it; move both hands out, ending with the index fingers pointing forward. ("REPLY" and "RESPONSE" are often made with "R"s.)
Usage: *answer* my letter; a quick *reply;* an intelligent *response*

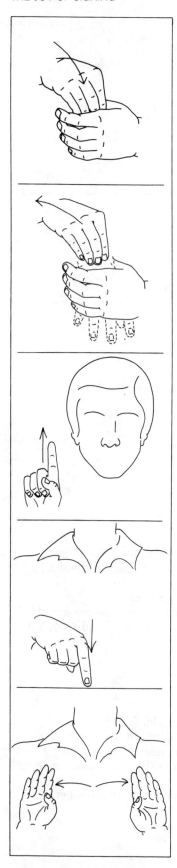

IN

Place the closed fingertips of the right hand into the left "C" hand.
Origin: placing something in the left hand
Usage: You live *in* America.

OUT, OUTSIDE

The right open "AND" hand, facing the body and pointing down, becomes a closed "AND" as it is drawn up through the left "C," which then closes.
Origin: moving out of the left hand
Usage: Republicans are *out,* Democrats are in.
　　　　Play *outside.*

UP

Point up with the index finger.
Usage: The cat is *up* in the tree.
Note: This sign is often omitted, substituted, spelled, or included within the context of another sign. Examples: stand *up* (omit); sun*up* (sign "SUNRISE"); time's *up* (sign "TIME" and "FINISH"); look *up* (the sign for "LOOK" is directed upward and the sign for "UP" is omitted).

DOWN

Point down with the index finger.
Origin: a natural gesture, used in the sense of descending, going down or downward
Usage: *down* in the valley
　　　　Who lives *downstairs?*
Note: This sign is often omitted, substituted, spelled, or included within the context of another sign. Examples: sit *down* (omit); sun*down* (sign "SUNSET"); look *down* (the sign for "LOOK" is directed downward and the sign for "DOWN" is omitted).

OPEN

Place both open hands side by side and draw the hands apart. The sign for "OPEN" varies, depending on what is being opened. Often the sign imitates the actual motion, as in opening a window, the mouth, the eyes, etc.
Origin: Hands move apart as if opening a door.
Usage: The White House is *open* to visitors.

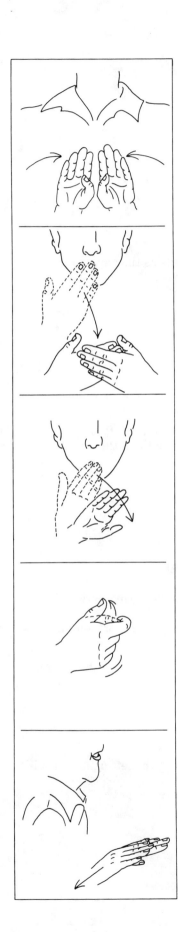

CLOSE, SHUT

Draw both open hands toward each other until the index fingers touch. The sign for "CLOSE" or "SHUT" varies depending on what is being closed.
Origin: Hands come together as if a door is closing.
Usage: I'm cold, please *close the door.*

GOOD, WELL

Touch the lips with the fingers of the right hand and then move the right hand forward placing it palm up in the palm of the left hand.
Origin: It has been tasted and smelled and offered as acceptable.
Usage: *good* food
doing *well* at work

BAD

Touch the lips with the fingers of the right hand and then turn the palm down.
Origin: It has been tasted and smelled and turned down.
Usage: That tastes *bad.*

FAST, QUICK, RAPID, IMMEDIATELY, SUDDENLY, RIGHT AWAY

The right thumb is snapped out of the curved index finger as if shooting a marble. This sign may be made with both hands.
Origin: as fast as shooting a marble
Usage: *fast* train; *quick* thinking; *rapid* growth; needs help *immediately;* storm came *suddenly;* children obeyed *right away*

SLOW

Stroke down the back of the left hand slowly with the right hand.
Origin: The hand is moving slowly.
Usage: a *slow* learner
Slow down, I can't understand your fingerspelling.

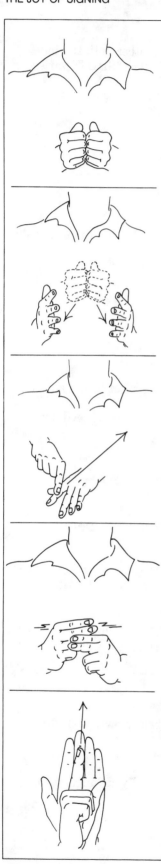

WITH, ACCOMPANY

Place the "A" hands together, palm to palm.
Origin: one hand with the other
Usage: Come *with* your friend.
I'm afraid; will you *accompany* me?

WITHOUT

Sign "WITH"; then open the hands as they are separated.
Origin: hands no longer together
Usage: He acted *without* a reason.

LONG

Draw the right index finger up along the left arm.
Origin: The finger is measuring length on the arm.
Usage: a *long* time

SHORT (in length), SOON, BRIEF

Rub the middle finger of the right "H" hand back and forth
along the index finger of the left "H."
Origin: The short movement indicates a short length.
Usage: a *short* story
coming *soon*
a *brief* visit

TALL

Pass the right index finger up along the left palm which is
pointing upward.
Origin: Upward movement indicates height.
Usage: a *tall* man

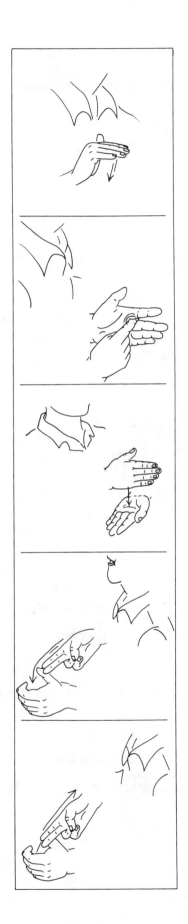

SHORT (in height), LITTLE, SMALL

Hold the right open hand in front of you, palm facing
down; lower it slightly.
Origin: The lowered hand indicates short stature.
Usage: a *short* man
　　　 a *little* girl
　　　 a *small* boy

START, BEGIN, COMMENCE

The tip of the right index makes a half-turn between the
index and middle fingers of the left open hand.
Origin: indicating a screw or a key being turned
Usage: *Start* the car.
　　　 Begin a new job.
　　　 It will *commence* at 2 o'clock

STOP, CEASE, QUIT

The little-finger side of the right open hand is brought
down sharply to a position across the left open palm.
Origin: The right hand is placed emphatically on the left to
form a barrier.
Usage: All the noise *stopped.*
　　　 His breathing *ceased.*
　　　 The men *quit* working at 3 o'clock.

PARTICIPATE, JOIN

Place the right "U" into the left "C."
Origin: placing yourself in a situation
Usage: Would you like to *participate?*
　　　 Come on, *join in!*

QUIT, RESIGN

Place the right "U" into the left "C" and then pull it out
again in a quick motion.
Origin: taking yourself out of a situation
Usage: I *quit!*
　　　 The president *resigned.*

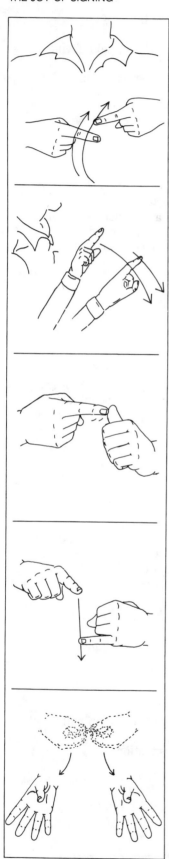

COME

Index fingers rotating once around each other move toward the body. Or use the open hand in a beckoning motion.
Origin: using the hands in a natural motion
Usage: When can you *come* to my home?
Come, I'm waiting for you. (Use second description.)

GO, GOING, WENT, ATTEND

The hands in the index-finger position are swung forward, one behind the other. For "ATTEND" the motion is repeated.
Usage: I *go* to work every night.
Go! (Sign this with vigor.)
She's *going* home tomorrow.
The doctor *went* to the hospital this morning.
He *attends* meetings regularly.

FIRST

Hold up the left "A" hand with the thumb pointing up and strike it with the tip of the right index. For second, third, fourth, and fifth, touch the tip of the respective fingers.
Origin: The thumb represents the first of the fingers.
Usage: in the *first* place

LAST, FINAL, END

With a downward motion strike the end of the little finger of the left "I" hand with the right index finger (or little finger).
Origin: The little finger is the last finger of the hand.
Usage: *last* day of the week
the *final* decision
the *end* of the world

LOSE, LOST

Both hands in the "AND" position, fingernails touching and palms facing up, are dropped and opened.
Origin: the open hands dropping something
Usage: always *lose* my umbrellas
lost your car keys

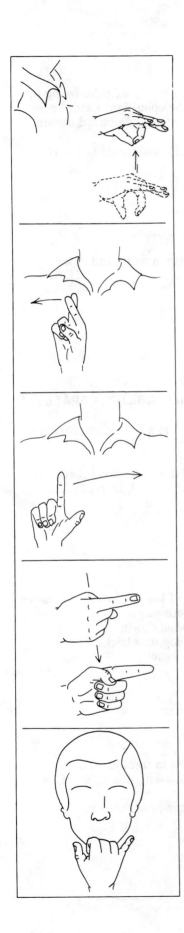

FIND, DISCOVER

Place the open hand in front of you, palm down; draw the thumb and forefinger together and lift up as if picking up something.
Origin: the natural motion of picking up something
Usage: can't *find* the check
  found time for his family
  discovered a bird's nest

RIGHT

Direct the "R" hand toward the right.
Origin: showing a rightward direction
Usage: Sit on the *right.*

LEFT

Direct the "L" hand toward the left.
Origin: showing a leftward direction
Usage: *left* at the next corner

RIGHT, CORRECT, PROPER, APPROPRIATE

The little-finger edge of the right "G" hand is placed on the index of the left "G" hand so that both index fingers point forward, one above the other. For "PROPER" and "APPROPRIATE" make the sign twice.
Usage: That's *right.*
  correct answer; *proper* clothing; *appropriate* behavior

WRONG, MISTAKE, ERROR

The "Y" hand touches the chin, palm facing in.
Usage: the *wrong* way
  made a *mistake*
  my *error*

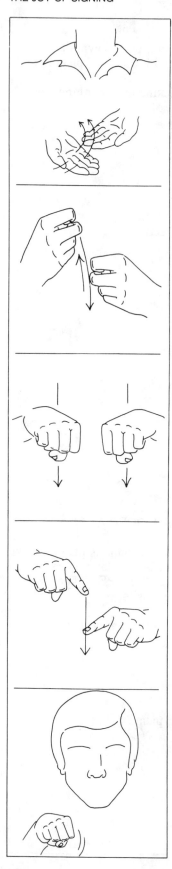

EASY, SIMPLE

Place the curved left hand in front of you, palm facing up. Using the little-finger side of the open right hand, brush under the fingertips of the left hand and upward several times.
Origin: The fingertips of the left easily yield to the right.
Usage: *easy* lesson
      a *simple* answer

DIFFICULT

Both bent "V"s strike each other in an up and down movement.
Usage: a *difficult* exam

CAN, COULD, POSSIBLE, ABLE, ABILITY, CAPABLE

Move both "S" hands downward in a firm manner (palms down).
Origin: The fist indicates power.
Usage: *can* sign well; we *could* if we had time; that's not *possible;* not *able* to understand; he really has *ability;* a very *capable* person

CAN'T, COULDN'T

The right index strikes the tip of the left index and passes it in a downward movement, both palms down.
Origin: The finger can't be pushed down.
Usage: You *can't* teach an old dog new tricks.
      I *couldn't* believe what I saw.

YES

Shake the right "S" up and down in front of you. Agreement is also indicated by shaking the right "Y" up and down.
Origin: The fist, representing the head, nods in agreement.
Usage: *Yes,* I will go.

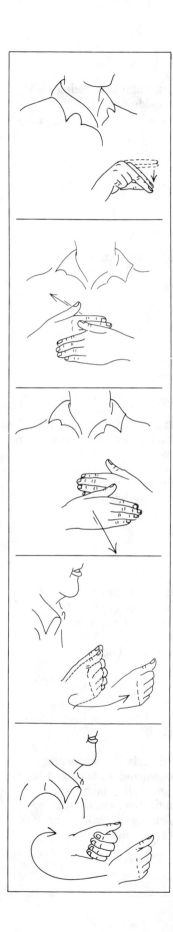

NO

Make an abbreviated "N" and "O" by bringing the index, middle finger, and thumb together in one motion.
Usage: *No,* I won't.

BEFORE, IN ADVANCE

With open hands facing you the right is drawn away from the left toward the right shoulder.
Origin: Back over the shoulder always indicates the past.
Usage: the day *before* yesterday
come *ahead* of time
Buy your ticket *in advance.*

AFTER, THEREAFTER, FROM NOW ON

Place the left open hand in front of you, palm facing you and fingers pointing right; place the right palm against the back of the left hand and then move the right forward, away from the left.
Origin: Indicates forward movement from a fixed point in time.
Usage: Come *after* 7 o'clock.

AHEAD

Place the "A" hands close together facing each other and move the right "A" in front of the left "A."
Origin: one in front of the other
Usage: *ahead* of me in line

BEHIND

Place the "A" hands close together facing each other and move the right "A" behind the left "A." To indicate that one is behind in accomplishment, place the right "A" behind the left "A" and draw the right back some distance.
Usage: hiding *behind* the door
I was *behind* in my studies. (Use second description above.)

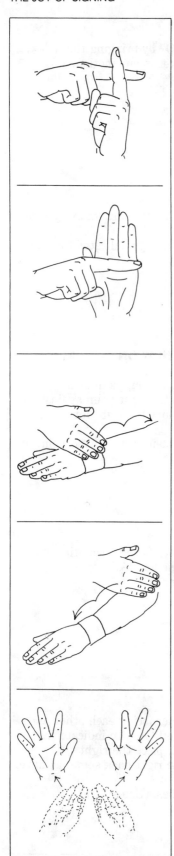

POSITIVE, PLUS

Place the left index in front of you, palm side facing right; cross it with the right index (palm side down).
Origin: natural sign
Usage: Think *positively*.
That's a real *plus*.

NEGATIVE, MINUS

Face the left open palm outward, tips pointing up; place the right index across the left palm (palm side down).
Origin: indicating the minus sign
Usage: a *negative* attitude
His grade was *A-*.

IMPROVE

Place the left arm in front of you and strike the little-finger side of the right open hand on the left wrist; move it up in stages, striking the arm each time.
Origin: moving upward in stages
Usage: Your interpreting is *improving* every day.
She was very sick but is *doing better* now.

WORSEN, DETERIORATE

Place the left arm in front of you and strike the little-finger side of the right open hand at the inside of the left elbow, moving it down in stages and striking the arm each time.
Origin: going downhill
Usage: The patient's condition is *worsening*.
His health *deteriorated*.

LIGHT, BRIGHT, CLEAR, OBVIOUS

Both "AND" hands point forward, index tips touching; open the fingers as the hands are moved upward and to the sides, ending in a "FIVE" position, palms facing forward.
Origin: opening of the fingers indicates rays of light
Usage: no *light;* a *bright* day; *clear* signs; make your meaning *clear; obvious* to everyone

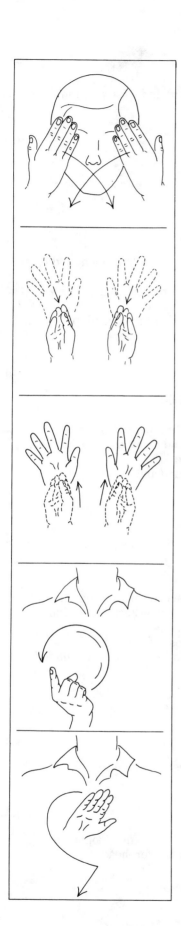

DARK, DIM

The open hands, palms facing you and pointing up, are crossed in front of the face.
Origin: indicates darkness when eyes are covered
Usage: a very *dark* night
　　　The room was *dim.*

LIGHTS OUT, TURN OFF THE LIGHT

The "FIVE" hands are brought down to the closed "AND" positions (palms forward).
Origin: opposite of light; rays of light fade away
Usage: *Lights out,* please.
　　　It's time to *turn off the lights.*

LIGHTS ON, TURN ON THE LIGHT

The closed "AND" hands are opened to "FIVE" positions, palms forward.
Origin: Rays of light are seen.
Usage: The *lights are on.*
　　　Turn on the lights, please.

ALWAYS, EVER

Describe a clockwise circle in front of you with the index finger, palm facing up.
Origin: A circle is never ending.
Usage: *always* learning
　　　ever present

NEVER

Move the right open hand, palm down, in a circular movement in front of the body as follows: up-right-down-left; then move the hand abruptly off to the right.
Origin: adapted from the natural gesture
Usage: *never* satisfied

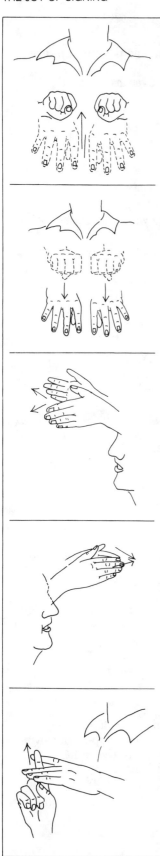

ADOPT, ASSUME, TAKE UP

Lift the open hands (palms down) and close them into "S" positions.
Origin: taking hold of something
Usage: *adopt* children
  assume responsibility
  take up where he left off

DROP

Place the "S" hands in front of you (palms down) and open them as they suddenly drop.
Origin: opening the hands as if dropping something
Usage: The waiter *dropped* a tray.
  I was angry and *dropped* my membership.

BROAD-MINDED, OPEN-MINDED

Place the open hands pointing forward in front of the forehead; move them forward and away from each other.
Origin: indicating an open mind
Usage: My friend is *broad-minded* and won't object.

NARROW-MINDED

Place open hands at side of forehead, fingers together and pointing forward, palms facing each other; move hands forward and toward each other.
Origin: indicating the narrowness of the mind
Usage: His conversation showed he was *narrow-minded.*

APPEAR, SHOW UP, POP UP

Bring the right index up between the index and middle fingers of the left hand.
Origin: suddenly appearing
Usage: He seemed to *appear* from nowhere.
  Jim finally *showed up.*
Note: To indicate that a thought suddenly "popped up" in your mind, make this sign near the forehead.

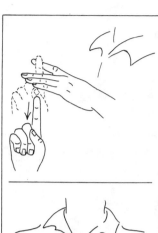

DISAPPEAR, DROP OUT

The right index finger pointing up is placed between the index and middle fingers of the left hand, which has the palm facing down; the right index is then drawn down.
Origin: dropping out of sight
Usage: He *disappeared* suddenly.
    dropped out of society
    It *slipped my mind.* (Sign is made near the forehead.)

CONDENSE, SUMMARIZE, ABBREVIATE

Bring the "C" hands toward the center and close them into "S" positions as the right little-finger edge is placed on the forefinger-thumb edge of the left fist.
Origin: as if squeezing something together
Usage: Your story is too long; *condense* it.
    a *summary* of the news
    an *abbreviated* version
Note: The sign for "short" is sometimes used to show abbreviation.

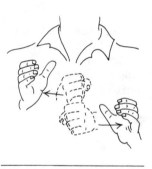

EXPAND, SWELL

Place the little-finger edge of the right "S" on the left "S" and draw them apart into a "C" position, the left palm facing right and the right palm facing left.
Origin: indicates enlargement
Usage: Present your ideas and then *expand* on them.
    Moisture causes wood to *swell.*

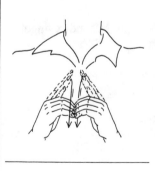

COLLAPSE, BREAKDOWN, CAVE-IN

Place the tips of the hands together; then let them suddenly move downward to a bent position.
Origin: from an upright to a collapsed position
Usage: The building *collapsed.*
    He had a nervous *breakdown.*
    The coal mine *caved in.*

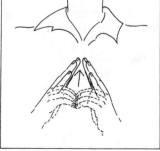

SET UP

Place the tips of both hands together, pointing down; then move them upward until the tips, still together, point upward.
Usage: We *set up* the tent.

9

Location and Direction

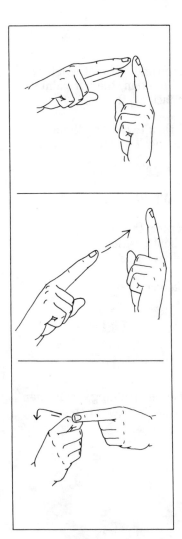

TO (As a preposition)

Direct the right index finger toward, and then touch, the left index fingertip which is pointing up. IMPORTANT: The sign for "TO" is omitted in the infinitive form.
Origin: heading toward the object and touching it
Usage: going *to* California; from sunrise *to* sunset; give the book *to* him
Note: like *to* walk (omit or fingerspell "TO")

TOWARD

Direct the right index finger toward the left index fingertip which is pointing up, but do not touch it.
Origin: heading toward an object
Usage: We are working *toward* a peaceful solution.

FROM

Point the left index finger to the right, palm facing in; then place the right "X" (palm facing left) against the left index and pull it toward you and down.
Origin: as if moving away from a fixed point
Usage: *from* east to west

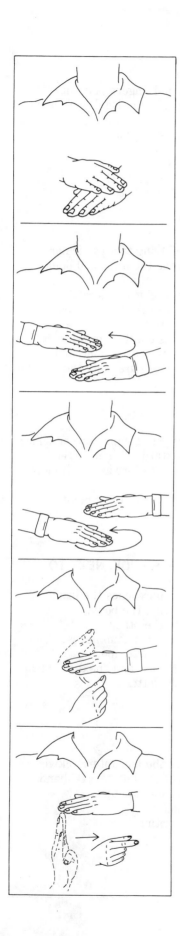

ON

The palm of the right open hand is placed on the back of the left open hand, both palms down.
Origin: one hand on top of the other
Usage: The food is *on* the table.
Note: When "on" means "forward," sign it that way. (See page 124.)

ABOVE, OVER

Hold the right open hand above the left open hand, both palms down; move the right in a counterclockwise circle.
Origin: indicating one thing above the other
Usage: A family lives *above* us.
a roof *over* their heads

BELOW, BENEATH, UNDER, BASIC, UNDERLYING

Hold the right open hand under the left open hand, both palms down; move the right in a counterclockwise circle.
Origin: indicating something beneath
Usage: *below* the surface
beneath the ground
under the table
basic to your studies
the *underlying* cause

UNDER

Move the right "A" (thumb pointing up) under the left downturned palm (or circle the "A" under the left).
Origin: representing that which is under or affected by someone or something
Usage: *under* the law
under supervision
under obligation

BACKGROUND

Form the right "B" and "G" under the left downturned palm.
Origin: based on the sign for "below"
Usage: We need to know your *background* first.

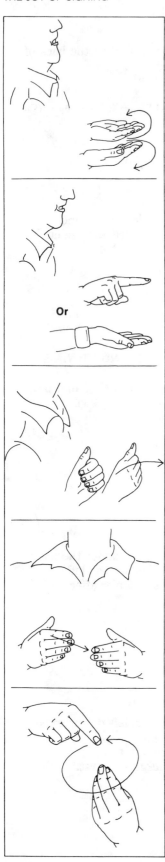

HERE, WHERE

With both open hands palms up and fingers pointing forward, move the right hand in a clockwise direction and the left hand counterclockwise.
Origin: indicates that which lies before you
Usage: *Here* I am.

Where there's life, there's hope.
Note: For the question "where" see page 31.

THERE

Point with the index finger if referring to a particular location. When used vaguely, circle the upturned open palm slightly toward the right.
Usage: The library is *over there* (point to a location).

There she is, Miss America (use the open hand in a larger and more poetic sense).
Note: In many instances "there" is omitted, as when it precedes the verb. Example: *There* are 12 months in a year. While speaking the words *there are,* only the sign for "are" is made.

FAR

Place both "A" hands in front of you, thumbs up, knuckles touching; move the right "A" forward. (When a great distance is indicated, the right moves forward with more effort and also a greater distance.)
Origin: indicates the distance from a starting point
Usage: not *far* from home

Stars are *far* from the earth.

NEAR, CLOSE TO, APPROACH, BESIDE, NEXT TO

The back of the right bent hand approaches the inside of the left bent hand, both palms facing the body.
Origin: one hand coming close to the other
Usage: sits *near* me; live *close to* town; summer is *approaching;* sits *beside (next to)* me.
Note: To differentiate between "near" and "next to" make the sign closer to the body for the latter.

AROUND, SURROUNDING

With the right index finger, describe a counterclockwise circle around the upturned tips of the left "AND" hand.
Origin: indicating movement around an object
Usage: flowers all *around* the house

people *surrounding* the victim

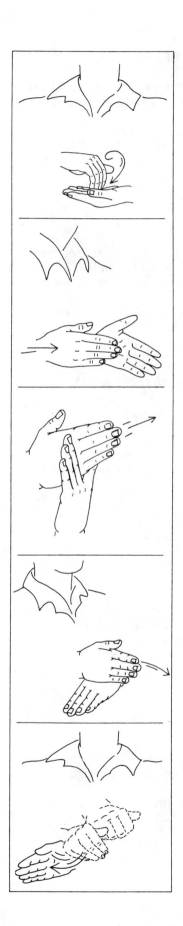

CENTER, MIDDLE

With the right bent hand make a clockwise circle over the left palm and then place the right fingertips in the center of the left palm.
Origin: in the center of the hand
Usage: *center* of attention
in the *middle* of the story

AGAINST, SUE

Strike the tips of the right open hand, palm facing you, against the left palm which is facing to the right.
Origin: coming against something
Usage: *against* the law
After the accident, she wanted to *sue* the driver.

THROUGH

Move the right open hand forward between the index and middle fingers of the left hand which is facing you.
Origin: moving through the fingers
Usage: driving *through* town

ACROSS, CROSSING, OVER

The little-finger edge of the right open hand passes across the back of the left open hand which is facing palm down.
Origin: indicates movement from one side over to the other
Usage: *across* the country
crossing the river
over the mountain

AWAY

Moving away from the body, the "A" hand opens and faces out.
Origin: moving the hand away
Usage: a vacation *away* from everybody

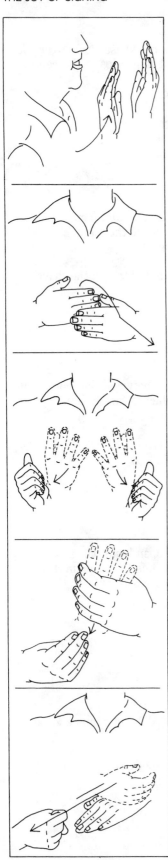

BEFORE, IN THE PRESENCE OF, TO FACE

The left open hand is held up, fingers pointing up and palm facing in; the right open hand moves up to face the left.
Origin: hands facing each other
Usage: He stood *before* (in front of) the class.
Sign the paper *in the presence of* two witnesses.
Face the judge.

BEYOND

Place the left open hand in front of you, fingers pointing right, palm toward you. Place the right open hand, palm toward you, between the body and the left hand; pass it over the left, down and forward.
Origin: on the other side and a little distance farther
Usage: The old man lives *beyond* that mountain.

DISAPPEAR, VANISH, FADE AWAY, DIE AWAY, DISSOLVE

Hold up both "AND" hands, palms facing you and tips pointing up. As hands are drawn apart to the sides, pass the thumb along the fingertips, ending in "A" positions.
Origin: something large becoming smaller and fading away
Usage: The snow *disappeared.*
The food *vanished* when the hungry boys arrived.
The rainbow *faded away.*
The music *died away.*
Sugar *dissolves* in water.

GONE, ABSENT, MISSING

The right open "AND" hand, facing the body and pointing up, becomes a closed "AND" as it is drawn down through the left "C" which then becomes an "O."
Origin: That which was in the hand is gone.
Usage: *gone* with the wind
absent twice a week
Who's *missing?*

ALL GONE

Place the right "C" on the back of the left open hand which is pointing right; draw the "C" quickly to the right into an "S" position.
Origin: That which was on the surface has moved away.
Usage: The pie is *all gone.*

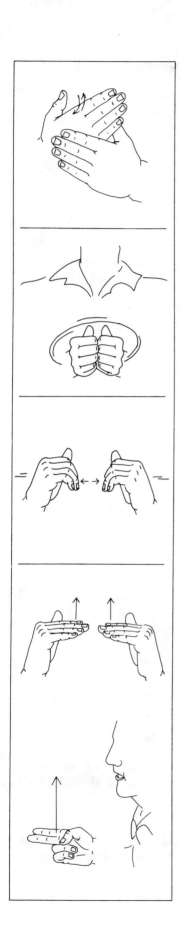

BETWEEN

Place the little-finger side of the right open hand between the thumb and fingers of the left open hand and move it back and forth between the thumb and index finger.
Origin: between the thumb and fingers
Usage: Let's keep it *between* us.

TOGETHER

Place the "A" hands together, palm to palm; move them right-forward-left in a semicircle.
Origin: moving along with another
Usage: We can accomplish a lot if we work *together*.

SEPARATE, APART

Both curved hands with fingers back to back, palms down, are pulled apart.
Origin: That which has been together is separated.
Usage: in *separate* groups
　　　　Keep them *apart*.

HIGH, ADVANCED, PROMOTION

Both bent hands, tips pointing toward each other and palms facing down, are moved upward in stages.
Origin: being elevated
Usage: a *high* position
　　　　advance to a better job
　　　　receive a *promotion*

Note: The sign for "HIGH" is sometimes made by raising the right "H." This is the sign most often used for feeling "high." Example: He was *high* on drugs.

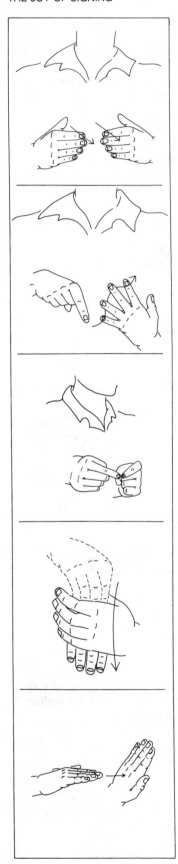

ONWARD, ON, FORWARD, ADVANCE

Both bent hands, tips pointing toward each other and palms facing you, are moved away from the body.
Origin: natural motion forward
Usage: *onward* to battle
We will go *on.*
They marched *forward.*
The army *advanced.*

AMONG

Hold up the left "FIVE" hand and pass the right index finger in and out between the fingers of the left hand.
Origin: in and out among the fingers
Usage: Are there any experts *among* us?

CORNER

Touch the tips of both index fingers at right angles.
Origin: showing a corner
Usage: the *corner* of a room

INTO, ENTER

Place the tips of the right "AND" hand into the left "C" hand, pushing the right hand through and forward.
Origin: indicates movement to the inside of something
Usage: Come *into* the house.
That idea never *entered* my head.

AT (Usually omitted or fingerspelled)

Hold the left hand in front of you, palm out. Strike the back of the left with the tips of the right hand, both hands pointing upward.
Usage: *at* the end of the way
at the close of the day
Note: In poetry and music the sign may be used if needed. However, in most cases "at" is omitted or fingerspelled.

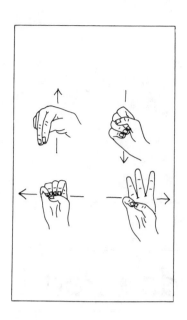

NORTH, SOUTH, EAST, WEST

Move the initial in the appropriate direction as if a map were before you.

Usage: the *north* pole
      going *south* for the winter
      wind is from the *east*
      Go *west,* young man.

Note: When giving directions, it is often better to use the initial in the direction of the compass. That is, if you are facing south and you tell someone to drive west, you would move the "W" to the right.

10

Verbs and Related Words • Part I

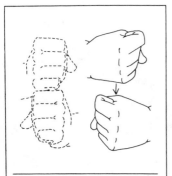

MAKE

Place the right "S" (palm facing left) on the left "S" (palm facing right). Turn them so the palms face you and strike them together again. Repeat several times.
Origin: twisting and pounding
Usage: He *made* the table and chairs in his shop.

BREAK

Hold the "S" hands side by side, palms down, and give them a sudden outward twist.
Origin: holding an object in the hands and breaking it in two
Usage: He didn't mean to *break* the window.

MUST, NECESSARY, NEED, OUGHT, SHOULD, HAVE TO, SUPPOSED TO

The crooked index finger, pointing down, moves downward forcefully.
Usage: I *must* take care of that today. Sleep is a *necessity*. What do you *need* now? Laws are *necessary*. We *should* obey them. We *ought to* investigate. Do you *have to* leave now? Eileen *has to* study tonight. Dan *had to* leave yesterday. They're *supposed to* go tomorrow.

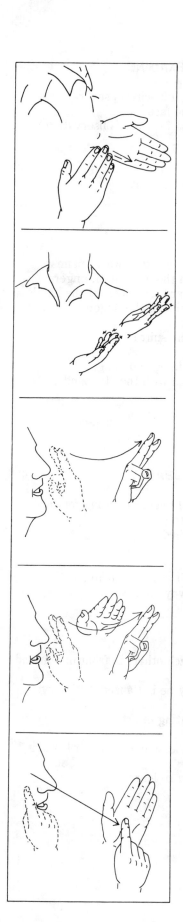

EXCUSE, FORGIVE, PARDON, EXEMPT, WAIVE

Stroke the edge of the left palm with the right fingertips.
Origin: wiping off the guilt
Usage: *Excuse* me, please. He asked *forgiveness.* The governor granted a *pardon.* The organization is tax *exempt.* Your course is *waived.*

WAIT

Hold the left open hand, palm up, a little away from the left side. Hold the right hand in the same position nearer the body, fingers pointing toward the left wrist. Wiggle the fingers of both hands.
Usage: Ray *waited* patiently for Joyce.

LOOK, WATCH, OBSERVE, SURVEY

Place the "V" in front of the face, palm in; turn the "V" so the fingertips point forward. (Or make with both hands.)
Origin: Fingertips represent the eyes looking out.
Usage: *Look,* it's raining. *Watch* the children for me. Astronomers *observe* the stars. The principal *surveyed* the situation (move the "V" hands back and forth). *Look at* me (turn tips toward self). *Looking at* each other ("V" tips pointing toward each other).

PREDICT, FORECAST, FORESEE, PROPHESY

Make the sign for "LOOK," passing it under the left open hand, palm down. For "PROPHET" add the "PERSON" ending.
Origin: looking into the future
Usage: *predict* bad storms; weather *forecast; foresee* a problem; to *prophesy* war

NOTICE, RECOGNIZE, SPOT (Detect)

Point to the eye with the right index finger and then touch the left palm.
Origin: to see and show
Usage: *Notice* the difference.
  I *recognized* Jim as he got off the plane.
  The teacher *spotted* (detected) the problem.

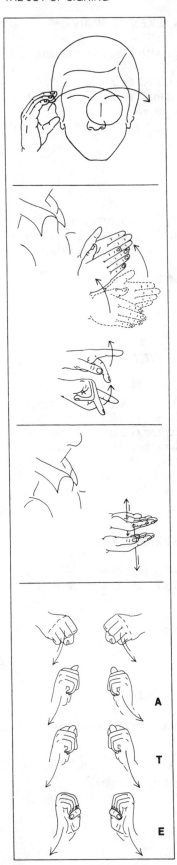

SEARCH, SEEK, LOOK FOR, EXAMINE

The "C" hand, with palm facing left, circles several times up-left-down-right in front of the face.
Origin: using a magnifying glass for closer observation
Usage: He *searched* everywhere.
People *seek* happiness.
She *looked for* her keys.
The doctor *examined* the patient.

ALLOW, LET, MAY, PERMIT

Both open hands with fingers pointing forward, palms facing in, are bent upward from the wrist until fingers point slightly upward and outward (the heels of the hands being closer together than the tips of the fingers).
Usage: We don't *allow* that.
Let me help you with the suitcase.
You *may* go now.
Pets are not *permitted* in our building.
Note: "PERMIT" is often signed with the "P" hands.

MAYBE, MAY, PERHAPS, PROBABLY

Both open hands, facing up and fingers pointing forward, are raised and lowered alternately.
Origin: The idea is being weighed.
Usage: *Maybe* I can go too.
It *may* rain tomorrow.
Perhaps your check will get here today.
We will *probably* go away next week.

TRY, ATTEMPT, EFFORT

Place both "S" hands, facing each other, in front of you and push them forward with effort.
Note: The following words may be initialized: "T"—try; "A"—attempt; "E"—effort
Origin: pushing forward indicating effort
Usage: It's not easy but I'll *try*.
I *attempted* to communicate even though I was a beginner.
She made a great *effort* to learn.

HELP, ASSIST, AID

Place the right open hand under the left "S," which is facing to the right; lift both hands together.
Origin: offering a helping hand
Usage: Please *help* me.
I need your *assistance*.
The Red Cross came to their *aid*.

REHABILITATION

Place the left open hand under the right "R"; lift them both.
Origin: based on the sign for "help"
Usage: The client was ready for *rehabilitation*.
Note: The term "vocational rehabilitation" is often signed with the initial letters "V" and "R."

DO, DID, DONE, DOES, ACTIVITY, CONDUCT, DEEDS

Place both "C" hands in front of you, palms down; move both hands to the right and left several times.
Origin: hands in active motion
Usage: What will you *do* now? We've *done* a lot. Is that all he *does*? Let's plan some *activities*. Claude is a man of *action*. His *conduct* is admirable. He is thoughtful in word and in *deed*.
Note: This sign should not be used when it does not refer to activity. In the following sentences it should either be omitted or spelled: *Do* you like chocolate? *Did* Mel leave Minnesota? *Does* Rita still live in Tennessee?

BEHAVIOR

Place the "B" hands in front of you, palms forward, and swing them back and forth.
Origin: The "do" sign is initialized.
Usage: The psychologist observed Andy's *behavior*.

USE, UTILIZE

Circle the right "U" in a small clockwise motion.
Usage: *Use* both signs and fingerspelling.
We *utilized* old lumber for the project.
He studied word *usage*.

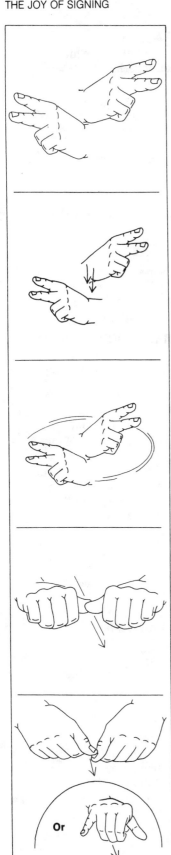

KEEP

Place the right "V" hand, palm leftward, on the wrist of the left "V" hand, palm rightward.
Origin: hands in the position of "seeing," represented by four eyes watching
Usage: Will you *keep* that car for a while?

CAREFUL

Make the sign for "KEEP" and strike together several times at the wrist.
Origin: a combination of watching and warning
Usage: If you aren't *careful* you'll fall on the ice.

TAKE CARE OF, SUPERVISE

Make the sign for "KEEP" and circle it from right to left.
Origin: four eyes watching over an area
Usage: Virginia will *take care of* the children.
  Grace is a good *supervisor*. (Add the "PERSON" ending.)

CONTINUE, ENDURE, LASTING, PERMANENT, PERSEVERE, KEEP ON

Place the thumb of the right "A" on the thumbnail of the left "A" and move both forward.
Origin: one thumb pushing the other forward
Usage: The story will *continue*. Gold *endures* forever. Will the speech *last* long? He has no *permanent* address. *Persevere* until you succeed. *Keep on* trying!

STAY, REMAIN, STAND

Place the thumb of the right "A" on the thumbnail of the left "A" and push downward slightly. Or direct the right "Y" hand downward in a short motion.
Origin: One thumb holds the other down.
Usage: *Stay* here—don't leave!
  His wife *remained* at home.
  The rule *stands*.

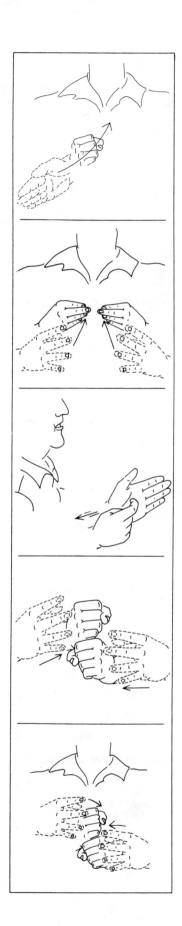

TAKE

Draw the open hand from right to left (palm facing left), ending in an "S" (or an "A") position.
Origin: taking hold of something
Usage: Can you *take* me home?

ACCEPT

The open "AND" hands point toward each other, palms facing the body. Move the hands toward the chest, closing them into the "AND" position, the fingers touching the body.
Origin: taking it to oneself
Usage: I am happy to *accept* your invitation.

DEMAND, REQUIRE, TAKES

Place the tip of the bent index finger in the left palm, which is facing right; draw both hands toward the body. (The sign for "DEMAND" is made more emphatically.)
Origin: as if demanding that something be placed in the palm
Usage: The officer *demands* attention.
    The English class is *required.*
    It *takes* a lot of patience to become skilled.

GET, OBTAIN

Both open "FIVE" hands, palms facing each other, close into "S" hands, the right on top of and touching the left.
Origin: grasping hold
Usage: How did you *get* that answer?
    We *obtain* knowledge through study and experience.

RECEIVE

Sign "GET" and draw it toward yourself.
Origin: grasping something and taking it to yourself
Usage: Joy *received* her M.A. degree in counseling.

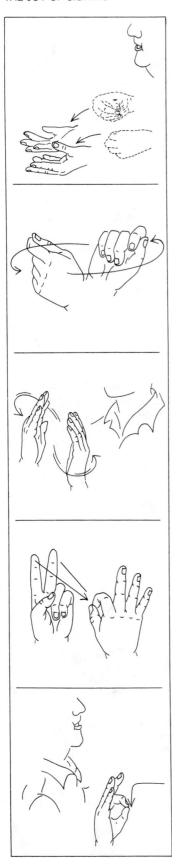

GIVE, DISTRIBUTE

Both "AND" hands facing down are turned in-up-forward, ending with palms open and facing up. For "DISTRIBUTE" the sign is broadened at the end.
Origin: opening the hand in a gesture of giving
Usage: I'll *give* what I can.
   Miss Rumford *distributed* the papers.
Note: This sign can be directed toward you to show someone is giving to you. (It may also be signed as in "gift," p. 212.)

CHANGE, ADJUST, ADAPT

Using a modified "A" position in both hands, place the right "A" so the palm faces forward, with the left "A" facing it. Twist the hands around until they have reversed positions. For "ADAPT" the "A" hands may be used.
Origin: hands changing positions
Usage: *changed* my mind; *adjust* the motor (use short quick motions back and forth); *adapt* to a new environment.

BECOME, GROW, GET

Place slightly curved open hands in front of you, the right palm facing forward and the left facing it; turn hands so they reverse positions.
Origin: The hands change positions as in "change."
Usage: Jerry *became* a father.
   She *grew* weary of all the complaints.
   Mike *got* sick after the party.

CHOOSE, CHOICE, SELECT, PICK

With the thumb and forefinger of the right hand make a motion as if picking something from the "V," which is facing you. (Sometimes made with only the right hand.)
Origin: making a choice between two items in front of you
Usage: *chose* her friends carefully; a wise *choice; selected* a green dress; *picked* his partner

APPOINT

Extend the right hand and close the forefinger and thumb; draw the hand back and down in this position.
Origin: choosing and putting it down
Usage: He was *appointed* as a member of the Supreme Court.

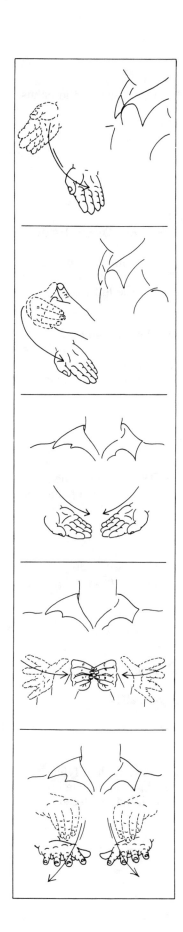

WELCOME

Bring the right open hand toward the body, palm facing up.
Origin: extending the hand in an invitation to come
Usage: Today we *welcome* our visitors from Japan.

INVITE

Touch the back of the left hand with the palm of the right and then bring the right toward the body, palm facing up.
Origin: a combination of the signs for "call" and "welcome"
Usage: *invited* to a party; the *invitation* arrived late

INTRODUCE

Hold both open hands in front of you, somewhat apart, with palms up; bring hands toward each other, tips pointing toward each other.
Origin: bringing two people together
Usage: Let me *introduce* you.

MEETING, ASSEMBLE, GATHER

Bring both open "AND" hands together from the sides into closed "AND" positions so the fingertips are touching and the palms are facing each other.
Origin: everyone coming together
Usage: The *meeting* began at 8:00.
The students *assembled* early.
We all *gathered* together.

SCATTER, SPREAD

Place both "AND" hands together in front of you, palms down, and direct them forward and toward each side as fingers open.
Origin: Fingers spreading represent people scattering.
Usage: The meeting was over and the people *scattered*.
The news *spread* rapidly.

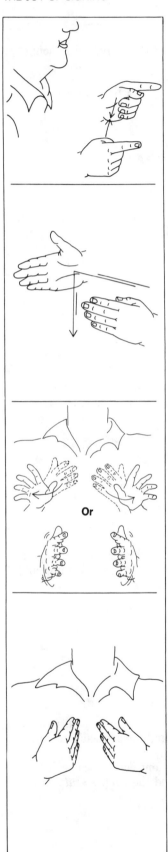

MEET

Bring both "G" hands together from the sides so the palms meet.
Origin: two persons coming together
Usage: Glad to *meet* you!

COMPLETED, FINISHED, DONE, ENDED, OVER, HAVE

Hold the left "B" hand in front of you, palm toward you; move the little-finger edge of the right open hand, palm facing left, along the forefinger edge of the left hand, dropping off at the edge.
Origin: cut off at the end
Usage: He *completed* his program. She *finished* college. When will you be *done?* The search is *ended.* Class is *over* at 3:00. Visitors *have* arrived.
RESULT—The above sign movement made with the right "R" is sometimes used, as in the final *result.*

FINISHED, ALREADY

This less formal sign for "FINISHED" is made by holding the "FIVE" hands in front of you, palms in, then palms out in a quick twisting movement. Or shake the "FIVE" hands (palm toward palm) several times.
Usage: He *finished* working.
People are *already* arriving.
Note: This sign is often used as an affirmative reply, as: Q: Have you been to the store? A: *Finished* (meaning, "Yes, I've already been there").

HAVE, HAS, HAD, POSSESS

Place fingertips of both bent hands against the chest, palms facing you.
Origin: holding the object against oneself
Usage: We *have* a large office.
Retha *has* six children.
Pete *had* a Volkswagen.
Solomon *possessed* great wisdom.
Note: In educational settings the following identifying letters are sometimes used when making the above sign: "V"—have; "S"—has; "D"—had. The initial is placed against the chest.

Victory

PRAISE, APPLAUD, CLAP, OVATION

Clap the hands several times.
Origin: a natural sign
Usage: The basketball coach *praised* his team.
People stood and *applauded* for the winner.
The students *clapped* for 5 minutes.
We gave the speaker a standing *ovation.*

CONGRATULATE

Sign "GOOD" and then clap the hands to indicate praise.
Or clasp the hands as if in a handshake.
Usage: *Congratulations,* we're proud of you!

CELEBRATE, TRIUMPH, VICTORY, FESTIVAL, HAIL, HOORAY, ANNIVERSARY

Swing the right modified "A" above the side of the head.
The "V" hands are often used for "VICTORY."
Origin: waving a banner
Usage: *celebrate* a birthday; *triumph* over the enemy;
game ended in *victory;* cherry blossom *festival; hail*
to the chief; *hooray,* we won! 25th *anniversary*

WIN

Sign "GET" and "TRIUMPH."
Usage: Who will *win* today?

SUCCEED, EFFECTIVE, FINALLY

Point both index fingers toward each other, palms in. Turn
and raise both hands so the index fingers point up with
palms facing out; repeat several times, higher each time.
Origin: going higher and higher on the ladder
Usage: a *successful* person
effective training
Finally! I found it!

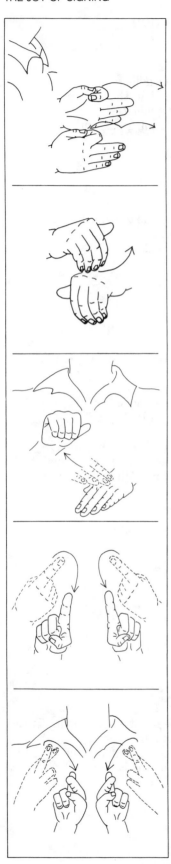

POSTPONE, PROCRASTINATE, DELAY, PUT OFF

Place both "F" hands in front of you, palms facing each other and fingers pointing forward; lift them up, forward, and down. Repeat and move farther away from you each time.

Origin: The decision is moved farther and farther away.
Usage: *postpone* the game; we *procrastinate; delay* a decision; don't *put off* until tomorrow what you can do today

SEND

Place the fingertips of the right bent hand on the back of the left and lift the right hand, straightening it into the open position, palm down.
Usage: Earl *sent* Betty some roses.

CALL

Place the palm of the right open hand on the back of the left open hand and draw the right up into an "A" position.
Origin: A deaf person is called by tapping him.
Usage: The meeting is now *called* to order.

HAPPEN, OCCUR

Point the index fingers up with the palms facing you, then twist them forward so the palms face down.
Usage: Something interesting *happened* recently.
Eclipses do not *occur* often.

RESULT

Sign "HAPPEN" with the "R" hands.
Usage: What are the test *results?*

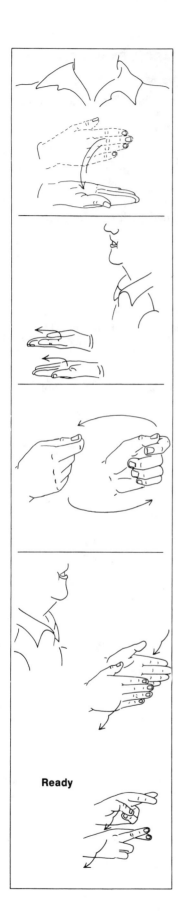

Ready

WILLING

Place the open palm on the chest; move it away from the body and turn the palm up.
Origin: My heart is extended to you.
Usage: Are you *willing* to assume responsibility?

OFFER, PRESENT, PROPOSE, SUGGEST, RECOMMEND, MOTION

Place the open hands in front of you, palms up and fingers pointing forward; move the hands up and forward in this position.
Origin: lifted and offered
Usage: *offered* a job; want to *present* an idea; *propose* a new plan; What can you *suggest?* Whom do you *recommend?* I make a *motion.*

EXCHANGE, TRADE, INSTEAD OF, SWITCH, REPLACE, SUBSTITUTE

Using the modified "A" position for both hands, place the right "A" behind the left; draw it under and place it in front of the left, while circling the left up and back, so that the hands have changed relative positions.
Origin: One hand changes places with the other.
Usage: *exchanged* the gift; *trade* stamps with me; coffee *instead of* tea; quickly *switched* places; men are *replaced* by machines; a *substitute* for sugar

PLAN, ARRANGE, PREPARE, IN ORDER, READY

The open hands, facing each other and pointing forward, are moved toward the right in several short sweeping motions.
Origin: everything in stacks, all arranged
Usage: Make *plans* early.
　　　　Arrange to leave soon.
　　　　Prepare the food.
　　　　everything *in order*
　　　　Are you *ready?*
Note: "READY" is often signed with the "R" hands.

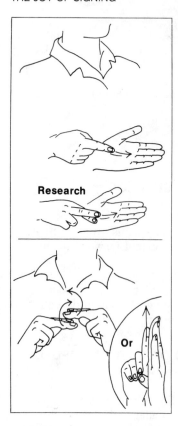

Research

Or

INVESTIGATE, INSPECT, RESEARCH, EXAMINE, CHECK

Place the tip of the right index into the left palm and move it forward toward the fingertips.
Origin: as if digging into the matter
Usage: Let us *investigate*.
   inspected by the government
   a *research* project
   He *examined* the dollar bill carefully.
   They had to *check* my background.
Note: "RESEARCH" is often signed with the right "R."

DEVELOP

Using the index and middle fingers of both hands, place them on top of each other alternately as if building. Or place the right "D" against the left palm and move the "D" upward.
Usage: *develop* a curriculum
   a recent *development* (Add the "MENT" ending after the upward "D.")

11

Verbs and Related Words • Part II

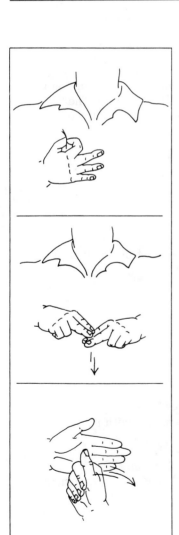

VOLUNTEER, APPLY

With the thumb and forefinger of the right hand grasp
your lapel (or clothing) and pull it forward.
Origin: putting oneself forward
Usage: Dennis *volunteered* to chair the committee.
      If you want a job you'll have to *apply* for one.

DEPEND, RELY

Place the right index and middle fingers on the back of the
left index and middle fingers, both palms down, and push
down slightly. (Can be made using only the index fingers.)
Origin: one is leaning on the other
Usage: It all *depends* on the weather.
      We *rely* on the newspaper for lots of information.

IMPRESS, EMPHASIZE

Press the thumb of the right "A" hand into the left open
palm and move the hands forward slightly.
Usage: *impressed* on my mind
      emphasize the need for more cooperation
      make a good *impression*
      I am *impressed*. (Move the sign toward self.)

INCLUDE, INVOLVE

The right "FIVE" hand (palm up) is moved up, turns over with fingers coming together, and is placed into the left "C" hand.
Origin: as if taking something and placing it inside
Usage: Please *include* me!
          Would you like to be *involved*?

ANALYZE

Place the bent "V" hands in front of you, facing each other with palms down; move them away from each other several times.
Origin: taking things apart
Usage: Let's try to *analyze* the problem.

BLAME, FAULT, ACCUSE

Place the right "A" hand, with thumb pointing up, on the back of the left closed hand. YOUR FAULT—The "A" is directed outward. MY FAULT—The "A" is directed toward self.
Usage: Who's to *blame*?
          Is it *my fault* or *your fault*?
          Why did Nancy *accuse* Jim?

INNOCENT

Place the "U" hands (palms in) in front of the mouth; move them toward the sides, palms up.
Usage: I'm *innocent!*

ENCOURAGE

Move the open hands forward in stages with palms out as if slightly pushing.
Origin: gently pushing in stages
Usage: The president *encouraged* farming.
          Sue seems depressed and needs *encouragement*.

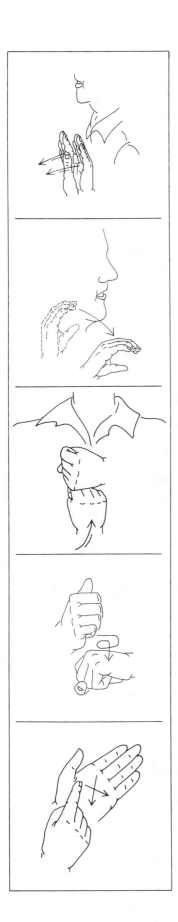

PUSH

Move the open hands forward, palms out, as if pushing an object.
Origin: natural motion of pushing
Usage: Three men *pushed* the car.

FORCE, COMPEL

Place the right "C" (pointing forward) below the cheek and push forward.
Usage: No one likes to be *forced.*
      You can't *compel* a person to love his neighbor.
Note: To show that you are the receiver of the action, bring the right "C" over the left wrist toward self.
Example: He *forced* me to take action.

SUPPORT, IN FAVOR OF, ADVOCATE

Place the right "S" under the left "S" and push upward.
Origin: The right hand supports the left
Usage: He *supports* a large family.
      All *in favor,* say aye.
      The governor *advocates* building better roads.
REINFORCE—Place the right "R" under the left "S" and push upward.

ESTABLISH, FOUNDED, BASED, SET UP

Using the right "A" make a clockwise circle and then place the little-finger edge firmly on the back of the left fist.
Origin: firmly planted on a rock
Usage: *established* in 1864
      founded in the 16th century
      a statement *based* on fact
      set up a new program

CANCEL, CRITICIZE, CORRECT

Draw an "X" in the left palm with the right index finger.
Origin: An "X" is used to cancel out something.
Usage: *Cancel* my appointment.
      He was quick to *criticize* the boy.
      The teacher *corrected* test papers after school.

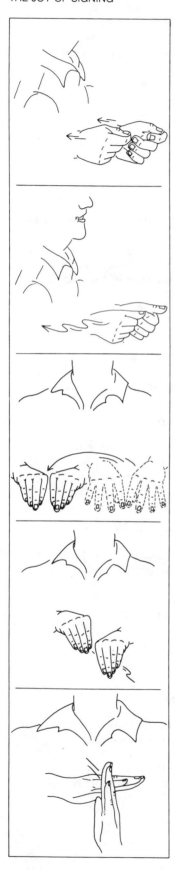

URGE, PERSUADE, COAX

Using the modified "A" hands, place the right behind the left and pull the hands toward the body in stages, as if pulling something toward you with effort.
Usage: *Urge* your friend to support you.

They almost *persuaded* me.

Jennifer *coaxed* her mother to let her go to the party.

AVOID

Place the right "A" behind the left "A"; swing the right wrist back and forth as it draws back and away from the left.
Origin: trying to get away from something
Usage: He was trying to *avoid* me.

PUT, MOVE

Place the open "AND" hands in front of you, palms down, and lift them slightly, changing to the "AND" position as you move them to the right and down.
Origin: An object is lifted and placed.
Usage: *Put* the children's toys away.

Are you *moving* to Georgia?

MOVE, MOVEMENT

Move the "AND" hands forward (pointing down), one behind the other in a zigzag motion.
Origin: moving things around
Usage: The dancers *moved* across the stage gracefully.

I thought I saw something *moving!*

PREVENT, BLOCK

Place the little-finger edge of the right open hand (palm down) against the forefinger of the left open hand (palm right) and push both hands forward.
Origin: Something is blocking movement.
Usage: You can't *prevent* that.

He *blocked* my plans.

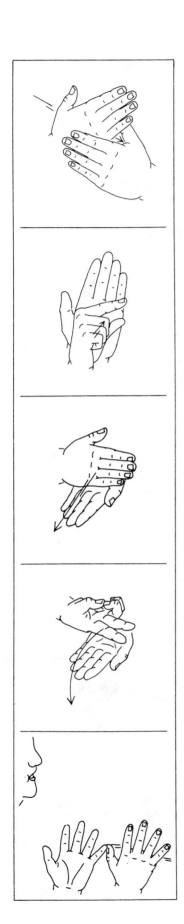

BOTHER, INTERFERE, DISTURB, INTERRUPT

Place the little-finger edge of the right open hand between the thumb and forefinger of the left open hand and strike it several times.
Origin: the right hand coming between
Usage: Don't *bother* me.

Something *interfered* with our plans.
The noise *disturbed* us.
A young woman *interrupted* the meeting.

FORBID

Throw the side of the right "G" hand against the left palm which is pointing up and facing right.
Usage: Smoking is *forbidden* in elevators.

REJECT

Place the little-finger side of the right hand on the open left palm; push the right hand out toward the fingertips. Or place the fingertips of the right hand into the left palm and push outward.
Origin: pushing something off the palm
Usage: The Army *rejected* Sue's brother.

FAIL, FAILURE

Place the back of the right "V" in the left open palm and slide it forward and off.
Origin: falling over the edge
Usage: If you *fail*, try again.

Do you sometimes feel like a *failure?*
FLUNK (Colloquial)—Strike the thumb side of the right "F" against the left palm. Example: She *flunked* the final exam.

LINE UP

Place the "FIVE" hands in front of you, pointing up, right palm facing left and left palm facing right; the right thumbtip touches the tip of the little finger on the left hand.
Origin: The fingers represent people standing in line.
Usage: The children *lined up* for ice cream cones.

Everyone please *get in line*.

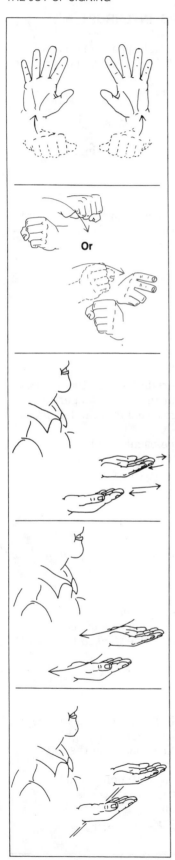

SURRENDER, GIVE UP, YIELD, SUBMISSION

Place both "A" hands in front of you, palms down; move them forward and up into "FIVE" positions with palms facing out.
Origin: hands thrown up in surrender
Usage: The enemy refused to *surrender.*
   Why not *give up?*
   The prisoners *yielded* to the police.
   Submit to authority.

CONQUER, OVERCOME, DEFEAT, BEAT

Place the wrist of the right "S" against the side of the wrist of the left "S"; push the right forward and down. Or reverse the movement if you are the receiver (have been defeated).
Origin: Right hand conquers the left.
Usage: Napoleon wanted to *conquer* all of Europe. Brad couldn't *overcome* his fear. We *defeated* the enemy. Our team *beat* Teachers College. (In this usage it is common to use the right "TWELVE" hand as in the second drawing.)

SERVE, SERVANT, WAITER

With both palms facing up, move the hands alternately back and forth. Add the "PERSON" ending where needed.
Origin: as if carrying a tray while walking
Usage: He *served* his country.
   He was a faithful *servant.*
   Call the *waiter.*

BRING

Bring both open hands toward you, palms facing up, one hand behind the other. (This sign should be moved in the intended direction; toward self, or toward another.)
Usage: *Bring* me some soap (toward you).
   I will *bring* you some more blankets (away from you).
   Who *brought* the flowers? (either direction).

CARRY

Both open hands, palms up, move from right to left in front of the body.
Origin: Hands move as if carrying something.
Usage: Jamie loves to *carry* the kitten around.

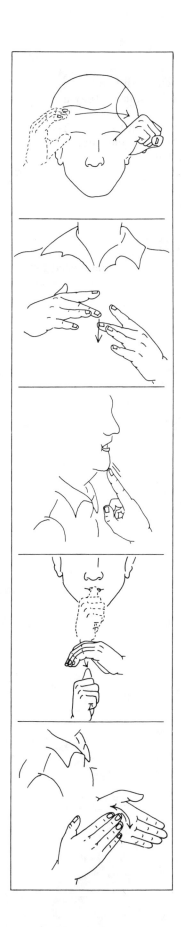

MISS (Fail to catch)

Place the right "C" near the right side of the forehead (palm left) and pass the hand quickly to the left, ending with the "S" position.
Origin: Something went by quickly.
Usage: I *missed* the train.
He *missed* the point of the joke.

MISS (Fail to meet)

The right middle finger strikes the tip of the left middle finger and passes it in a downward movement (both palms down).
Usage: She *missed* classes often
He *cut* classes every Friday afternoon.

MISS (Feel the absence of)

Touch the chin with the right index finger.
Origin: This sign is used for "disappointed"; if you miss someone you are disappointed he has not come.
Usage: I'll *miss* you when you move away.

HIDE

Place the thumb of the right "A" hand against the lips and then move the "A" hand under the left palm, which is held in front of you.
Origin: a secret that is hidden
Usage: Children enjoy playing *hide*-and-seek.

RUB

Rub the tips of the right hand against the palm of the left.
Origin: natural motion of rubbing
Usage: My shoes are *rubbing* and my feet hurt.

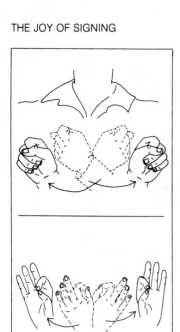

SAFE, SAVE, RESCUE

Cross the "S" hands in front of you, both hands facing you as if bound at the wrists; turn both hands so they are separated and facing forward.

Origin: First the hands are bound, then they are free.

Usage: We arrived *safely* after our long journey.
The fireman *rescued* the baby.

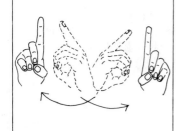

FREE

Sign as for "SAVE," using the "F" hands.

Usage: President Lincoln will always be remembered for *freeing* the slaves.

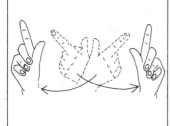

DELIVER

Sign as for "SAVE," using the "D" hands.

Usage: *Deliver* us from evil.

LIBERTY

Sign as for "SAVE," using the "L" hands.

Usage: sweet land of *liberty*

INDEPENDENT

Sign as for "SAVE," using the "I" hands.

Usage: a very *independent* young man

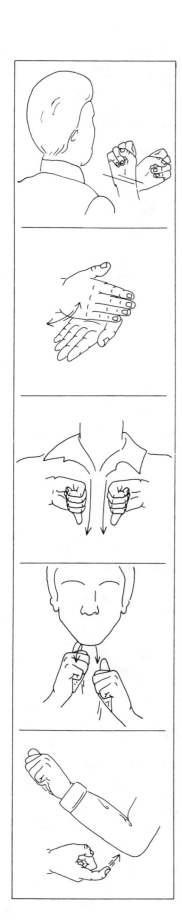

BOUND, BIND

Place the wrist of the right "S" (palm up) on the wrist of the left "S" (palm up) and push down slightly.
Origin: as if wrists are tied
Usage: prisoners *bound* in chains
Marriage vows are *binding.*

SHARE

Place the little-finger side of the right open hand crosswise on the left palm and move it back and forth between the left wrist and fingertips.
Origin: as if dividing something that is in the hand and saying, "Some for you and some for me"
Usage: Let's *share* the lunch.

DENY (Self-denial)

With both hands in the "A" position, thumbs pointing down, push the hands down the chest a short distance.
Origin: The inner feelings that would rise are pushed down.
Usage: She *denied* herself all candy during Lent.

DENY (To declare not to be true)

Place the thumb of the right "A" hand under the chin and push it forward; repeat with the left "A" and alternate several times.
Origin: repeating the sign for "NOT" several times
Usage: He *denied* everything when he was accused.

TEMPT

Tap the left forearm near the elbow with the right index finger.
Origin: tapping someone to entice him
Usage: Rich food is a great *temptation* to people on a diet.

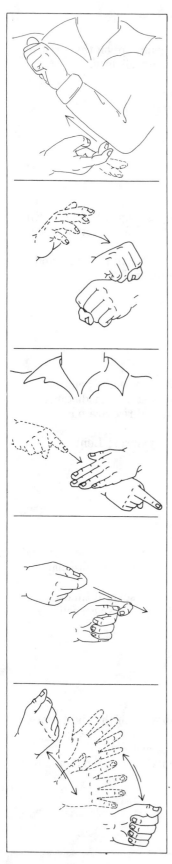

STEAL

Place the right "V," palm facing up, under the left elbow and bend it as it is drawn toward the wrist.
Origin: as if using a hook to secretly pull something out from underneath an object
Usage: Someone *stole* my beautiful new car.

CAPTURED, CATCH

The right curved "FIVE" closes quickly into an "S" position on the back of the left closed hand.
Origin: as if grasping and holding
Usage: The prisoner was *captured*.
The police *caught* the thief.
Quick, *catch* him!

KILL, SLAY, MURDER

Slide the right index finger under the left palm and out toward the left with a twist. The right "K" may be used as an initial sign for "KILL."
Origin: as if inserting and twisting a knife
Usage: Several people were *killed* in the accident.
Soldiers were *slain* in battle.
He was in jail for *murder*.

PERSECUTE, TEASE, RUIN, SPOIL, DAMAGE

Slide the right modified "A" across the top of the left modified "A." When used for "TEASE" the motion is repeated several times.
Usage: The patient thought everyone was *persecuting* her. The boys *teased* the little girls. The rain *ruined* my shoes. The child is *spoiled*. That could *damage* his reputation.

DESTROY, DEMOLISH, DAMAGE

Place both slightly curved "FIVE" hands in front of you facing each other, the right lower than the left. The hands change to "A" positions as they brush past each other, the right one moving toward the body and the left away. The hands then pass each other again, ending in the original position.
Origin: as if tearing up paper
Usage: *destroyed* by fire; completely *demolished;* heavy *damage*

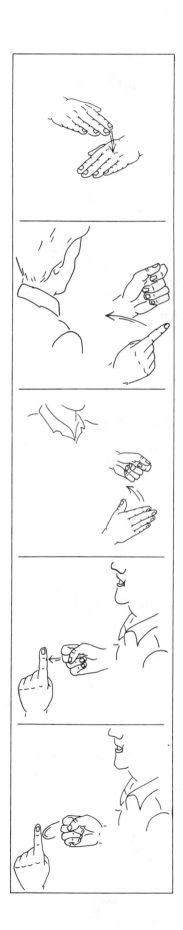

WARN

Tap the back of the left hand several times with the right open hand. Sometimes the right index finger is also raised as if in warning.
Origin: as if tapping someone quickly to give warning
Usage: The policeman gave the driver a *warning*.

PUNISH, PENALTY

Hold the left modified "A" hand in front of you as if holding an imaginary culprit; move the right index finger down quickly just below the left arm.
Usage: The judge determined the *punishment*.
        There is a $10 *penalty* for driving too fast.

SPANK

Hold the left modified "A" in front of you; move the right open hand as if giving a spanking.
Origin: natural motion of spanking a child
Usage: He really needs a *spanking*.

HIT, IMPACT, STRIKE

Strike the left index finger (which is pointing upward) with the right "S" (palm-side left).
Origin: striking an object
Usage: His words really *hit* me hard.
        The president's speech had a strong *impact*.
        A car *struck* the pole.

BEATING

Strike the left index finger (which is pointing upward) with the right "S" from left to right several times.
Origin: as if beating on someone
Usage: The gang gave him a *beating*.

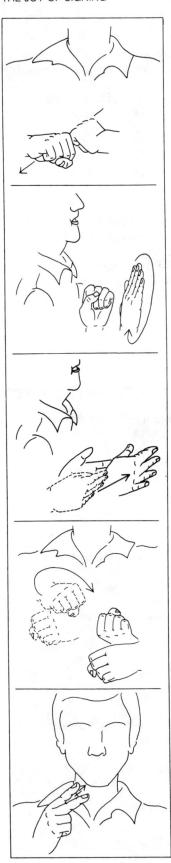

DEFEND, PROTECT, GUARD

Place the left "S" behind the right "S" and push hands out slightly.
Origin: pushing away or resisting danger
Usage: Soldiers *defend* our country.
They *protect* us from danger.
Men were *guarding* the property.

SHIELD, SHELTER

Place the left "S" in front of you. The right open hand (palm out) moves clockwise as if shielding the left fist.
Origin: raising a shield for protection
Usage: The mother always *shielded* the child.
a *shelter* in the storm

REFLECT

Place the tips of the right closed "AND" hand against the left palm; open the right as it moves away from the left.
Origin: light reflecting from a surface
Usage: The strong *reflection* bothered our eyes.

LOCK

Make a small circle with the right "S" hand and then place the back of the right wrist on the wrist of the left "S," which is facing right.
Usage: All doors should be *locked*.

STUCK, TRAPPED

Place the tips of the right "V" against the neck (palm down).
Origin: as if sticking a fork in the neck
Usage: We were *stuck* in the mud.
The thief was *trapped*.

TURN

Hold up the left index finger; point the right index finger down and circle it around the left index in a counterclockwise motion, the left index turning slightly.
Origin: shows turning away from the original position
Usage: The men *turned* against their leader.

"TURN" takes on various meanings when combined with other words. It is then signed according to its meaning in the sentence. The following are a few examples:

Turn off the motor (turn a key to the left).
Turn off the light (the open "AND" position closes to show lights going off).
doing a *good turn* (a good deed)
Take turns (twist the right "L" back and forth).
turn down an offer (thumbs down)
rain *turned to* snow (changed to)
It *turned* his stomach (sign "UPSET," hands flip over near stomach).
turned over in her sleep ("V" hand turns over from palm-down to palm-up)
turn loose (sign "CONNECT" and then open the fingers)
Everyone *turned out* (came).
He *turned out to be* a successful doctor (became).
He *turned over* the business to his son (gave).
leaves *turned* in the fall (changed)
She *turned* pale (became).

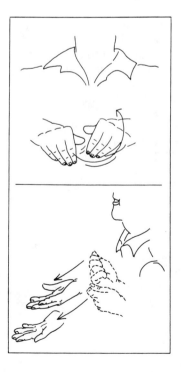

COVER

Slide the right curved hand over the back of the left curved hand from right to left, both palms facing down.
Origin: covering the hand
Usage: ground *covered* with snow

CAUSE

Place the "A" hands in front of you, thumbs pointing up; throw the hands leftward as they open, palms up and open.
Origin: as if throwing something into the air or into existence
Usage: Floods *cause* destruction.
The combination of sun and rain *caused* the rainbow.

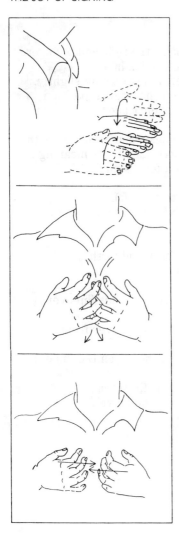

BET

Place the open hands in front of you several inches apart, palm facing palm; turn both palms down in a quick motion.
Origin: placing the cards face down on the table
Usage: He made a *bet* of $5.

MESH, FIT TOGETHER, FALL IN PLACE, MERGE, BLEND, INTEGRATE, WORK OUT

Place both curved "FIVE" hands in front of you, palms facing you, and interlock the fingers beginning with the little finger (as gears fit together).
Usage: We couldn't understand what happened but suddenly everything *fit together (meshed, fell in place).* Two businesses *merged.* The colors *blended.* The school was *integrated.* Everything *worked out* well.

MATCH, FIT

Bring the curved "FIVE" hands together so the fingers interlock (palm facing self).
Usage: Joel's coat *matches* his pants.
The test included true-false, multiple choice, and *matching* questions.
The punishment should *fit* the crime.

Note: Some use this sign for "roommate."

"MATCH" and "FIT" take on various meanings depending on the context. A few examples are listed here:
MATCH: You can't *match* his skill (come up to or meet).
The twins wore *matching* dresses (same).
The tennis *match* was exciting (game).
I never saw her *match* (never saw anyone her equal).
The young man is a good *match* for my daughter. (Fingerspell, or use the sign pictured above.)
Do you have a *match?* (Mime striking a match in the left palm.)

FIT: *fit* food for animals (right food)
It is *fit* that we give thanks (right, proper).
young men, *fit* for duty (prepared)
feeling *fit* now (well, healthy)
He had a *fit* about it (was angry).
The dress *fits* perfectly (fingerspell).
a house not *fit* to live in (reword or fingerspell)
having a *fit* (a seizure, fingerspell)

12

Quality, Kind, and Condition

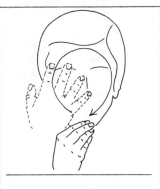

BEAUTIFUL, PRETTY, LOVELY, GORGEOUS

Place the right "AND" hand in front of the chin, palm facing you; open the fingers and circle the hand in front of the face from right to left, ending in the original position.
Origin: attention is drawn to the face
Usage: a *beautiful* sunset; a *pretty* girl; a *lovely* smile; a *gorgeous* dress

WONDERFUL, MARVELOUS, GREAT, FANTASTIC, A WONDER

Throw both open hands up, palms facing forward.
Origin: Hands are thrown up in wonder.
Usage: The trip to Australia was *wonderful.*
    a *marvelous* invention
    a *great* person
    a *fantastic* place
    the *wonders* of the world

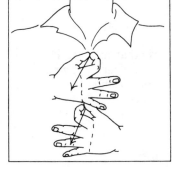

INTERESTING

Place the thumbs and index (or middle) fingers against the chest, with the other fingers extended, and draw the hands away from the body, closing the indexes and thumbs.
Origin: The heart is drawn toward the object.
Usage: The speaker told an *interesting* story.
    People have different *interests.*

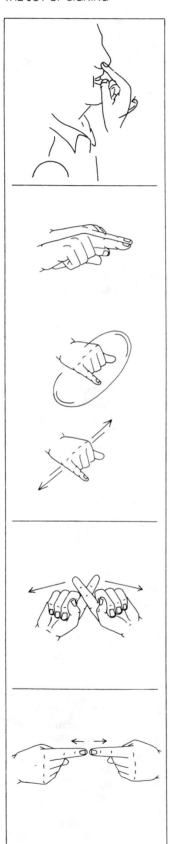

BORING, TEDIOUS, DULL

Place the tip of the index finger against the side of the nose and twist the finger slightly.
Origin: nose to the grindstone
Usage: Students get *bored* with their studies.
a long and *tedious* journey
a *dull* evening
Note: Some prefer to sign "DRY."

SAME, LIKE, ALIKE, SIMILAR, UNIFORM, STANDARD, IN COMMON

Place both index fingers side by side, touching each other with palms down.
Origin: Both fingers are alike.
Usage: at the *same* time; he looks *like* his father; they have *similar* ideas (sign "SAME" twice)

Or place the "Y" hand in front of you palm side down and move it around in a counterclockwise circle.
Usage: they all have *similar* ideas; a *uniform* temperature throughout the house; that's *standard* procedure in each department; we have one thing *in common*

Or move the "Y" hand back and forth between yourself and another person, indicating similarity between the two of you.
Usage: Look, we both have the *same* shoes.
The twins sure look *alike.*

DIFFERENT, DIFFER

Cross the index fingers and pull them apart.
Origin: Instead of keeping the fingers together as in "same," they are pulled apart to show a difference.
Usage: The first house was *different* from all the others.
You and I *differ* in our opinions.

OPPOSITE, OPPOSE, ENMITY, AT ODDS, CONTRARY

Both index fingers, pointing toward each other, are pulled apart.
Usage: He sat *opposite* her. I *oppose* that motion. The two words have *opposite* meanings. There is *enmity* between them. They once were friends but now are *at odds.* That is *contrary* to fact.

PARALLEL

Place both index fingers side by side but not touching, palms down; move them forward.
Origin: side by side
Usage: His thinking *parallels* mine.

VARIETY, VARIOUS, DIVERSE, ETC.

Place the index fingers in front of you, pointing straight ahead; move the fingers up and down several times as the hands move apart. (Or sign "DIFFERENT.")
Usage: a great *variety* of things
We wanted *various* people to give opinions.
He is a man of *diverse* interests.
His suitcase contained clothes, books, papers, *etc.*

KIND (Variety)

Circle the right "K" around the left "K" while the left one also circles slightly.
Usage: What *kind* of food do you like?
Note: Some prefer to use the sign for "variety" in this context.

EXACT, PRECISE

Bring the fingertips of the right modified "A" hand toward the left modified "A" and touch the tips together.
Origin: hitting the nail on the head
Usage: Give me the *exact* word.
We need *precise* measurements.

PERFECT, PERFECTION

Bring the middle fingertips of the right "P" hand toward the left "P" and touch the middle fingertips.
Origin: using the initial letter and hitting the nail on the head
Usage: a *perfect* plan
That's *perfectly* clear.
striving for *perfection*

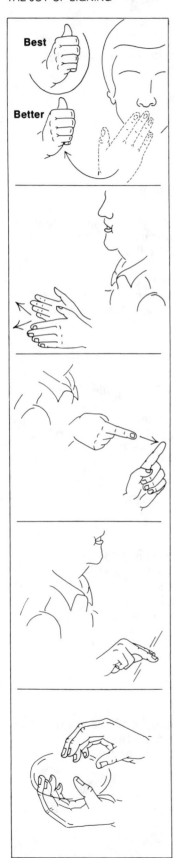

BETTER, BEST

Place the open hand in front of the mouth, palm facing in and fingers pointing left; draw it up into an "A" position. For "BEST" the "A" is moved higher than for "BETTER."
Origin: good to a greater degree
Usage: Your signs are *better* than mine.
       best in the world

GENERAL (As opposed to SPECIFIC)

Place the tips of the open hands together; then move the hands apart, wrists bending back (hands point forward).
Origin: Broadening out the hands indicates the meaning.
Usage: This television program is of *general* interest.

SPECIFIC, POINT

Place the left index in front of you, palm side facing right; direct the right index toward the tip of the left and touch it.
Origin: The left index represents a specific item that is pointed out.
Usage: a *specific* requirement
       That's a good *point.*

NEUTRAL

Shake the right "N" in front of you.
Note: This sign will usually be understood only in context.
Usage: I'm neither for nor against your idea; I'll remain *neutral.*

CONFUSION, MIXED UP

The left curved "FIVE" is held in front of you, palm facing up; the right curved "FIVE," with palm down, circles counterclockwise above it.
Origin: everything going in circles
Usage: There was a lot of *confusion* after the game.
       We couldn't find anything—everything was *mixed up.*

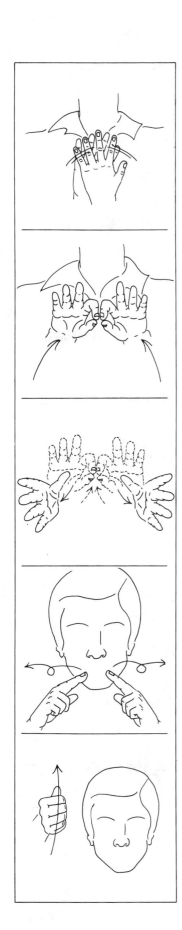

VAGUE, OBSCURE, BLURRY

Rub the right palm back and forth against the left palm, both hands in the "FIVE" position, the back of the right hand facing you.

Usage: Your explanation is *vague;* I don't understand it.
Legal language is sometimes *obscure.*
The picture is *blurry.*

IMPORTANT, WORTH, WORTHY, PRECIOUS, VALUABLE, MERIT, SIGNIFICANT

Draw the "F" hands up from the sides toward the center until they touch.

Origin: brought to the top

Usage: *important* people; *worth* a hundred dollars; an action *worthy* of praise; gold is *precious;* a *valuable* old book; your plan has *merit;* a *significant* decision

WORTHLESS

Sign "WORTH" (as above) and drop the open hands from the center to the sides.

Origin: worth nothing

Usage: We thought the old coin would be valuable but discovered it was *worthless.*

FAMOUS

Index fingers touch the lips and move away from the face, describing small circles in the air.

Origin: It has been told abroad.

Usage: a *famous* president

PROMINENT, CHIEF, HIGH

Lift the right "A" hand, thumb pointing up.

Origin: high up

Usage: a *prominent* lawyer ("FAMOUS" could be used here)
chief of staff
high in government

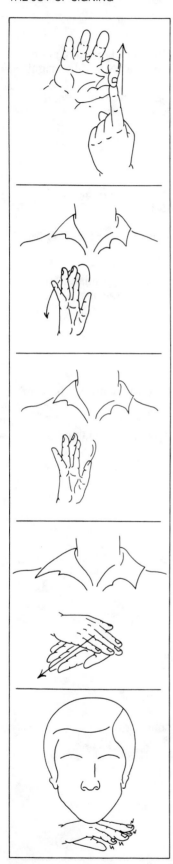

SPECIAL, EXCEPTIONAL, EXCEPT, UNIQUE, OUTSTANDING

With the right thumb and index finger grasp the end of the left index finger, which is pointing up, and pull up.
Origin: One is singled out for special attention.
Usage: He requires *special* food.
      an *exceptional* child
      All were here *except* Joe.
      an intelligent and *unique* person
      outstanding skills

FINE

Place the thumb of the "FIVE" hand at the chest, palm facing left, and move the hand slightly up and forward.
Origin: representing ruffles
Usage: a *fine* man
      feeling *fine,* thank you
Note: For informal use the fingers are wiggled while the thumb is against the chest.

POLITE, COURTEOUS, MANNERS, FANCY, FORMAL, ELEGANT

Place the thumb of the "FIVE" hand at the chest, palm facing left, and move the hand slightly up and forward several times.
Usage: a *polite* young woman
      a *courteous* answer
      Where are your *manners?*
      fancy dress
      formal party
      elegant drapes

CLEAN, NICE

The right open palm is placed on the left open palm and is passed across it.
Origin: All the dirt is rubbed off.
Usage: a *clean* house
      a *nice* girl
      cleaning the window (when used to show action, as in this case, rub the hands in a circular motion)

DIRTY, FILTHY

The back of the right hand is placed under the chin and the fingers wiggled.
Origin: Similar to the sign for "pig."
Usage: *dirty* hands
      The street was *filthy.*

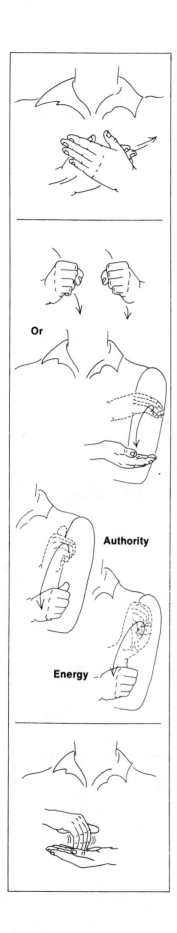

NEW

The left open hand faces up; the back of the right open hand brushes across the heel of the left from right to left.
Usage: a *new* town and *new* friends

STRONG, POWERFUL, MIGHTY, AUTHORITY, ENERGY

Bring the "S" hands down with force. Or use the right open hand to indicate the size of the left arm muscle.
Note: Sometimes "authority" and "energy" are initialed over the muscle as in the second description.
Origin: The fists and muscles represent power.
Usage: a *strong* wind
a *powerful* nation
a *mighty* army
authority to sign the paper
an *energy* program

WEAK, FEEBLE

Place the four fingertips of the right hand in the left palm; then bend the fingers of the right hand.
Origin: weak in the knees
Usage: a *weak* foundation
old and *feeble*

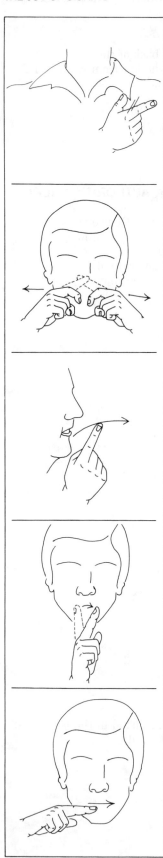

LAZY

Strike the right "L" against the left shoulder, palm in. (Sometimes made with both hands at opposite shoulders.)
Origin: hands crossed on the chest in a resting position
Usage: It was a *lazy* afternoon.

UGLY

Cross the index fingers in front of the nose, palm facing palm; then pull them apart and bend the index fingers as they cross the face.
Origin: face is pulled out of shape
Usage: an *ugly* duckling

TRUE, TRULY, REAL, REALLY, ACTUAL, SURE, GENUINE, INDEED

Touch the tip of the right index finger to the mouth, palm facing left, and move it slightly up and forward.
Origin: speaking straightforwardly
Usage: a *true* friend; love you *truly;* Oh, *really?* it *actually* happened; a *sure* proof; a *genuine* diamond; war is *indeed* terrible

FALSE, ARTIFICIAL, FAKE

The right index finger, pointing up with palm facing left, is brushed across the lips from right to left.
Origin: The truth is brushed aside.
Usage: *false* teeth
     artificial flowers
     The painting was a *fake.*

LIE

Right index finger, palm facing down, passes across the lips from right to left.
Origin: not straightforward, but to the side
Usage: He *lied* in the courtroom.

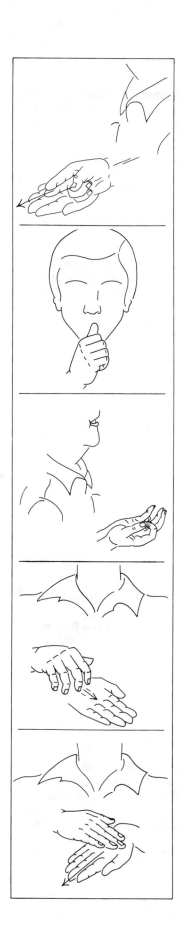

HONEST, TRUTH

Place the middle finger of the right "H" on the left palm near the wrist and move it forward toward the fingertips.
Origin: divided in half honestly
Usage: an *honest* man
   tell the *truth*

SECRET, PRIVATE, CONFIDENTIAL

Place the thumbnail of the right "A" against the lips.
Origin: The lips are sealed.
Usage: hidden in a *secret* place
   private conversation
   confidential papers

FINE (In small particles)

Rub the thumb and index finger together, while the other fingers are extended.
Origin: Rubbing a grain of sand between the fingertips.
Usage: very *fine* sand
   fine dust

ROUGH, SCRATCH, RUGGED

Place the fingertips of the right curved hand against the left palm and move it forward with a wavy motion.
Origin: indicating the surface is rough
Usage: The wood is *rough.*
   Shoes *scratched* the floor.
   a *rugged* path

SMOOTH

Place the open hands palm to palm at right angles and draw the right one across the left slowly.
Origin: showing a smooth surface
Usage: a *smooth* board

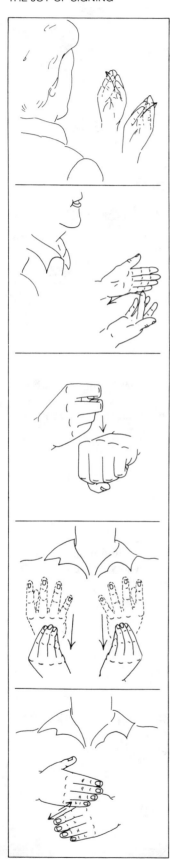

SMOOTH, FLUENT

Hold out both "AND" hands and draw the thumb along the tips of the fingers in the direction of the index fingers, at the same time moving the hands slightly away from each other.
Origin: Fingers feel smooth.
Usage: Everything went *smoothly*.
Robin uses signs *fluently*.

SHARP

Pass the tip of the middle finger of the right hand along the little-finger edge of the left open hand (as if feeling a sharp edge) and give the right hand a quick turn so the palm faces down.
Origin: as if feeling the edge of a knife
Usage: need a *sharp* knife

HARD

Strike the middle finger of the right bent "V" on the back of the left "S."
Origin: back of the hand is hard
Usage: *hard* as a rock

SOFT

Both open "AND" hands point upward; then draw them down into the closed "AND" position.
Origin: as if feeling something soft between the fingers
Usage: a *soft* bed
*soft*hearted

MEDIUM

Place the little-finger edge of the right open hand crosswise on the index-finger edge of the left open hand. Move the right toward the tip of the left index and back several times.
Origin: indicating an area not as long as the finger, sort of medium in length
Usage: boiled eggs—hard, soft, or *medium*

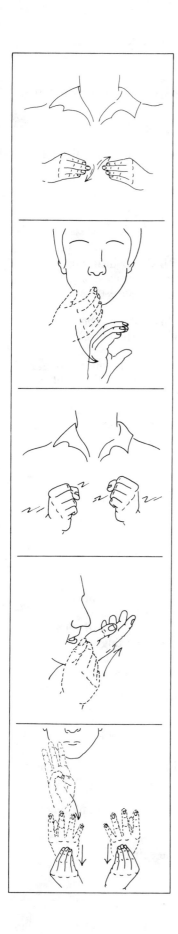

FLEXIBLE

Place the closed "AND" hands in front of you, tips pointing toward each other; move them in and out alternately.
Origin: as if showing that something can be bent
Usage: easy to work with and *flexible*

HOT, HEAT

Place the right "C" at the mouth, palm facing in; give the wrist a quick twist so the palm faces out.
Origin: something hot quickly taken from the mouth
Usage: *hot* water
      Can you feel the *heat?*

COLD

Shake both "S" hands, palms facing each other.
Origin: as if shivering
Usage: A *cold* day in January.

WARM

Place the "A" hand in front of the mouth, palm in, and open the hand gradually as it moves slightly up and out.
Origin: blowing into the hand to warm it
Usage: *Warm* yourself at the fireplace.

WET

Sign "WATER" ("W" at right side of mouth) and "SOFT."
Origin: feeling the water between the fingers
Usage: We had a leak and everything was *wet.*

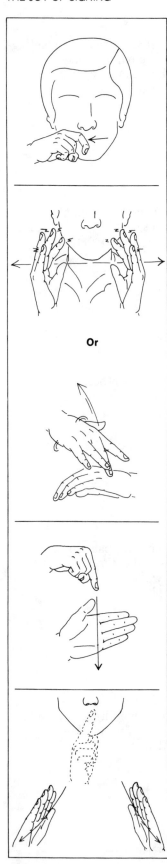

Or

DRY

Bent right index finger is drawn across the lips from left to right.
Origin: The lips are dry.
Usage: The ground was *dry.*
a *dry* lecture (the sign for "boring" may also be used in this instance)

SHINING

Open palms facing each other with tips pointing up are drawn apart to the sides while the fingers are wiggling.
Origin: The movement of the fingers represents shimmering light.
Usage: Susan's eyes *shone.* (In this instance the sign should be made at the sides of the eyes.)

Or touch the back of the left hand with the middle finger of the right open hand; then draw it up and to the right with a shaking motion from the wrist.
Origin: Back of the left hand represents the surface; movement of the right represents the shimmering effect.
Usage: The kitchen floor is *shiny.*

DEEP

Using the right index position, push the side of the index finger straight down along the inside of the left palm, which is facing right with tips pointing forward. (The greater the depth, the farther the index finger moves downward.)
Origin: The finger moving down indicates depth.
Usage: The ocean is *deep.*
I studied the subject in *depth.*

QUIET, CALM, STILL, TRANQUIL, SERENE

Place the index finger against the mouth, palm facing left; draw both open hands down and toward the side, palms facing down.
Origin: Hands moved downward represent a quieting effect.
Usage: a *quiet* man; a *calm,* sweet voice; *still* waters; a *tranquil* morning; a *serene* spirit

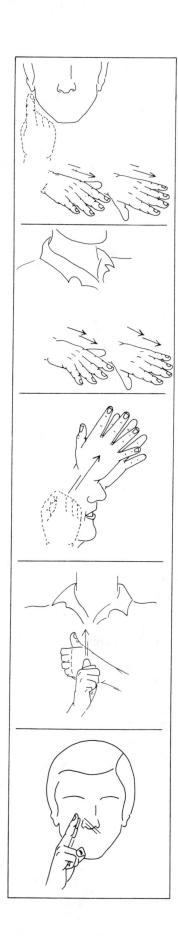

NOISY, SOUND, LOUD

Touch the tip of the ear with the index finger; direct both "FIVE" hands toward the left, right behind left, palms down.
Origin: the ear and the vibrations
Usage: What was that *noise?*
      I hear the *sound* of singing.
      very *loud* talking

VIBRATION

Place the "FIVE" hands in front of you, palms down, and move them back and forth alternately.
Origin: indicating movement
Usage: I felt the *vibration* in the floor.

AWFUL, FEARFUL, TERRIBLE, DREADFUL, HORRIBLE

Hold the "O" hands at the sides of the face and direct them upward while opening the hands into "FIVE" positions, the palms facing in.
Origin: hair standing on end
Usage: an *awful* storm; a *fearful* animal; *terrible* suffering; a *dreadful* place; a *horrible* crime

DANGER

Place the thumb of the right "A" hand at the back of the left hand; brush the right "A" hand upward several times.
Usage: a *dangerous* stunt.

FUNNY, HUMOROUS

Brush the tips of the "U" fingers off the end of the nose.
Usage: That's not *funny.*
      a *humorous* story

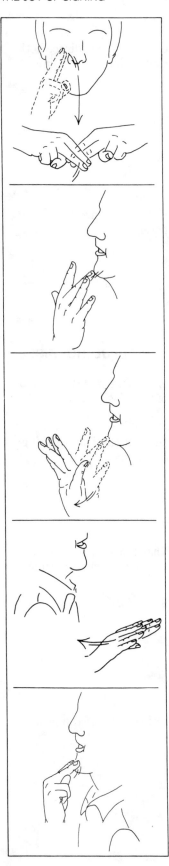

FUN

Brush the tip of the nose with the tips of the "N" fingers;
then brush off the tips of the left "N" with the tips of the
right "N" and reverse.
Usage: all in *fun*

FAVORITE

Touch the chin several times with the right middle finger.
Usage: What is your *favorite* dessert?

LUCKY

Touch the chin with the middle finger; then turn the hand
quickly with the palm facing out.
Usage: You're a *lucky* person!

PET

Stroke the back of the left hand with the palm of the right
hand.
Origin: as if petting an animal
Usage: *Petting* a child too much may not do him any good.
This is my *pet*.

CUTE

Draw the tips of the "U" fingers down the chin once or
twice.
Usage: That's a *cute* little girl.

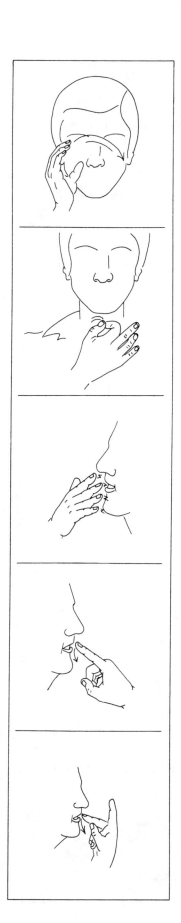

ODD, QUEER, STRANGE

Place the right "C" in front of the face; then give the wrist a quick downward twist.
Usage: a very *odd* fellow
a *queer* person
A *strange* thing happened.

CURIOUS

Grasp a bit of skin at the neck with the right index and thumb, other fingers extended; twist back and forth slightly.
Origin: The neck is extended in curiosity.
Usage: *curious* about other people's business
satisfy your *curiosity*

COLOR

Place the "FIVE" hand in front of the mouth and wiggle the fingers as the hand moves away very slightly.
Usage: The *colors* of our flag are red, white, and blue.

RED

Draw the inside tip of the right index finger down across the lips (sometimes made with an "R").
Origin: red as the lips
Usage: Joy has a new *red* Cutlass.

PINK

Draw the middle finger of the "P" hand down across the lips.
Origin: pink as the lips
Usage: The bride carried *pink* roses.

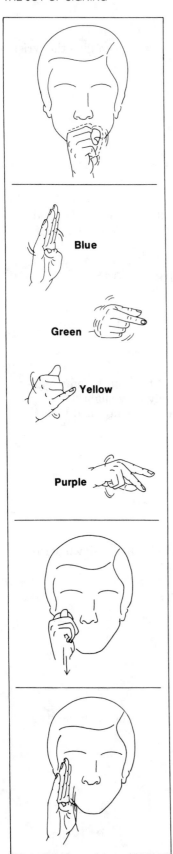

Blue

Green

Yellow

Purple

ORANGE

Squeeze the "S" hand once or twice.
Origin: as if squeezing an orange
Usage: The playroom was painted white and *orange.*

BLUE, GREEN, YELLOW, PURPLE

Draw the initialed hand to the right with a shaking motion.
Usage: *blue* sky
      green field
      bright *yellow* moon
      a combination of pink and *purple*

TAN

Draw a "T" down the cheek.
Usage: came home from Florida with a nice *tan*
      a *tan* raincoat

BROWN

Draw the index-finger side of the "B" hand down the right cheek.
Usage: a *brown* dog

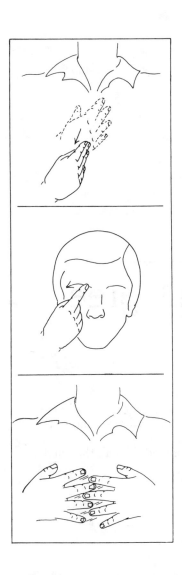

WHITE

Place fingertips of the open "AND" hand against the chest and draw the hand forward into the "AND" position.
Usage: *white* elephant sale

BLACK

Draw the index finger across the right eyebrow from left to right.
Usage: a *black* cat sitting in the window

GRAY

Place the "FIVE" hands in front of you, palms in; pass them back and forth through the open fingers.
Origin: showing a mixture
Usage: a *gray* flannel suit
Note: This word is frequently fingerspelled.

13

Quantity, Size, and Degree

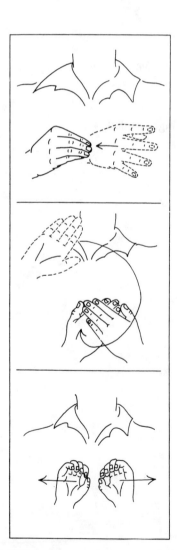

AND

Place the right hand in front of you, fingers spread apart and pointing left (palm facing you); draw the hand to the right, closing the tips.
Origin: "And" indicates something additional; the hand is preparing for the "add" sign.
Usage: bread *and* butter

ALL, WHOLE

The left open hand faces the body. Make a circle with the right hand going out and around the left hand, ending with the back of the right hand in the palm of the left.
Origin: The sweeping movement of the right hand includes everything.
Usage: *all* the world; the *whole* school

NONE, NO

Place the "O" hands in front of you, palms facing out; bring both hands to the sides, still in the "O" position.
Origin: Two zeros indicate the absence of any quantity.
Usage: We have *none*.
　　　We have *no* money for a new car.

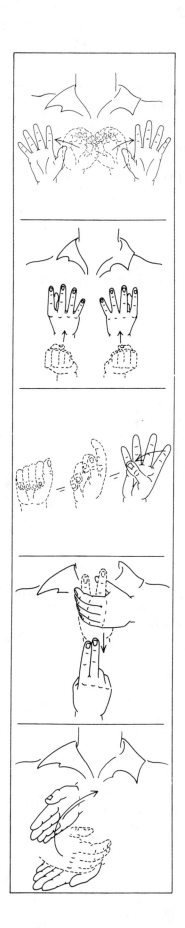

NOTHING

Place the "O" hands in front of you, palms facing out; bring both hands to the sides, opening into the "FIVE" position, palms forward.
Origin: Hands open completely to indicate there is nothing in them.
Usage: I have *nothing* to hide.

MANY, LOTS

Hold both "S" hands in front of you, palms facing up, and open them quickly several times.
Origin: All the fingers opening up indicate a great number.
Usage: *many* paintings in the museum
　　　Lots of people watched the parade.
Note: This sign is used for "How many?" along with a questioning look on the face.

FEW, SEVERAL

The right "A" hand, with palm facing up, opens slowly as the thumb passes along the inside of the opening fingers.
Origin: A small number is indicated by opening the fingers one by one.
Usage: a man of *few* words
　　　Several days passed.

BOTH

Pass the right "TWO" hand down through the left "C"; right hand ending with the two fingers coming together (both palms facing self).
Origin: indicates two becoming one unit
Usage: *both* are in college

SOME, PART, PORTION

Place the little-finger side of the right curved hand into the left palm; draw the right hand toward self and straighten it.
Origin: indicating a part of the whole
Usage: *some* of the books
　　　part-time work
　　　a *portion* of my time

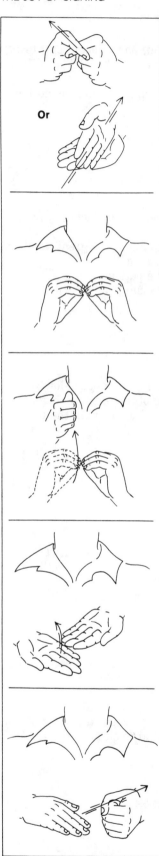

HALF

Hold out the left index finger, pointing toward the right, palm in; place the right index across it and draw it back toward self.

Or place the little-finger edge of the right open hand across the left palm and draw it back toward self.
Origin: half the finger, or half the hand
Usage: *Half* is enough.
　　　 half the pie

MORE

Bring the tips of both "AND" hands together.
Origin: adding to a quantity (Similar hand positions are used for "add.")
Usage: *more* than enough

MOST

Sign "MORE"; then lift the right "A" hand, with thumb pointing up.
Origin: "MORE" plus the "EST" ending
Usage: *Most* plants require sun.

ALMOST, NEARLY

With both open palms facing up, place the little-finger edge of the right under the fingertips of the left and draw up.
Origin: barely touching the fingertips
Usage: *almost* fell
　　　 nearly missed the plane

FULL, FILL

Place the right open hand on the left "S" (palm facing right) and brush across it to the left.
Origin: filled to the brim
Usage: The elevator was *full.*
　　　 People *filled* the room.

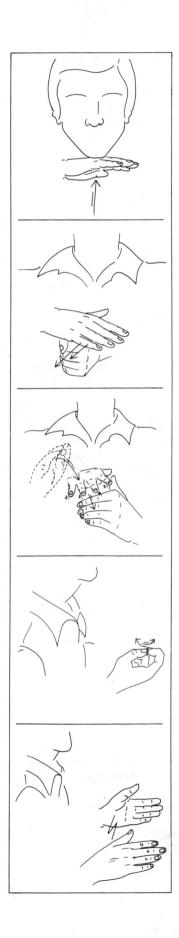

FULL, FED UP

Place the top of the right open hand under the chin.
Origin: filled up to the chin
Usage: I'm *full* and can't eat any more.
I'm *fed up* with her gossip.
Note: In the slang usage the sign is made with great emphasis.

ENOUGH, PLENTY, SUFFICIENT, ADEQUATE

Place the right open hand on the left "S" which is facing right; brush across it to the right several times.
Origin: filled to the brim and starting to run over
Usage: money *enough* for everything
plenty of time
sufficient proof
His wages are *adequate.*

OVERFLOW, RUNNING OVER

Place the right "AND" hand against the left palm; move the right hand up to the index-finger edge and then over the side, fingers wiggling.
Origin: running over the edge
Usage: The tub is *running over.*

LITTLE, BIT, SLIGHTLY

Using an "X" position, rub the end of the thumb against the end of the index finger, palm facing up.
Origin: as little as might be on a fingertip
Usage: feel a *little* hungry
a *bit* doubtful
felt *slightly* dizzy

SMALL, LITTLE

Hold both slightly curved hands in front of you, palm facing palm, and push hands toward each other several times.
Origin: Hands pushed toward each other indicate smallness.
Usage: a *small* country; a *small* animal; a *small* house; a *little* baby; a *little* kitten

173

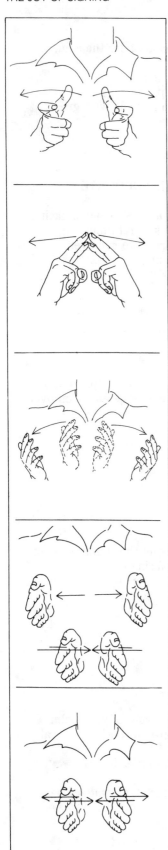

LARGE, GREAT, BIG, ENORMOUS, HUGE, IMMENSE

The "L" hands, facing each other, are drawn apart. (The size of the sign indicates the intended degree.)
Origin: Hands are drawn apart to indicate great size.
Usage: a *large* house; a *great* field; *big* business; *enormous* ship; *huge* elephant; an *immense* national debt
Note: The "L"s are frequently modified by crooking the index fingers.

VERY

Place the tips of the "V" hands together and pull them apart.
Origin: Hands are drawn apart to indicate the degree.
Usage: *very* good work

MUCH, A LOT, LOTS

Hold both hands in front of you, palm facing palm, with fingers slightly spread and curved; draw hands apart.
Origin: Hands drawn apart indicate a large amount.
Usage: *much* confusion; heard *a lot* about that; *lots* of trouble
Note: This sign is used for "How much?" along with a questioning look on the face.

WIDE, BROAD—NARROW

Place both open hands in front of you, palm facing palm, and draw them apart. For "NARROW" bring them toward each other.
Usage: 3 feet *wide*
a *broad* street
a *narrow* road

WIDTH

Place both open hands in front of you some distance apart, palm facing palm; move them toward each other and out again several times.
Origin: The in-out-in movement indicates questionable width.
Usage: Is that the *width* you want?

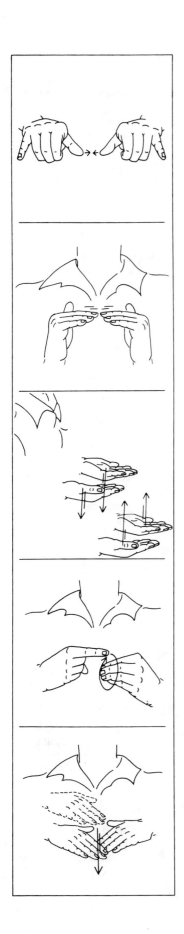

MEASURE

Place the "Y" hands in front of you, palms facing down, and touch the thumb tips together several times.
Origin: Using the thumb and little finger to measure.
Usage: *Measure* your windows before buying drapes.
The *measurements* of the living room are 15' x 18'.

EQUAL, FAIR

Place bent hands in front of you, palm sides down; bring tips together several times.
Origin: One is on the same level with the other.
Usage: *equal* work, *equal* pay
The judge was *fair.*

HEAVY—LIGHT

Place both open hands in front of you, palms facing up, and drop the arms slightly as if holding too heavy an object. For "LIGHT" raise the hands slightly as if bouncing a light object.
Usage: He's not *heavy,* he's my brother.
My suitcase was very *light.*

ABOUT (Concerning, in connection with)

Place the left "AND" hand in front of you pointing right; circle the right index around the tips, clockwise.
Usage: a book *about* animals

ABOUT (Approximately, around)

The right flat hand, palm down, circles in a counterclockwise movement.
Usage: Meet me *about (around, approximately)* 4 o'clock.

THAN

Place the left open hand in front of you, palm down, and brush the index-finger edge of the right open hand off the fingertips of the left and down.
Origin: This word is used in a comparative sense and the sign shows that what follows is of a lower degree.
Usage: older *than* I am

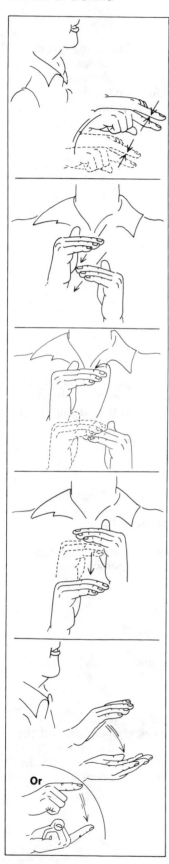

TOO, ALSO

Sign "SAME" twice, once in front of you and again to the left.
Origin: Something is the same as the other.
Usage: Are you going *too?* I'm *also* making plans.
Note: There is no sign for "too" when it refers to something beyond what is desirable, such as *too* long. In such a case the word following "too" is given greater emphasis.

LIMIT, RESTRICT

Place the right bent hand several inches above the left bent hand; bring both hands forward a short distance.
Origin: The position of the hands indicates how high one can go.
Usage: a time *limit*
    Membership is *restricted* to 20.

ABOVE, OVER, EXCEED, MORE THAN, TOO MUCH

Place the fingers of the right bent hand on the back of the left bent hand; lift the right and move it straight up, palm still facing down.
Origin: The left hand represents a limit; the right hand goes beyond the limit.
Usage: *above* the fifth floor; *over* 21; *exceed* the speed
    limit; ate *too much*

BELOW, UNDER, LESS THAN

Place the right bent hand, palm down, under the left open hand (top of right hand touching palm of the left); lower the right hand a few inches.
Origin: one hand lower than the other
Usage: 30° *below* zero
    boys *under* 18
    less than $5

DECREASE, LESS, REDUCE, DIMINISH, LOWER

Hold the open hands in front of you some distance apart, right above left, palms facing each other, and bring them toward each other.

Or use index fingers to make the sign.

Origin: less and less distance between hands
Usage: Cars *decrease* in value. *Less* noise, please.
    Earnings were *reduced.* Savings *diminished.* Taxes
    are *lower.*

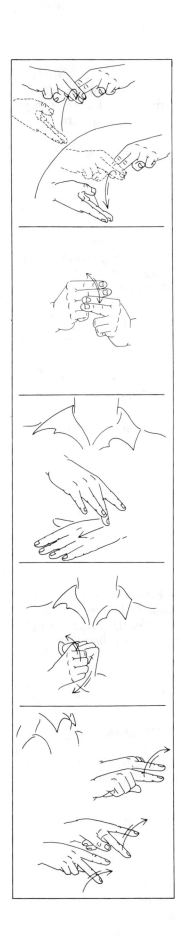

INCREASE, A RAISE, GAIN WEIGHT/TAKE OFF WEIGHT

Hold the left "U" in front of you, palm facing down; bring the right "U" from a palm-up to a palm-down position on the left "U"; repeat several times. For "TAKE OFF WEIGHT" make the sign in reverse (move the right "U" off the left).

Usage: an *increase* (a *raise*) in pay; an *increase* in the number present; *gained* another pound; *took off* 5 pounds

WEIGH

Place the middle finger of the right "H" across the index of the left "H" and balance the right "H" on the left, similar to the motion of a seesaw.

Origin: indicating a scale balancing
Usage: turkey *weighed* 18 pounds
illness caused a *weight* loss

EMPTY, VACANT, BARE, NAKED, BALD, BLANK

Move the middle fingertip of the right "FIVE" hand along the back of the left open hand.

Origin: as bare as the back of your hand
Usage: *empty* closet; house is *vacant;* room is *bare; naked* children; *bald* head (move the fingertip in a circular movement on the back of the left fist, which represents the head); fill in the *blanks;* my mind is *blank* (for this usage the fingertip passes across the forehead)

CROWDED, CRUSHED

Place the "A" hands together, palm to palm; while they are touching, twist the right hand toward you and the left hand away from you.

Origin: squeezed together
Usage: The room was *crowded.*
My clothes were *crushed.*

AS

Place the index fingers side by side several inches apart, palms down, and move them over to the left in this position.

Origin: Similar to the sign for "same."
Usage: white *as* snow

PROPORTION

Sign as above using the "P" hands.
Usage: Pay is in *proportion* to work done.

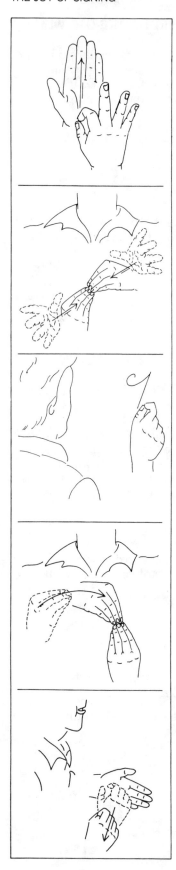

COUNT, ACCOUNTING

Move the tips of the "F" hand up the center of the left palm, which is facing right and pointing up. For the noun "ACCOUNTING" repeat the sign (i.e., two upward movements of the right hand).
Usage: *Count* the number of people in the room.
Ralph majored in *accounting*.

TOTAL, SUM, ALTOGETHER

Hold the open "AND" hands in front of you, one above the other (palms facing each other); bring them together, closing into "AND" positions as the fingertips touch.
Origin: Everything is brought together.
Usage: The *total* cost is $24.50.
The *sum* of 10 and 10 is 20.
Altogether we had 25 people.

PERCENT, INTEREST

Using the "O" hand, draw a percent sign in the air.
Usage: 60 *percent* of the people voted.
The bank pays high *interest*.

ADD

Place the tips of the right "AND" hand on the tips of the left "AND" hand, which has the palm facing up; repeat, bringing the left hand higher each time. (Or bring the right "AND" hand under the left, which is in a palm-down position, and touch tips.)
Origin: adding something to the pile
Usage: *Add* to your knowledge.

SUBTRACT, REMOVE, DEDUCT, ELIMINATE

Place the fingertips of the right curved hand (palm down) against the left palm and move it down, ending in an "A" position.
Usage: *Subtract* 3 from 10.
Remove the paper from the table.
deductions from paychecks
Eliminate several names.

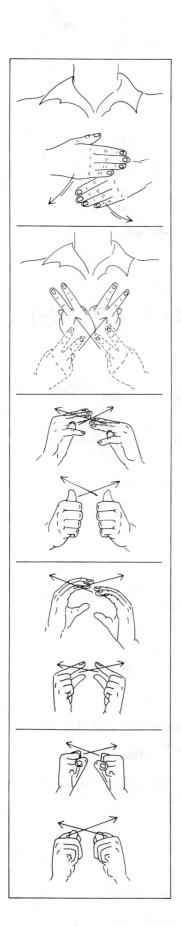

DIVIDE

Place the little-finger edge of the right open hand
crosswise on the index-finger edge of the left open hand;
draw both hands to the sides, ending with palms down.
Origin: as if splitting something
Usage: *Divide* 40 by 5.
        Divide the class in half.

FIGURE, ARITHMETIC, MULTIPLY, WORSE

Place both "V" hands in front of you, palms facing you, and
cross them so that the back of the right "V" passes across
the palm of the left.
Usage: *Figure up* the bill.
        Arithmetic is taught in school.
        Multiply 5 x 6.
        Traffic problems are *worse*.

MATHEMATICS

Sign as for "FIGURE" using the "M" hands.

ALGEBRA

Sign as for "FIGURE" using the "A" hands.

CALCULUS

Sign as for "FIGURE" using the "C" hands.

GEOMETRY

Sign as for "FIGURE" using the "G" hands.

STATISTICS

Sign as for "FIGURE" using the "S" hands.

TRIGONOMETRY

Sign as for "FIGURE" using the "T" hands.

14

Communication and Government

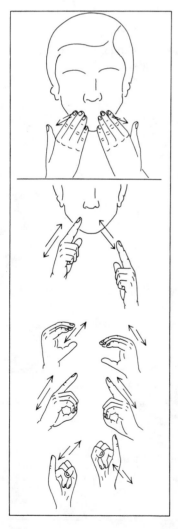

THANK, THANK YOU, YOU'RE WELCOME

Place the tips of the open hands against the mouth and throw them forward, similar to throwing a kiss. (May be made with one hand.)
Usage: Esther *thanked* Will for the flowers.
Thank you for the birthday card.
You're welcome.

CONVERSATION, TALK

Place the tips of the index fingers on the lips and move them forward and backward alternately.
Origin: talking back and forth
Usage: Let's *talk* for a while.

COMMUNICATE—Make the above sign with the "C" hands.
Usage: Good *communication* is important.

DIALOGUE—Make the above sign with the "D" hands.
Usage: It was an interesting *dialogue.*

INTERVIEW—Make the above sign with the "I" hands.
Usage: Make an appointment for the *interview* at 3:00.

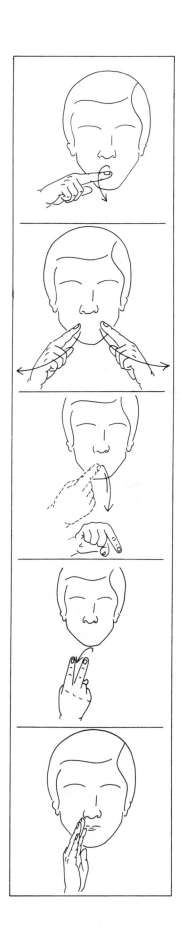

SPEAK, SAY, TELL, SPEECH

The index finger, pointing to the left, is held in front of the mouth and rolls forward in a circular movement.
Origin: words proceeding from the mouth
Usage: Actions *speak* louder than words.
What did you *say?*
Tell me about it.
She has good *speech.*

ANNOUNCE, PROCLAIM, DECLARE

Index fingers touch the lips and are drawn forward and out, away from the face.
Origin: The sign for "tell" is enlarged.
Usage: *Announce* the winner.
He *proclaimed* a holiday.
The president *declared* an emergency.

COMMAND, ORDER

Point the right index finger toward the mouth; turn it outward and down in a strong motion.
Origin: telling with force
Usage: The captain gave a *command.*
He *ordered* his men to march.

VOICE, VOCAL

Place the tips of the "V" at the throat and draw them up toward the chin.
Origin: indicating the throat with the initial
Usage: a high *voice*
your *vocal* cords

WHISPER

Place the right curved hand at the right side of the mouth, palm facing left.
Origin: hiding the mouth while talking
Usage: She *whispered* her secret.

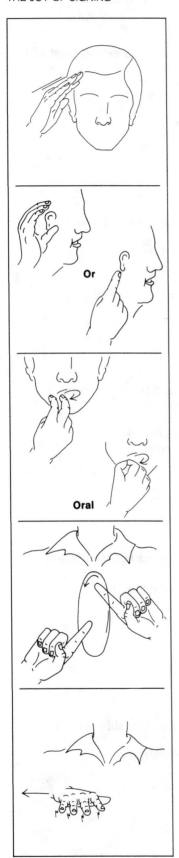

HELLO, HI

The right hand in an open position moves outward from
the forehead, almost as if saluting.
Origin: The natural gesture used in greeting people.
Usage: *Hello,* how is everybody?
      Hi, David, where have you been? ("HI" is
      frequently fingerspelled.)

LISTEN, HEAR

Place the "C" against the right ear; or place the tip of the
index finger at the ear.
Origin: cupping the hand over the ear to hear
Usage: *Listen,* the birds are singing.
      Do you *hear* what I *hear?*

SPEECHREADING, LIPREADING, ORAL

Describe a circle around the lips with the bent "V," palm
facing in. (Some use an "O" for "ORAL.")
Origin: The sign for "read" is directed to the lips.
Usage: *Speechreading* is not easy.
      Some people are easier to *lipread* than others.
      She comes from an *oral* background.

SIGNS (The language of)

Cross the index fingers in front of you, palms facing out,
and circle the arms alternately toward the body.
Origin: Hands are moved, representing signs.
Usage: *Signs* represent concepts.
      Study *sign* language.

FINGERSPELLING, SPELL

The right "FIVE" hand with palm down moves from left to
right, fingers wiggling.
Origin: indicating the movement of fingers spelling
Usage: *Fingerspell* your name.
      a poor *speller* (add the "PERSON" ending)

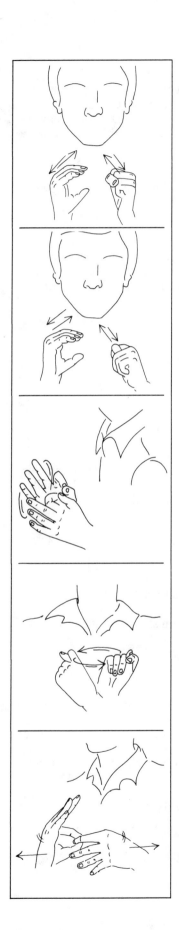

SIMULTANEOUS COMMUNICATION

Make an "S" with one hand and a "C" with the other; move them forward and backward alternately, just below the mouth.

Usage: All of our teachers use *simultaneous communication.*

Note: Use the "S" and "M" hands for "simultaneous method."

TOTAL COMMUNICATION

Make a "T" with one hand and a "C" with the other; move them forward and backward alternately, just below the mouth.

Usage: *Total communication* helps deaf children.

INTERPRET

Make the sign for "CHANGE" using the "F" hands.

Origin: Hands in the original "language" position make the sign for "change." (In other words, interpreting is language that is changed.)

Usage: *Interpreting* requires great skill.

Good *interpreters* are in demand. (Add the "PERSON" ending.)

TRANSLATE

Make the sign for "CHANGE" using the "T" hands.

Origin: Translating refers to changing.

Usage: We *translate* word for word.

CAPTIONS

The thumb and index fingertips of both hands (with other fingers extended) are pulled apart in a twisting motion.

Usage: *Captioned* films are enjoyed by deaf people.

Many television programs are now close-*captioned* for hearing-impaired persons.

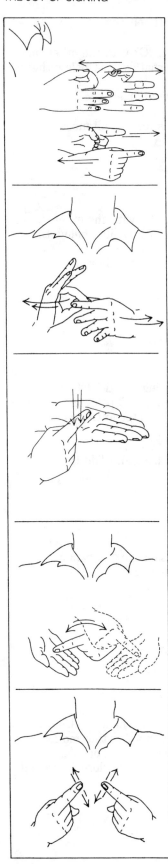

EXPLAIN, DESCRIBE, DEFINE

Place the "F" hands in front of you, palms facing each other and fingers pointing forward; move the hands forward and backward alternately. (The "D" hands may be used for "DESCRIBE" and "DEFINE," with index fingers pointing forward.)
Usage: *Explain* your problem.
      Describe the place.
      a clear *definition*

STORY

The thumb and index fingertips of both hands (with other fingers extended) are pulled apart several times.
Usage: Our children look forward to their bedtime *story.*

DISCUSS, ARGUE

Strike the side of the index finger into the left palm several times.
Usage: a *discussion* about politics
      The senator *argued* for a new policy. (Used in this sense the index can remain on the left palm while both hands are moved back and forth.)

DEBATE

Make the sign for "DISCUSS" alternately with the right and left hands.
Usage: a *debate* about capital punishment

QUARREL

Point both index fingers toward each other, palms facing you, and shake the hands up and down from the wrists simultaneously.
Origin: imitation of roosters fighting
Usage: Stop *quarreling!*

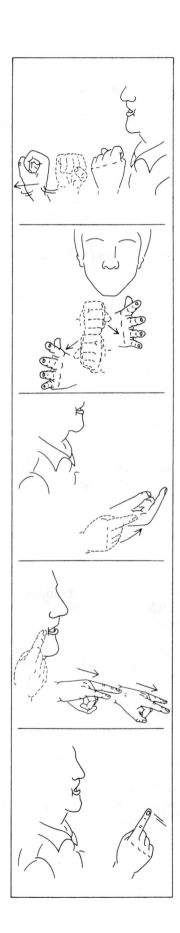

EXAGGERATE

Place the right "S" in front of the left "S" (both palms down) and move the right "S" away in a twisting motion, as if stretching and pulling.
Origin: stretching the story
Usage: That story seems *exaggerated*.

BAWL OUT

Place one "S" hand above the other, palm sides out. The hands snap open as they move forward.
Usage: She *bawled out* the student.

INSULT

The index finger twists as it moves forward and slightly up.
Origin: piercing with a knife and twisting it
Usage: That's an *insult* to my intelligence!

MOCK, SCORN, RIDICULE

Draw the right index finger back from the mouth and direct both hands forward (right behind left), with the index and little fingers extended.
Origin: laughing and pointing fingers in derision
Usage: The children *mocked* Jimmy.
They *scorned* the traitor.
The little boys *ridiculed* Fern.

SCOLD

Shake the index finger in a natural motion of scolding.
Origin: a natural sign
Usage: Mrs. Robertson *scolded* the boys.

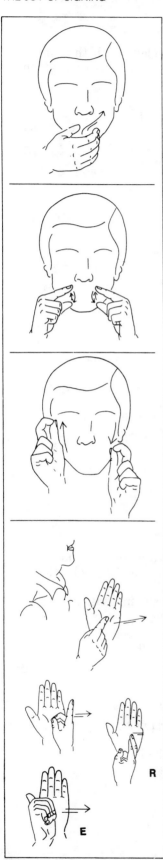

SCREAM, SHOUT, CRY OUT, ROAR

Place the right "C" hand at the mouth, palm facing you, and move it upward in a wavy motion.
Origin: indicating the cry coming from the mouth
Usage: Girls *scream.*
Boys *shout.*
People *cried out.*
The lion *roared.*

GOSSIP

The thumb and index fingertips of both hands (with other fingers closed) face each other and open and close.
Origin: two mouths opening and closing
Usage: spreading *gossip*

EXPRESSION (Facial)

Place both modified "A" hands at the sides of the face, palms facing each other; hands alternate in short up-and-down movements.
Origin: The face is pulled into various expressions.
Usage: Facial *expression* is important when signing.

SHOW, REVEAL, FOR EXAMPLE

Place the tip of the right index into the left open hand, which is facing out, and move both hands forward.
Origin: as if pointing to something in the hand
Usage: *Show* me how to do it.
Her words *revealed* her ignorance.
One word can have several meanings, *for example . . . .*

DEMONSTRATE, REPRESENT, EXPRESS

These words may be signed "SHOW" as above, or they may be initialed as shown here.
Usage: The teacher *demonstrated* the use of the machine.
Sue *represented* her class in the meeting.
Some people find it difficult to *express* their feelings.

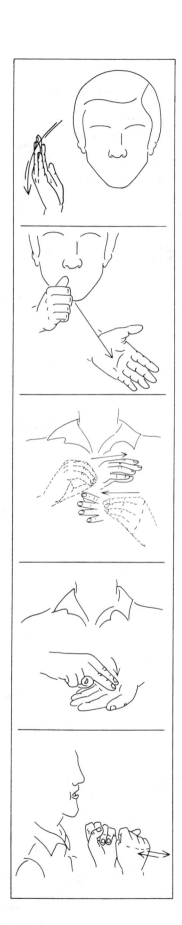

LECTURE, SPEECH, TESTIMONY

Hold the right open hand to the side with palm facing left and fingers pointing up; move the hand from the wrist forward and backward several times.
Origin: a gesture made in public speaking
Usage: The *lecture* was boring.
    a very interesting *speech*
    a *testimony* in court

LETTER, MAIL

Place the thumb of the right "A" hand against the mouth and then into the left palm.
Origin: stamping a letter
Usage: I received a *letter* from Bea and Hal.
    Any *mail* today?

CORRESPONDENCE

The right closed "AND" hand opens as it moves to the left; at the same time the left closed "AND" hand opens as it moves to the right, both hands passing each other.
Origin: sending in both directions
Usage: It took a lot of *correspondence* to solve the problem.

STAMPS

Place the right index and middle fingers on the palm of the left.
Origin: affixing the stamp
Usage: a collection of over 5,000 *stamps*

ADVERTISE, PUBLICIZE

Place the right "S" in front of the left "S" (palm sides down) and move the right "S" away and back again several times.
Origin: as if blowing a horn
Usage: *Advertise* in the newspaper.
    Actors receive a lot of *publicity*.

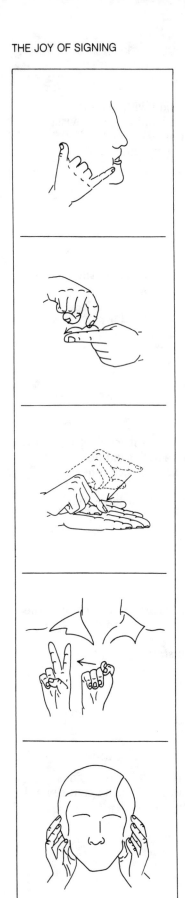

TELEPHONE, CALL

Place the thumb of the "Y" hand on the ear and the little finger at the mouth.
Origin: the natural position of a phone in use
Usage: The *telephone* can save time or waste time.
   Call me at home.
Note: The noun "telephone" has a double movement. The verb form "to call" or "to phone" has a single movement.

TELEGRAM

Using the right "X" make a series of dots along the edge of the left index finger, which is pointing right.
Origin: indicating dots and dashes
Usage: Send a *telegram.*

NEWSPAPER

The right "G" (palm down) picks imaginary type and places it in the left palm.
Origin: old-style typesetting
Usage: Did you read about the tax reform in the
   newspaper?

TELEVISION

Spell TV.
Usage: Which is your favorite *television* program?

RADIO

Hold the cupped hands over the ears.
Origin: the old-fashioned headsets used with radios
Usage: *Radio* means nothing to a deaf person unless he has
   an interpreter.

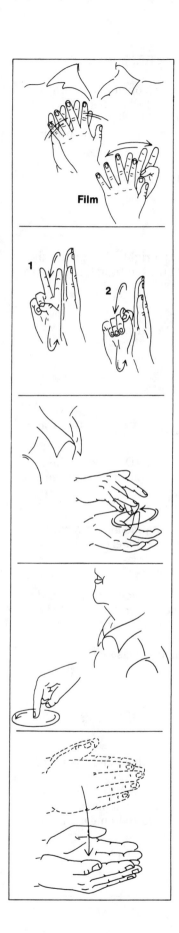

Film

MOVIE, FILM

Place the palm of the right "FIVE" hand against the palm of the left "FIVE" hand and move it back and forth slightly.
Origin: the shimmering effect of the screen
Usage: an old *movie* with captions
a 16 mm *film*
Note: "FILM" is sometimes signed with the right "F."

VIDEOTAPE

Place the side of the right "V" against the left open palm, which is pointing up and facing right; move the "V" forward-down-back-up in a circle. Repeat with the right "T."
Origin: indicating the movement of the reel
Usage: A *videotape* of yourself signing is helpful.

RECORD PLAYER

Place the right hand, palm down, above the left hand, palm up; point the middle fingers toward each other (leaving hands in the "FIVE" position). Move the right hand in a counterclockwise direction.
Origin: The left middle finger represents the spindle; the right represents the record going around.
Usage: I hear a *record player* in the next room.

TAPE RECORDING

Using the index finger pointing down, make a counterclockwise circle.
Origin: indicating the tape going around
Usage: We used *tapes* for practicing our signs.

BOOK

Place the open hands palm to palm; then open them as if opening a book.
Origin: indicating the closed and then the open book
Usage: *book* of the month

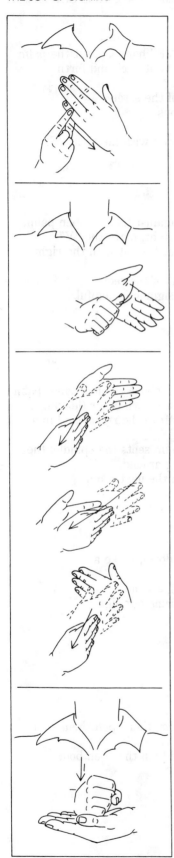

MAGAZINE, PAMPHLET, BROCHURE, LEAFLET

Grasp the little-finger edge of the left open hand with the thumb and forefinger of the right and slide them down the outside edge of the left hand. Note: The sign for "MAGAZINE" may be preceded by "BOOK"; the others may be preceded by "PAPER."
Origin: a book that is thin
Usage: He subscribes to several *magazines*.
pamphlets in the mail

PAGE, LOOK IT UP

Place the inside of the thumb of the right "A" against the palm of the open left hand and move the thumb slightly to the left several times.
Origin: paging through a book
Usage: What is the *page* number?
I will *look it up* in the dictionary.

COPY

This word may be signed in several ways. Note the usage in each one.

1. Place the tips of the right open "AND" hand against the palm of the left hand and draw the right away into the closed "AND" position.
Usage: Make a *copy* for me.

2. The right open "AND" hand, palm facing forward, is drawn toward the left open palm and fingertips close as they touch the left palm.
Usage: *Copy* the paragraph from his book.

3. Place the left open hand in front of you, palm toward you and fingers pointing right; then place the tips of the open "AND" hand against the back of the left, drawing away into the closed "AND" position.
Usage: Let's sing in signs together—please *copy*.

SEAL, STAMP

Strike the right "S" on the left palm, hold and then lift the right hand quickly.
Origin: as if making an imprint
Usage: The *seal* of the college is on your diploma.
The *stamp* of approval is required on each item.

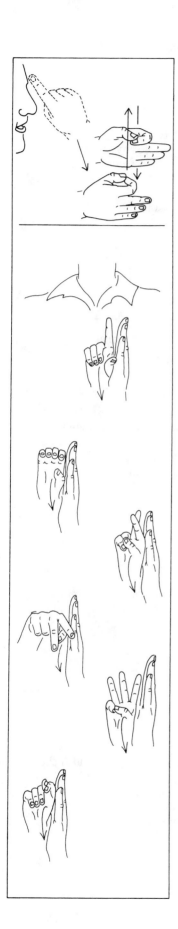

JUDGE, TRIAL, COURT

Touch the forehead with the index finger; then move both "F" hands up and down alternately (palms facing each other and fingers pointing forward).
Origin: Thoughts are being weighed in a balance.
Usage: *judge* and jury
       The *trial* is postponed.
       He will be *tried* in New York.
       Court begins at 9:00.

LAW, LEGISLATION, LAWYER, ATTORNEY

Place the right "L," with palm facing forward, against the palm of the left hand. Add the "PERSON" ending as needed.
Origin: "L" representing the law is on the books
Usage: the *law* of the land; new *legislation* requires interpreters; better see your *lawyer;* a tax *attorney* can help you

Initial signs are used for the following:

COMMANDMENTS, CONSTITUTION

Usage: Ten *Commandments*
       Constitution of the U.S.

RULES, REGULATIONS

Usage: *rules* of the game
       regulations of the institution

PRINCIPLES, PARLIAMENTARY, POLICY

Usage: a man of high *principles; parliamentary* procedure; our new school *policy*

WILL

Usage: his last *will* and testament

TESTAMENT

Usage: the Old *Testament*

Note: Often the letter is placed against the palm twice, the second time lower than the first.

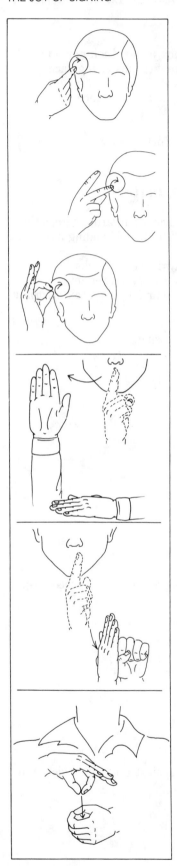

GOVERNMENT, GOVERNOR

Using the right index finger, describe a small circle at the right side of the temple and end by placing the point against the temple.
Origin: Authority is indicated at the head.
Usage: ". . . *government* of the people, by the people, and for the people, shall not perish from the earth" (Abraham Lincoln).

Initial signs are used for the following:

POLITICS, POLITICAL

Usage: involved in *politics*
studying *political* science

FEDERAL

Usage: Washington is often called the *federal* city.

VOW, SWEAR, OATH, LOYAL

Place the index finger at the mouth and then raise the right hand, palm facing forward, while the fingertips of the left hand (palm facing down) touch the right elbow.
Origin: Raising the right hand as if taking an oath.
Usage: made a *vow*
I *swear* to tell the truth.
president's *oath* of office
loyal to his party

PROMISE

Place the right index finger at the mouth and then place the right open palm on the index-finger side of the left "S" hand.
Usage: If you make a *promise,* keep it.

VOTE, ELECTION

Touch the thumb and forefinger of the right hand (other fingers extended) and place them in the left "O."
Origin: dropping a ballot in the box
Usage: We *vote* for our president.
Election Day is in November.

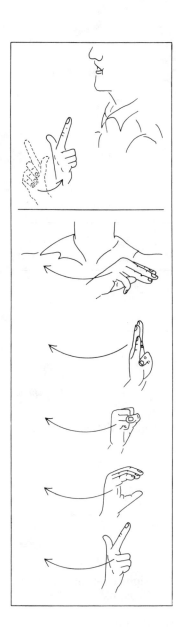

SECOND (As a motion)

Twist the right "L" in an inward motion.
Usage: A motion was made and *seconded.*

MEMBER

Place the right "M" at the left shoulder; then at the right.
Usage: a *member* of our club

Initial signs are also used for the following:

BOARD

Usage: *board* of directors

SENATE

Usage: attending a meeting of the *senate*

CONGRESS

Usage: listened to a speech by a *congress*woman

LEGISLATURE

Usage: The state *legislature* meets today.

NOTES:

DEMOCRAT, REPUBLICAN—Shake the right "D" or
"R." These are understood in context.
AMEND—Sign "CHANGE" using "A" hands or use the
sign for "ADD," as the case may be.
ALL IN FAVOR—Sign "SUPPORT" since this is the
meaning of the phrase ("All supporting the issue say aye").

15

Education

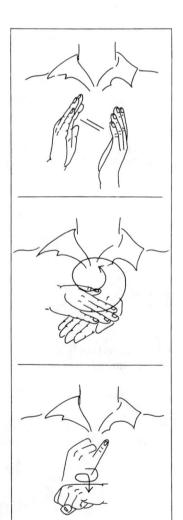

SCHOOL

Clap the hands twice.
Origin: The teacher claps for attention in the classroom.
Usage: *School* days are over.

COLLEGE

Clap the hands once, then circle the right open hand, palm down, counterclockwise above the left palm.
Origin: a school that is higher
Usage: a *college* program for deaf students

INSTITUTION, INSTITUTE, RESIDENTIAL SCHOOL

Make a small clockwise circle with the right "I" and place it on the back of the left closed hand.
Origin: the sign for "establish" made with the letter "I"
Usage: a well-known *institution*
the child development *institute*
Val attended the Michigan *School for the Deaf.*
Note: This sign is commonly used to refer to residential schools for the deaf.

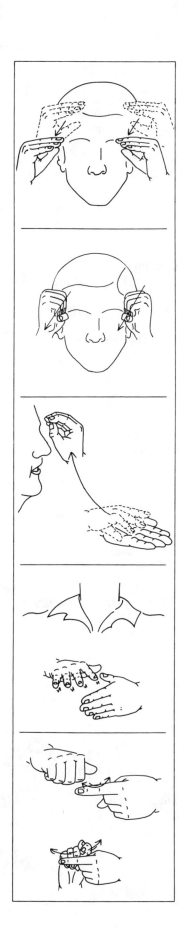

TEACH, INSTRUCT, EDUCATE

Place both open "AND" hands in front of the forehead, facing each other; bring them forward, away from the head, into closed "AND" positions.
Origin: taking something from the mind to pass on to others
Usage: *Teach* me to sign well.
　　　Instruct me to play tennis.
　　　Educate people in college.

EDUCATION

Place both "E" hands in front of the forehead, facing each other; move them away from the head and back several times. Or start with the "E" hands, changing to "D" hands.
Origin: derived from the sign for "teach"
Usage: received my *education* in England

LEARN, STUDENTS

Hold out the left hand, palm facing up, and with the right hand make a motion as if taking something out of the left hand and placing it on the forehead.
Origin: from the book into the mind
Usage: always interested in *learning* more
　　　a fine *student* (sign "LEARN" + "PERSON" ending)

STUDY

Point the fingers of the right hand, palm down, at the left open hand; wiggle the fingers of the right hand as it is moved toward and away from the left hand.
Origin: poring over a book
Usage: Success in college requires *study*.
Note: "Student" may be signed "STUDY" + "PERSON" ending.

PRACTICE, TRAINING

Rub the "A" hand back and forth along the outside edge of the left index finger. (Sometimes the "T" is used for "training.")
Origin: as if polishing something
Usage: *Practice* your interpreting.
　　　a valuable *training* program

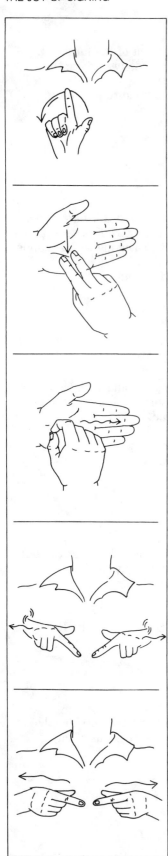

LIBRARY

The right "L" is circled.
Note: In particular settings, initials are frequently used as shortcuts. The "L" would be understood as "library" in an educational setting or context.
Usage: The *library* contains 75,000 books.

READ

Hold the left hand in front of you, palm up, fingers pointing to the right; point the "V" to the top and move downward.
Origin: Left hand represents book and right represents eyes scanning the page.
Usage: *"Reading* maketh a full man" (Francis Bacon).

WRITE

Pressing the tip of the right thumb and forefinger together, other fingers closed, write in the left palm.
Origin: natural motion of writing
Usage: *Write* to your congressman and support Line 21.

LANGUAGE, TONGUE

Place the two "L" hands in front of you, palms down; draw them apart in a twisting motion.
Usage: *Language* can be spoken or written.
  My native *tongue* is German.

GRAMMAR

Both hands in "G" positions are moved away from each other in a twisting motion.
Origin: the sign for "sentence" made with a "G"
Usage: studying English *grammar*

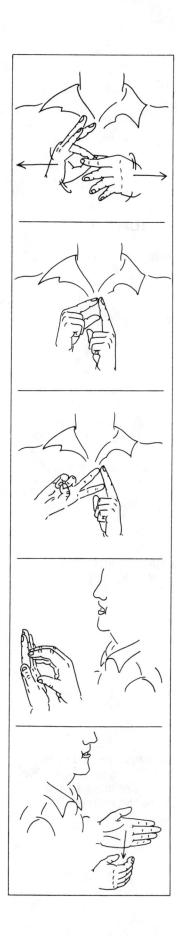

SENTENCE

The thumb and index fingertips of both hands (with other fingers extended) are pulled apart in a twisting motion.
Origin: The sign originated with the word "chain" and was used to indicate words linked together.
Usage: several *sentences* in a paragraph

WORD

Place the right index and thumb (with other fingers closed) against the left index which is pointing up, palm facing right. Note: Sometimes "VOCABULARY" is signed by repeating "WORD" several times.
Origin: one segment of a sentence
Usage: a man of few *words*

VOCABULARY

Place the right "V" (palm out) against the left index which is pointing up.
Origin: initialed sign for "word"
Usage: Deaf children often have a limited *vocabulary*.

PARAGRAPH

Place the curved right "FIVE" hand against the left open palm which is facing right and pointing upward.
Origin: The left hand represents a page and the right indicates the paragraph that is a portion of that page.
Usage: Read the first *paragraph*.

CHAPTER

Place the tips of the right "C" hand against the left palm and draw down.
Origin: indicating a long passage
Usage: Read the third *chapter*.

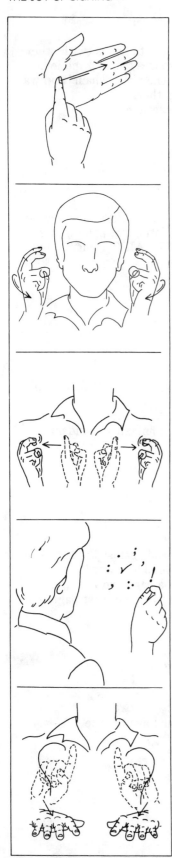

LINE

Run the right index finger across the left palm from heel to fingertips (left fingertips pointing right).
Origin: the finger underlining one line on a page
Usage: The fifth *line* is not clear.

QUOTE, THEME, TITLE, SUBJECT, TOPIC

Use the bent "V" hands, giving them a slight twist inward to make the quotation marks.
Usage: and I *quote*
　　　　theme of our play
　　　　title of the song
　　　　our *subject* today
　　　　the *topic* of conversation

IDIOM

Place the "I" hands in front of you, palms forward, and draw them apart; then make the sign for quotation marks, as above.
Usage: We must also learn the sign language *idioms*.

PERIOD, DECIMAL POINT, COMMA, SEMICOLON, COLON, EXCLAMATION, CHECK MARK, APOSTROPHE, THEREFORE

Use a modified "A" position and draw the desired mark in the air.

EXAMINATION, TEST, QUIZ

Draw question marks in the air with both index fingers; then direct the fingers of both "FIVE" hands forward. Or open and close index fingers as hands are moved down (as if there are questions from the top to the bottom of the page).
Origin: all questions coming at you
Usage: a difficult *exam*
　　　　a short *test*
　　　　a weekly *quiz*

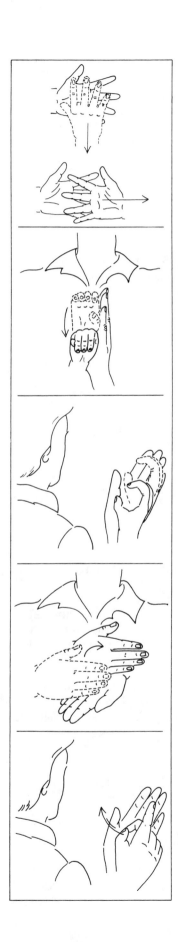

SCHEDULE

Move the right fingertips (fingers slightly spread) downward across the left palm which is pointing rightward; then turn the right palm inward and brush back of fingertips to the right across the left palm.
Origin: showing the paper ruled for a schedule
Usage: Prepare a *schedule* and follow it.

CURRICULUM

Hold the left palm in front of you; place the right "C" against it; lower the right hand slightly, form an "M" and place it against the left.
Usage: The *curriculum* includes math, English, and history.

COURSE

Hold the left palm in front of you; place the little-finger edge of the right "C" on the left hand near the fingertips, then in the center of the palm.
Origin: the sign for "lesson" made with a "C"
Usage: I'm taking four *courses* this semester.

LESSON

Hold the left palm in front of you; strike the little-finger edge of the right open hand across the fingers of the left and then again across the lower palm.
Origin: representing the portion of the page to be studied
Usage: Our *lesson* for tomorrow will be short.

DICTIONARY

Place the fingertips of the right "D" against the left palm; move it slightly toward self and repeat.
Origin: as if paging through a book
Usage: We cannot do without *dictionaries*.

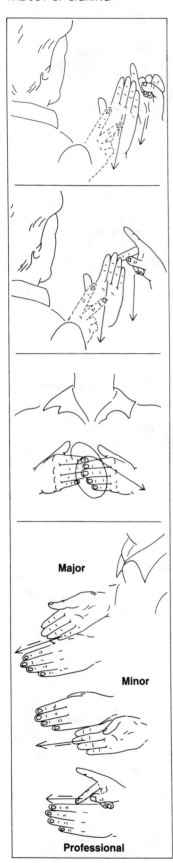

Major

Minor

Professional

PROJECT

Draw the middle finger of the right "P" down the left palm; then draw the right "J" down the back of the left hand (which is open with palm in, fingers pointing up).
Usage: a research *project* on the origin of signs

PROGRAM

Draw the middle finger of the right "P" down the left palm, then down the back of the left hand (which is open with palm in, fingers pointing up).
Origin: represents a program printed on both sides
Usage: planning a full *program*

PROCESS, PROCEDURE, PROGRESS, PROGRESSIVE

Both bent hands, tips pointing toward each other, circle over each other in a forward motion.
Origin: wheels of progress
Usage: the educational *process;* the correct *procedure;*
making *progress* in school; a *progressive* nation

MAJOR, SPECIALTY, SPECIALIZE, FIELD, AREA, LINE

Hold the left hand open in front of you, palm facing right, tips pointing forward; place the right open hand (palm left and pointing forward) on the left hand near the base of the index finger. Move the right hand forward on the left index.
Origin: following a specific line
Usage: My *major* is math. What is your *specialty,* doctor?
He *specialized* in pediatrics. His *field* is nuclear physics. My *area* is business administration. What's your *line* of work?

MINOR

Place the right open hand (palm left) under the little-finger side of the left hand, and move it forward.
Usage: His *minor* is music.

PROFESSION, PROFESSIONAL

Make the sign for "MAJOR" using the initial "P."
Usage: the legal *profession;* a *professional* interpreter

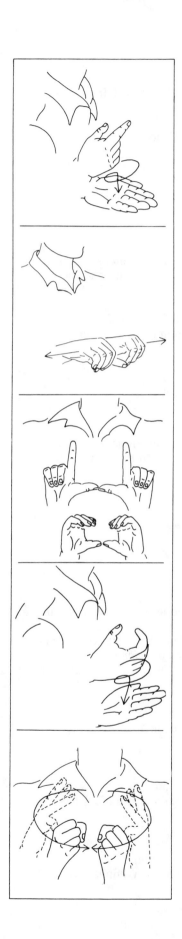

GRADUATE, GRADUATION

Describe a small clockwise circle with the right "G" hand and place it in the left palm.
Origin: placing the seal on the diploma
Usage: Carol will *graduate* from New York University.
Margaret Meade was our *graduation* speaker.

DIPLOMA, DEGREE

Place both "O" hands in front of you, palms down, and draw them apart. Or form the "O"s with the thumb and index finger, leaving the other fingers extended.
Origin: indicating the shape of the rolled diploma
Usage: received a *diploma* from high school
working for a college *degree*

LICENSE, CERTIFICATE

Place both "L" hands in front of you, palms out. For "CERTIFICATE" use the "C" hands.
Origin: indicates the shape of a license or certificate
Usage: driver's *license*
R.I.D. *certificate*

CERTIFY

Make a small clockwise circle with the right "C" hand and place it in the left palm.
Origin: placing the seal on the certificate
Usage: A *certified* interpreter is used in the courts.

WORKSHOP

Place the "W" hands in front of you; draw them apart to the sides and around, changing to "S" hands, ending with the little fingers of the "S" hands touching.
Origin: "GROUP" initialized
Usage: a *workshop* for vocational rehabilitation counselors

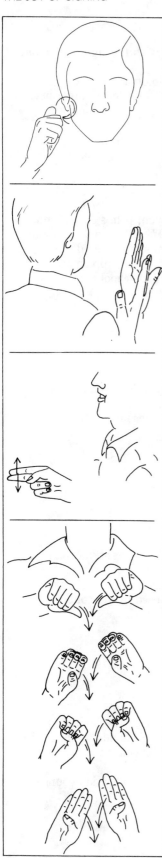

AUDIOLOGY

Circle an "A" at the ear. (For "AUDIOLOGIST" add the "PERSON" ending.)
Usage: His field is *audiology*.
Audiologists study the science of hearing.

PSYCHOLOGY

Hold the left open hand in front of you, fingers pointing up and palm facing right; place the right open hand (palm left, fingertips pointing up) at the separation of the thumb and index finger of the left hand.
Origin: the hands form the Greek letter *psi*
Usage: *Psychology* studies the mind and behavior.

HISTORY

Move the "H" up and down slightly.
Note: In the area of education, initial signs are frequently used. The "H" would be understood to mean "history" in this setting.
Usage: We studied American *history* in the ninth grade.

SCIENCE

Place both "A" hands in front of you, palms forward; alternately move the right to the left and down, and move the left to the right and down.
Origin: imitating the motion of pouring from containers
Usage: There are many branches of *science*.

CHEMISTRY

Use the "C" hands in the above motion.
Usage: Where is my *chemistry* book?

EXPERIMENT

Use the "E" hands in the above motion.
Usage: He demonstrated the *experiment* before the class.

BIOLOGY

Use the "B" hands in the above motion.
Usage: *Biology* class meets Mondays, Wednesdays, and Fridays.

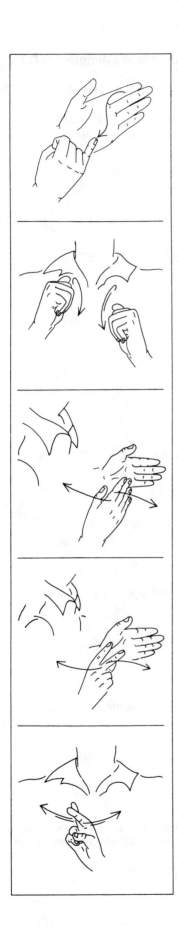

ART, DRAWING, DESIGN

Using the right "I" as an imaginary brush, draw a wavy line down the left palm. ("DESIGN" can be initialized.)
Origin: as if drawing a picture
Usage: a skilled *artist* (add the "PERSON" ending)
      drawing pictures
      a modern *design*

DRAMA, PERFORMANCE, ACTING, PLAY, THEATRE

Place the "A" hands in front of you (palm side out) near the chest and circle them toward the body alternately.
Origin: going through the motion of acting
Usage: a student of *drama*
      a good *performance*
      well known for her *acting*
      a Shakespearean *play*
      National *Theatre* of the Deaf

SING, SONG, MUSIC

Extend the left arm. Pointing the fingertips of the right hand to the left palm, wave the right arm back and forth.
Origin: directing the music
Usage: Let's *sing* in signs.
      an old *song* from the sixties
      the sound of *music*

POETRY

Extend the left arm. Pointing the fingertips of the right "P" toward the left palm, wave the right back and forth.
Origin: The sign for "music" is initialed.
Usage: "I think that I shall never see a *poem* lovely as a tree . . . ."

RHYTHM

Using the right "R," swing the arm back and forth in front of you in a rhythmic motion.
Origin: indicating the rhythm or beat
Usage: I've got *rhythm.*

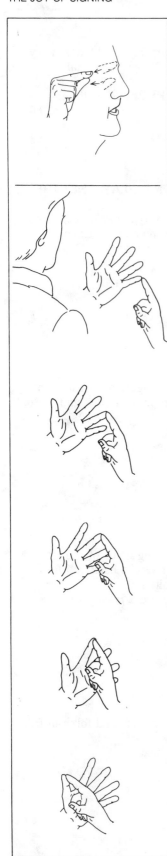

GALLAUDET (College for the deaf in Washington, D.C.)

Place the right "G" hand at the side of the eye and draw back, closing the fingers.
Origin: represents glasses worn by Rev. T. H. Gallaudet
Usage: The charter for *Gallaudet* College was signed by Abraham Lincoln.

PREPARATORY STUDENT

Point to the little finger of the left open "FIVE" hand.

FRESHMAN

Point to the fourth finger of the left open "FIVE" hand.

SOPHOMORE

Point to the middle finger of the left open "FIVE" hand.

JUNIOR

Point to the index finger of the left open "FIVE" hand.

SENIOR

Point to the thumb of the left open "FIVE" hand, or place the open right hand on the left thumb which is facing you.

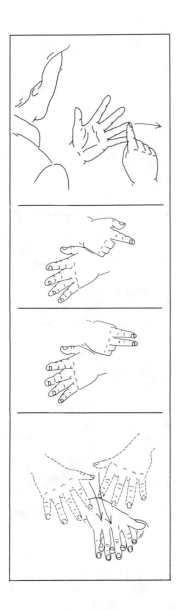

LEAVING COLLEGE

Leaving college during a particular year is indicated by using the index finger to touch and move away from the left-hand finger that represents the year in which the student left. The illustration shows that a student left during his freshman year.

FIRST-YEAR GRADUATE STUDENT

Place the right "G" on the left wrist.

SECOND-YEAR GRADUATE STUDENT

Place the side of the "TWO" hand on the left wrist.

MAINSTREAM

Both hands in the "FIVE" position, palms down, move toward each other and intertwine, palms remaining down and both hands moving forward.
Origin: coming together and moving ahead
Usage: Several deaf children were *mainstreamed.*

COLLEGES

The names of colleges are usually signed as they are spoken:
U.C.L.A.—Each letter is circled slightly.
New York University—"NEW YORK" + "U" (circled).
University of Illinois—"U" (circled) + "Ill." (fingerspelled).
George Washington University—G.W.U. (all are circled).

DEGREES

B.A., M.A., M.S., Ed.D., Ph.D., etc.—Fingerspell.
DOCTOR—When referring to a person who has a doctorate in a field other than medicine, "doctor" is abbreviated "Dr."
Examples: my teacher, *Dr.* Williams (fingerspell "Dr.")
our family *doctor* (use the medical-doctor sign, placing the "D" on the wrist)

16

Miscellaneous Nouns

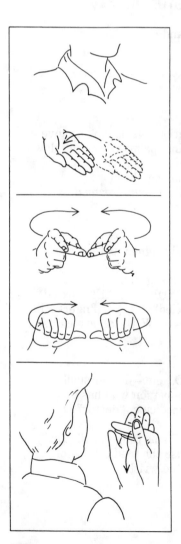

THING

Place the slightly curved open hand in front of you, palm facing up; move it to the right and drop it slightly.
Origin: an imaginary object in the hand
Usage: Many *things* must be done.
Note: Frequently an "E" is used for "EQUIPMENT" and an "M" for "MATERIAL" (palm-side up as in "THING").

PLACE, AREA

Touch the tips of the middle fingers of the "P" hands; draw them apart; circle them toward self and touch the fingertips again. "AREA" may be made with the "A" hands.
Origin: drawing a circle to indicate the limits of an area
Usage: Have you traveled to many *places?*
      a small *area* (use the "A" hands)
Note: An area may also be shown by circling the downturned right hand.

LIST

Hold the left palm in front of you, tips pointing up; strike the little-finger edge of the right open hand several times across the open left palm, slightly lower each time.
Origin: showing a list from the top to the bottom of a page
Usage: a long *list* of groceries

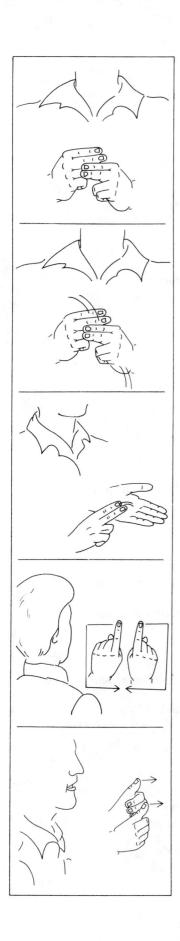

NAME

Place the middle finger of the right "H" across the index finger of the left "H."
Origin: Crossing the fingers to form an X represents the place where the name is to be signed.
Usage: Your *name* may have an interesting meaning.

NAMED, CALLED

Sign "NAME" and move the hands in this position slightly up-forward-down.
Usage: a man *named* Robertson
They always *called* her Penny.

SIGNATURE

Hold the right "U" in front of you, palm in, turn it and place it face down on the left palm which is facing up.
Origin: The left hand represents the paper, the right represents the signature.
Usage: I need your *signature.*
Please *sign* your name.

SIGN, POSTER

Draw a square in front of you with both index fingers.
Usage: We followed the *signs.*
a large, colorful *poster*

POSTING A NOTICE

Direct both "A" hands forward as if placing thumbtacks in a wall.
Usage: We wanted to inform everyone so we *posted a notice.*
We put it up on the bulletin board.

BELLS

Bells are signed by imitating the motion associated with them as described below:

1. CLAPPER STRIKING A BELL
Strike the left open hand with the inside of the right "A"; then opening the right to a "FIVE" position, shake it from the wrist while moving it away from the left.
Origin: represents the striking and the vibration
Usage: "I heard the *bells* on Christmas Day . . . ."

2. A BELL RUNG BY PULLING A ROPE
Hold the rope of an imaginary church bell and pull down once or twice.
Usage: The war was over and they *rang the bells* everywhere.

3. HANDBELLS
Hold the bell with the tips of the "AND" hand and shake it.
Usage: The teacher had a *bell* on her desk.

4. DINNER BELL
Hold the bell with the thumb and index fingers, other fingers open.
Usage: The gift was a beautiful china *dinner bell.*

5. DOORBELL
Using the thumb of the "A" hand, push an imaginary doorbell.
Usage: I think our friends are here; I hear the *doorbell.*

6. ALARM CLOCK, FIRE ALARM
Strike the side of the right index finger against the left palm several times.
Usage: My *alarm* rang but I didn't get up.
We heard the *fire alarm* and left the building.

7. LIGHT FLASHING
In the homes of many deaf people a flashing light is used as a doorbell and as an alarm clock. The sign is made by starting with the closed "AND" position, opening it and closing it again; repeat several times.
Usage: Look, the *doorbell;* I wonder who's coming so late.

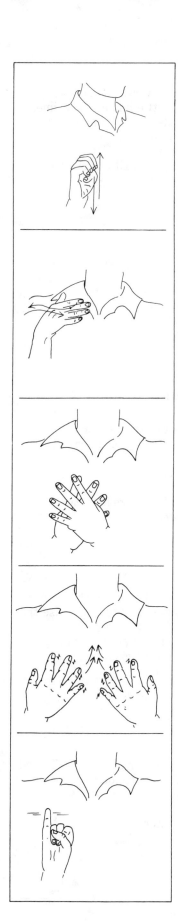

ELEVATOR

Move the right "E" up and down.
Origin: indicates the movement of the elevator
Usage: Take the *elevator* to the 13th floor.

FLAG

Place the right elbow in the left palm and wave the right hand.
Origin: the flag waving in the wind
Usage: Salute the American *flag*.

JAIL, PRISON, BARS, CAGE

Place the back of the right "FOUR" hand crosswise against the palm of the left "FOUR."
Origin: showing the prison bars
Usage: 3 days in *jail*
      to *prison* for life
      The man is behind *bars*.
      animals in a *cage*

FIRE, BURN

Place the bent hands in front of the body, palms facing up; with the fingers wiggling, move first one hand upward, then the other.
Origin: flames rising
Usage: a five-alarm *fire*
      a cozy *fire*place
      Paper *burns* easily.

INSURANCE

Move the "I" hand back and forth in front of you, palm out.
Usage: My car *insurance* payment is due.

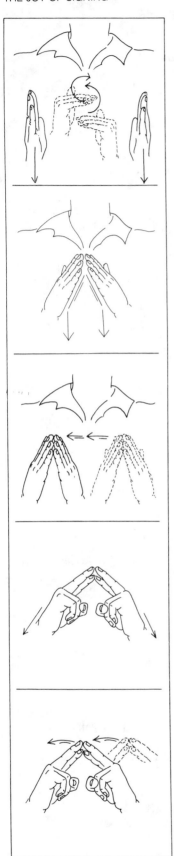

BUILDING

Place one bent hand on the other; reverse and repeat several times, raising the hands a little higher each time. Finish by outlining the top and sides of a building. For the verb form use the first part of this sign only.
Origin: placing one brick upon another
Usage: The Empire State *Building* is in New York City.

HOUSE

Place the tips of the open hands together and then trace the form of the roof.
Origin: a natural sign showing the roof of a house
Usage: What makes a *house* a home?

CITY, TOWN, VILLAGE, COMMUNITY

Touch the tips of the open hands together as for "HOUSE"; repeat several times, moving to the right.
Origin: showing a row of houses
Usage: Our *city* has a new mayor.
       We live in a small *town*.
       People have lived in the old *village* for years.
       Hillside is a small *community*.

TENT

Place the tips of the "V" hands together and draw them down and apart to indicate the shape of a tent. (Or use the index and little fingers.)
Origin: the shape of the tent beginning at the center pole
Usage: It was windy and our *tent* collapsed.

CAMP

Place the tips of the "V" hands together as in "TENT" and repeat several times while moving the hands to the right. (Or use the index and little fingers.)
Origin: a row of tents
Usage: Our *camp* was near the water.

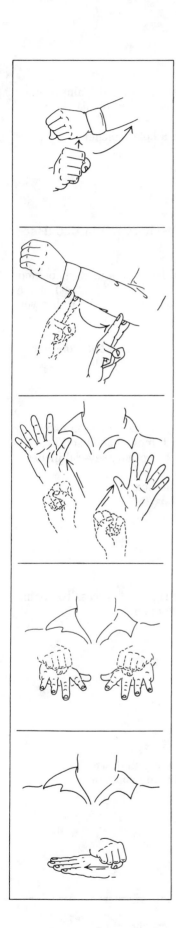

FOUNDATION

Place the right "S" under the left "S" and then under the left forearm.
Origin: showing the support under a building
Usage: first the *foundation,* then the house

BRIDGE

Place the tips of the right "V" under the left wrist and again against the arm farther to the left.
Origin: indicating the supports of a bridge
Usage: The Golden Gate *Bridge* is in northern California.

FIREWORKS

Place the "S" hands in front of you, palm sides forward. Move hands upward alternately, opening them into "FIVE" positions.
Origin: picturing sudden bursts of fireworks
Usage: Did you see the fantastic *fireworks* on the Fourth of July?

MAGIC

Place the "S" hands in front of you, palms down; move them forward and open them to "FIVE" positions, fingers pointing forward; repeat several times.
Usage: We always enjoy a *magic* show.

STAGE

Move the right "S" toward the right across the top of the left open hand, which is in a palm-down position.
Origin: indicating the surface of the stage
Usage: star of *stage* and screen

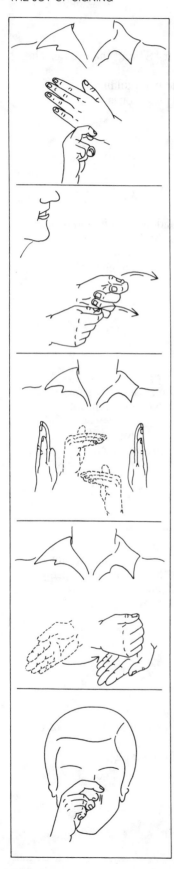

TICKET

Squeeze the lower edge of the left open hand (palm facing self) between the index and middle fingers of the right bent "V" hand.
Origin: punching the ticket with a hole puncher
Usage: *tickets* for the play
     got a *ticket* for speeding

GIFT, REWARD, PRESENT, CONTRIBUTION (Also used for GIVE)

Place both modified "A" hands in front of you, right behind left (right palm facing left and left palm facing right); move hands in a forward arc or toward yourself to show that you are the recipient.
Origin: presenting an imaginary gift
Usage: a birthday *gift*; a $10 *reward*; a *present* from her
     coworkers; a *contribution* to the Red Cross

BOX

Place the open hands in front of you, palms facing each other and fingers pointing upward; move hands so that both are palms down, one above the other, several inches apart (depending on the size of the box).
Origin: indicating the shape of the box
Usage: Pack the books in small *boxes.*

COLLECTION

Draw the little-finger side of the right "C" across the palm toward you and close to a slightly open "A."
Origin: gathering something in
Usage: a stamp *collection*

DOLL

Place the right "X" on the nose and pull down slightly.
Usage: a collection of *dolls* from many countries

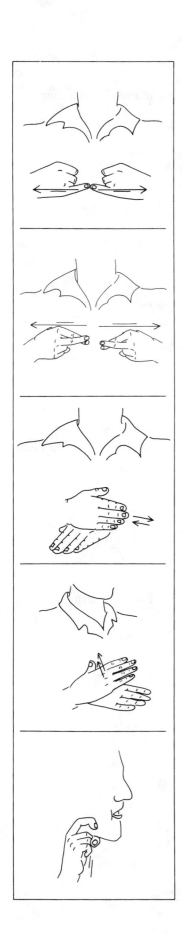

STRING, THREAD, LINE

Place the tips of the "I" fingers together and draw them apart.
Origin: as if string is pulled from a spool
Usage: *string* for a kite
use blue *thread*
My fishing *line* is tangled.

ROPE

Place the fingertips of the "R" hands together and draw them apart.
Origin: indicates the length and twisting of a rope
Usage: a strong *rope* for the tug-of-war

WOOD, SAW

Place the little-finger side of the right open hand on the back of the left open hand and make a short sawing motion. For "SAW" use a larger, longer motion.
Origin: as if sawing wood
Usage: *wooden* shelves
sawing logs

PAPER

The left open hand faces up; the heel of the right palm brushes leftward across the heel of the left palm twice.
Usage: *Paper* is becoming expensive.

RUBBER

Stroke the side of the right "X" down along the side of the chin.
Origin: indicating the gum
Usage: Much of our *rubber* comes from South America.

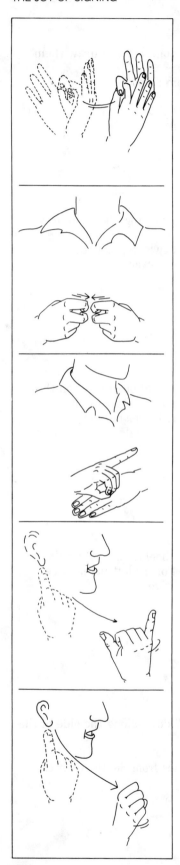

CHAIN

Link together the index and thumb of each hand (other fingers extended); repeat several times, first with the index side of the right hand up, then with the thumb side up.
Origin: fingers joined as links of a chain
Usage: The *chain* couldn't be broken.
   Chain your bicycle to the post.

ELECTRICITY, PHYSICS

Bend the index and middle fingers of both hands and strike the joints together. (Also made using only the bent index fingers.)
Origin: indicating the electrical charge
Usage: Lightning cut off our *electricity*.
   Physics is a science.

DIAMOND

Place the right "D" on the fourth finger of the left hand.
Usage: *Diamonds* are the hardest substance known to man.

GOLD

Touch the right ear with the index finger and bring it forward with a quick twist into a "Y" hand.
Origin: worn on the ear and yellow
Usage: the *gold* rush of 1849

SILVER

Touch the ear with the index finger and bring it forward with a quick twist into an "S" hand.
Origin: worn on the ear
Usage: *Silver* dollars are rare.

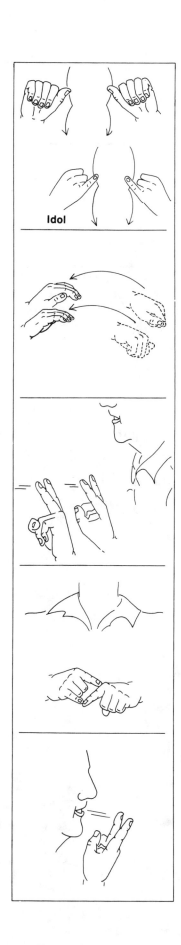

Idol

IMAGE, FORM, STATUE, IDOL, SHAPE

Trace an imaginary form in front of you with the "A" hands. The "I" hands are often used for "IDOL."
Usage: The ancient Greeks made *images* of their gods.
Some were in the *form* of animals.
the famous *Statue* of Liberty
idols of wood and stone
She saw a *shape* behind the curtain.

BURY, GRAVE

Place both "A" hands in front of you, palms facing down; draw hands back toward the body into a curved-hand position, palms still down.
Origin: showing the mound of earth
Usage: In New Orleans the dead are *buried* above the ground.
Kennedy's *grave* is visited by thousands of people.

FUNERAL

Place the right "V" behind the left "V" with both palms facing forward; move them forward, tips pointing up.
Origin: a procession moving forward slowly
Usage: His *funeral* service will be tomorrow.

CIGARETTE

Place the index and little finger of the right hand against the left index.
Origin: showing the size of the cigarette
Usage: Do you have any *cigarettes?*

CIGAR

Place the right "R" at the mouth, tips pointing away from the mouth.

SMOKING

Place the right "V" at the lips.
Origin: the natural motion of smoking a cigarette
Usage: *Smoking* in bed often causes fires.

MUSICAL INSTRUMENTS

Musical instruments are signed by imitating the movement associated with them. Pictured here are a few examples:

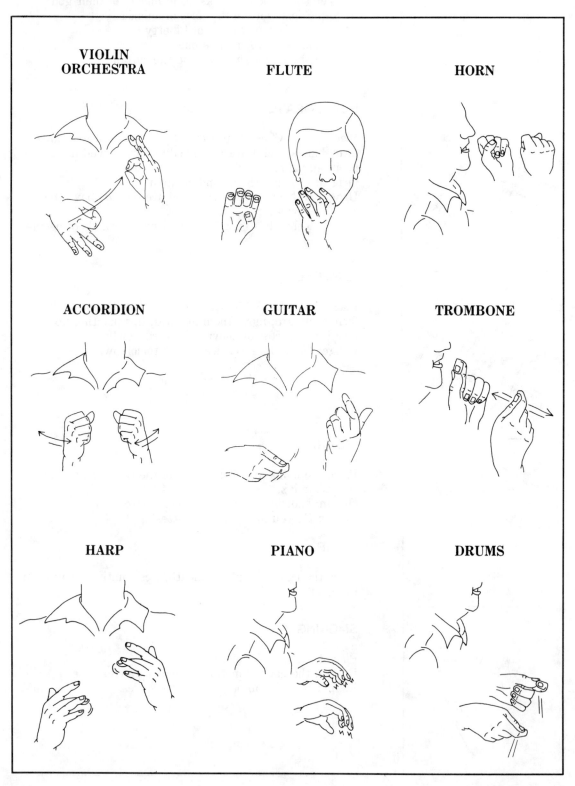

VIOLIN
ORCHESTRA

FLUTE

HORN

ACCORDION

GUITAR

TROMBONE

HARP

PIANO

DRUMS

17

Nature

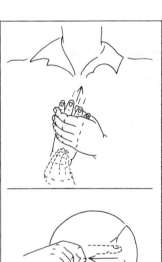

SPRING, GROW

The right "AND" hand opens as it comes up through the left "C," which is held in front of you with the palm facing right.
Origin: Right hand indicates that which is coming up out of the ground.
Usage: *Spring* begins in March.
  Flowers are *growing* everywhere.

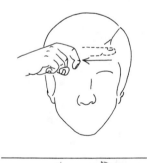

SUMMER

The right index finger is crooked and wiped across the forehead.
Origin: wiping the perspiration from the forehead
Usage: a long, hot *summer*

FALL, AUTUMN

The left open hand points upward toward the right. The right open hand brushes downward along the left forearm with the edge of the right index.
Origin: leaves falling off a tree
Usage: back to school in the *fall*
  Autumn leaves are colorful.

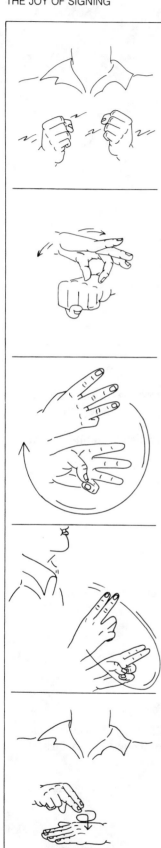

WINTER, COLD, CHILLY

Shake both "S" hands, palms facing each other.
Origin: shivering from the cold
Usage: in the middle of *winter*
      sleeping in a *cold* room
      feel *chilly* without a coat

EARTH, TERRESTRIAL

Place the thumb and middle finger of the right hand on the back of the left hand near the wrist and rock the right back and forth.
Origin: the earth rotating on its axis
Usage: The *earth* is 8,000 miles in diameter.
      on this *terrestrial* ball

WORLD

Circle the right "W" forward-down-up around the left "W" and place it on the thumb side of the left hand.
Origin: the world going around
Usage: He sailed around the *world.*

UNIVERSE

Sign "WORLD" using "U" hands.
Usage: The earth is a small part of the *universe.*

NATURE, NATURAL, NATURALLY, NORMAL

Circle the right "N" over the left hand and then place it on the back of the left hand.
Usage: the laws of *nature*
      natural beauty
      Naturally that's true. (Although not acceptable to all, this usage has become quite common.)
      It's *normal* for a boy to be active.

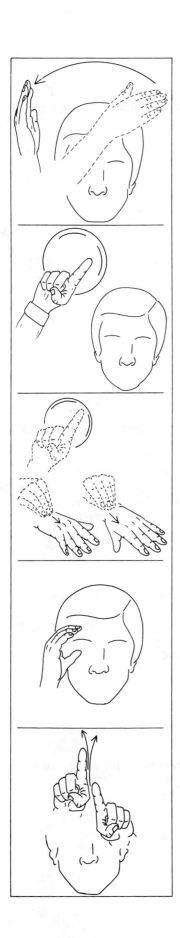

SKY, HEAVENS

Make a sweeping motion with the open hand from left to right, above eye level.
Origin: Indicating the vast expanse of the skies.
Usage: a starry *sky*
the blue *heavens*

SUN

Draw a clockwise circle in the air.
Origin: indicates the sun by a round circle overhead
Usage: The *sun* is bright.

SUNSHINE

Sign "SUN"; then place both "AND" hands high, right behind the left, and open the fingers as the hands are moved forward, palms facing down and fingers pointing forward.
Origin: the rays of the sun
Usage: The warm *sunshine* felt good.

MOON

Place the "C" hand over the right eye, palm facing left.
Origin: The "C" represents the crescent.
Usage: by the light of the *moon*

STAR

Using both index positions, palms facing forward and fingers pointing up, move the right index up along the side of the left index, alternating hands, and repeat several times.
Origin: index fingers striking each other like a flint to represent both the light and the twinkling
Usage: 50 *stars* in our flag

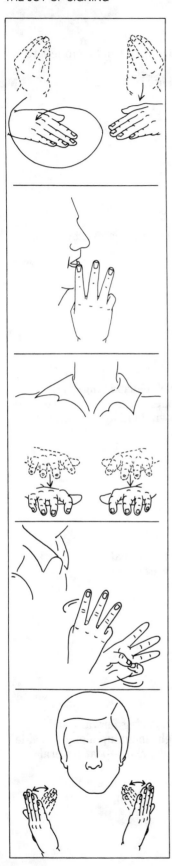

LAND, FIELD

Rub the fingertips of both hands with the thumb as if feeling soil; make a counterclockwise circle with the right open hand, palm down.
Origin: feeling the soil and indicating a large area
Usage: This is good farm *land.*
      walking through the *field*

WATER

Strike the side of the mouth several times with the index finger of the "W" hand.
Origin: the initial letter at the lips indicating drinking water
Usage: Man cannot live without *water.*

ICE, FREEZE

Place both "FIVE" hands in front of you, palms down, and drop them slightly, coming to a sudden stop as the fingers bend.
Origin: The water coming down suddenly freezes.
Usage: The rain is changing to *ice.*
      I'm *freezing* and want some hot chocolate.
      The lake is *frozen* and skating is allowed.

WEATHER

The "W" hands face each other and then twist back and forth.
Origin: adapted from the sign for "change," since the weather is subject to change
Usage: good *weather* for bicycling

PLEASANT, COOL

Place open hands in front of you at shoulder height, palms toward you; bend and unbend the hands several times.
Origin: The breeze is blowing at your face.
Usage: a *pleasant* day
      cool and comfortable

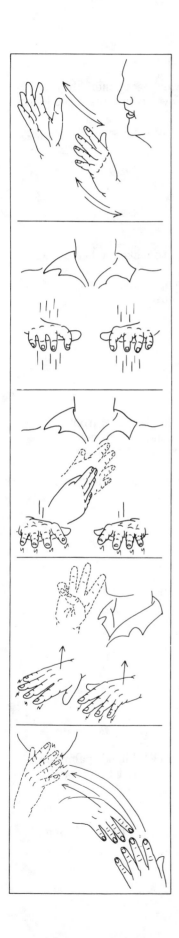

BREEZE

Place the open hands in front of you, tips pointing forward with palms in; wave them gently back and forth.
Origin: indicating a moving breeze
Usage: Without an occasional *breeze* we couldn't bear the heat.

RAIN

Sign "WATER"; then let both curved "FIVE" hands (palms down) drop down several times in short, quick motions. (The sign for "WATER" is sometimes omitted.)
Usage: Everything was dry and we needed *rain*.

SNOW

Sign "WHITE"; then lower both "FIVE" hands with palms down and fingers gently wiggling.
Origin: white flakes gently falling
Usage: Everyone wanted *snow* for Christmas.

FLOOD

Sign "WATER"; then place both "FIVE" hands in front of you, palms down and fingers pointing forward; wiggle the fingers as hands are raised.
Origin: The water level is rising.
Usage: The *flood* caused much damage.

RAINBOW

Sign "COLOR" (by placing the tips of the wiggling "FIVE" hands at the mouth and moving them away); then make a large arc from left to right with the right "FOUR" hand.
Origin: indicating the arch of colors in the sky
Usage: A *rainbow* has seven beautiful colors.

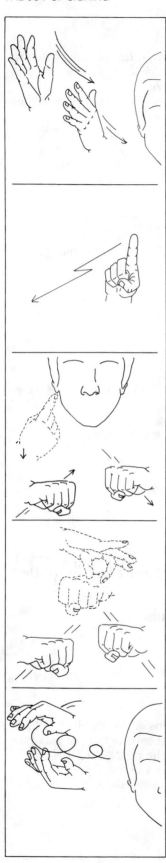

WIND

Hold the hands high, palms toward each other, the left slightly lower than the right; move them toward the left in several short sweeping motions.
Origin: sweeping movement of the wind
Usage: a cold northeast *wind*

LIGHTNING

Use the index finger pointing up to make a quick zigzag motion in the air.
Origin: the quick flash of lightning in the skies
Usage: The *lightning* struck a house.

THUNDER

Point to the ear, then place the "S" hands in front of you, palms down, bringing the right hand toward you and the left hand toward the side; reverse and repeat several times.
Origin: Movement of the fists represents vibrations.
Usage: That sounded like *thunder!*

EARTHQUAKE

Sign "EARTH" and finish with the "S" hands as in "THUNDER."
Origin: a natural combination of signs
Usage: *Earthquakes* are frightening.

CLOUD, STORM

Place the right slightly curved "FIVE" hand, palm down, above the left upturned slightly curved "FIVE" hand; swirl the hands around toward the left.
Origin: indicating billows of clouds
Usage: not a *cloud* in the sky
Note: The sign for "storm" is made in a large swirling motion.

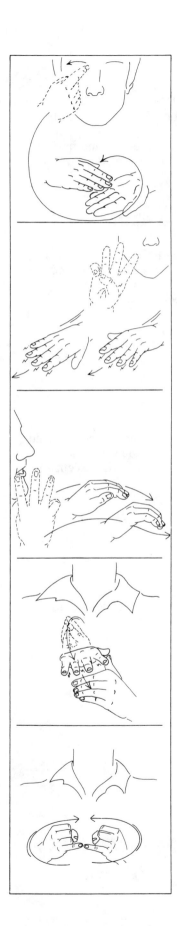

SHADOW

Sign "BLACK"; then make a counterclockwise circle with the right open hand, palm down, over the upturned left hand.
Origin: indicating something black overshadowing an object
Usage: We sat in the *shadow* of a large tree.

RIVER, FLOW

Sign "WATER"; then place the left hand behind the right, palms down, and wiggle the fingers as the hands are moved toward the right.
Origin: water that flows
Usage: The Amazon is the largest *river* in the world.
The *water flowed* past our house.

OCEAN, SEA

Sign "WATER"; then place the left hand behind the right, palms down, and move the hands up and down to indicate the waves of the ocean.
Origin: water and waves
Usage: The ship crossed the *ocean* in 3½ days.
across the *sea*

FOUNTAIN, SPRING

Push up the right "AND" hand (with palm facing left and fingers pointing up) through the left "C," opening it and wiggling the fingers as it is moved up, over, and down.
Origin: water rising from its source and flowing over
Usage: Watch the *fountain* change colors.
a health spa with mineral *springs*

ISLAND

Touch the tips of the "I" hands and move them away from each other, then toward you.
Origin: The "I" hands draw a circle to indicate the limits of an area.
Usage: No treasure was found on the *island*.

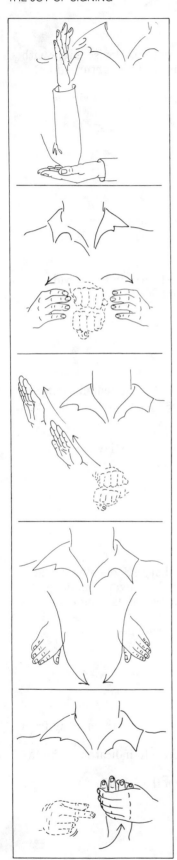

TREE, FOREST, WOODS

Hold the right arm up in front of you with the elbow in the left palm; shake the right "FIVE" hand in and out rapidly several times. For "FOREST" or "WOODS" the right "F" or "W" is sometimes used.
Origin: The arm and hand indicate the tree and branches.
Usage: a poem lovely as a *tree*; green *forest*; dark *woods*

ROCK, STONE

Strike the back of the left "S" with the palm side of the right "A"; place the "C" hands in front of you, facing each other, forming the shape of a rock.
Origin: The fist represents a rock; striking indicates hardness.
Usage: a large *rock*
  several small *stones* (use only the first part of the sign)

MOUNTAIN, HILL

Strike the back of the left "S" hand with the palm-side of the right "A"; then raise both open hands toward the side, one behind the other, as if indicating the side of a mountain. The same sign is used for "HILL" except the hands are not raised as high.
Usage: Climb every *mountain.*

VALLEY

Place both open hands high on each side, palms down; bring them down and together with index sides touching.
Origin: indicates sides of the mountains with the valley in the center
Usage: a green *valley*

GRASS

Sign "GREEN" and "GROW."
Usage: sitting on the *grass* eating our lunch

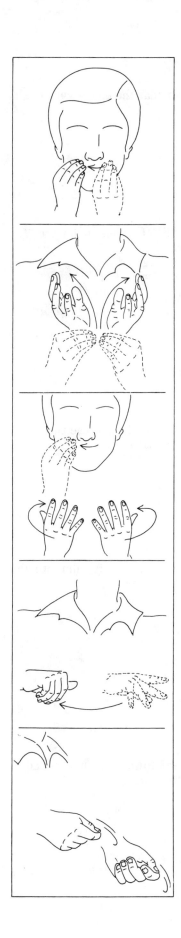

FLOWER

Place the tips of the "AND" hand first under one nostril, then under the other.
Origin: smelling the flowers
Usage: a variety of *flowers*

BLOOM, BLOSSOM

Place the tips of the "AND" hands together, then open them upward slowly, fingers slightly separated.
Origin: indicates the flower slowly opening
Usage: flowers in *bloom*
The cherry trees *blossomed* overnight.

GARDEN

Place the "FOUR" hands in front of you, palms in; move them away from each other toward the sides and then toward you. Add the sign for "FLOWERS" if this is appropriate.
Origin: indicating the fence and the flowers
Usage: Come and see my flower *garden.*

PLANT, SOW

With the fingers pointing down, pass the thumb across the inside of the fingertips from the little finger to the index finger and move the hand from left to right as if planting seeds.
Origin: planting seeds in a row
Usage: *plant* corn
sow wheat

HOEING, GARDENING

Using both modified "A" hands as if holding a hoe, go through the motion of hoeing.
Origin: indicating the natural movement of hoeing
Usage: They finished *hoeing* and then hoped for rain.
Gardening can be hard work.

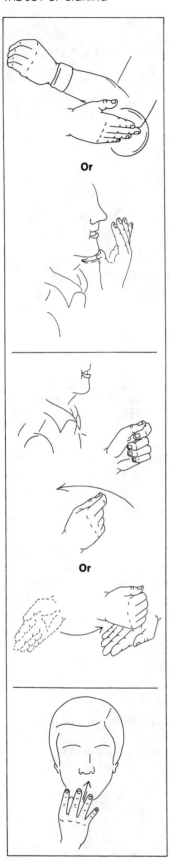

Or

Or

FARM, COUNTRY (Rural)

Rub the underside of the left arm near the elbow with the right open hand.

Or place the thumb of the right "FIVE" hand under the chin and move the hand to the right.
Usage: many small *farms* in New England
Our family lived in the *country*.

HARVEST, REAP

Use the left hand to hold imaginary stalks and use the right modified "A" to imitate the motion of cutting the stalks.

Or use the right open hand and sweep the left palm into an "A" position as if gathering in the harvest.
Usage: time for *harvesting*
We often *reap* what we sow.

HAY

Point the tips of the "FOUR" hand toward the mouth and move the hand toward the mouth.
Usage: *hay* for the animals

18

Body, Medicine, and Health

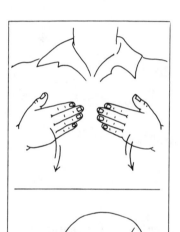

BODY, PHYSICAL

Place the flat hands on the chest; repeat slightly lower.
Origin: indicating the body area
Usage: Keep your *body* in good condition.
   a *physical* examination

HEAD

Place the fingertips of the bent hand at the side of the
head near the temple and then slightly lower.
Origin: indicating the temple area
Usage: My *head* feels hot.

FACE, LOOK

Using the index finger, trace a circle in front of the face.
Origin: indicating the whole face
Usage: a pretty *face*
   You *look* good today.

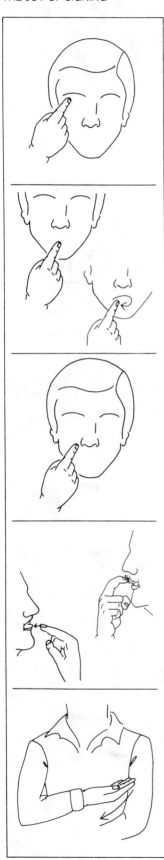

EYE

Point to the eye (or to both for the plural).
Usage: sparkling blue *eyes*

MOUTH

Point to the mouth.
Usage: The dentist looked into my *mouth.*

LIPS

Trace the lips with the index finger.
Usage: Your *lips* are easy to read.

NOSE

Point to the nose.
Usage: My nose is *cold.*

TEETH

Run the tip of the bent index finger across the teeth.
Usage: strong white *teeth*

TONGUE

Touch the tip of the tongue with the index finger.
Usage: A look at your *tongue* tells the doctor something.

ARM

Pass the back of the right fingertips down the left arm.
Usage: a baby in my *arms*

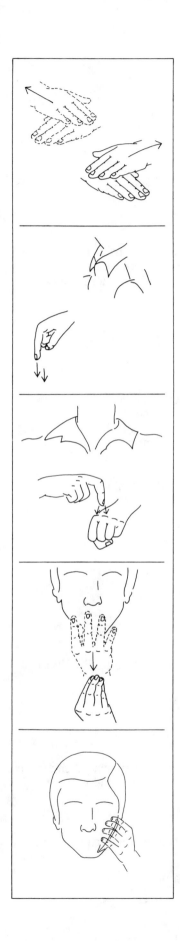

HANDS

Stroke the back of the left hand with the right and then stroke the right hand with the left.
Origin: indicating the hands up to the wrist
Usage: You have good *hands* for signing.

FEET

Point down twice.
Origin: indicating both feet
Usage: My *feet* hurt.

BONES

Tap the knuckles of the left hand with the curved index finger.
Origin: indicating the bones of the hand
Usage: a large-*boned* person

BEARD (Long)

Place the open "AND" hand under the chin and draw it down to a closed position, back of the hand down.
Origin: indicating the length of the beard
Usage: Uncle Sam has a long *beard.*

BEARD

Place the tips of the right curved hand at the right cheek and draw down the side of the cheek.
Origin: shows the heavy growth on the cheek and chin
Usage: a red *beard*

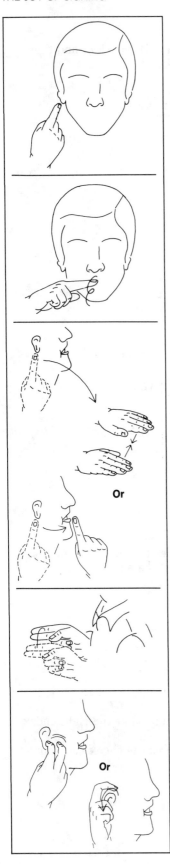

EAR, HEAR, SOUND

The right index finger touches the ear.
Usage: My *ear* aches.
   I *hear* you.
   Two words *sound* alike.

HEARING (A hearing person)

The index finger, pointing left, is held in front of the
mouth and rolls forward in a circular movement.
Origin: Hearing people can speak and are therefore called
speaking people.
Usage: Are you *hearing* or deaf?

DEAF

Touch the right ear and then sign "CLOSED."
Note: The sign for "DEAF" was formerly made by
touching the ear and then the mouth with the tip of the
index finger, representing the old concept of being deaf
and dumb or deaf-mute.
Origin: ears are closed
Usage: Helen Keller was both *deaf* and blind.

HARD-OF-HEARING

Make an "H" in front of you twice, moving it slightly to
the right the second time.
Usage: Ann is *hard-of-hearing.*

HEARING AID

Place the bent "V" at the ear and twist it several times. Or
place the bent index finger behind the ear and move it
back and down slightly.
Origin: placing the ear mold into the ear or placing the
hearing aid behind the ear
Usage: The *hearing aid* helped her to monitor her own
   voice.

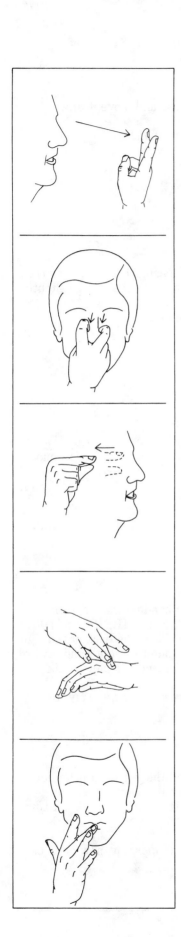

SEE, SIGHT, VISION

Place the "V" in front of the face, fingertips near the eyes, and move the hand forward.
Origin: fingertips pointing to the eyes looking out
Usage: Oh, say can you *see?*
      Sight is most important to deaf people.
      We *saw* the football game on television.
      He has poor *vision* (or *eyesight)* and needs glasses.

BLIND

Place the bent "V" in front of the eyes, palm in, and draw it down slightly.
Origin: eyes pulled shut
Usage: *Blind* people read Braille.

GLASSES

Draw the index finger and thumb together and back to show the frame of the glasses.
Origin: represents the frame from lens to ear
Usage: need new *glasses* soon

TOUCH

Touch the back of the left hand with the right middle finger, other fingers extended.
Origin: the natural motion of touching
Usage: Billy *touched* the hot stove and was burned.
      Keep in *touch* with me.
DWELL ON—In this position, the hands move in a circular motion (forward-down-back-up).
Usage: Let's not *dwell on* the subject any longer.

TASTE

Place the middle fingertip on the tip of the tongue, other fingers extended.
Origin: the finger placing something on the tongue to be tasted
Usage: That homemade soup *tastes* good.

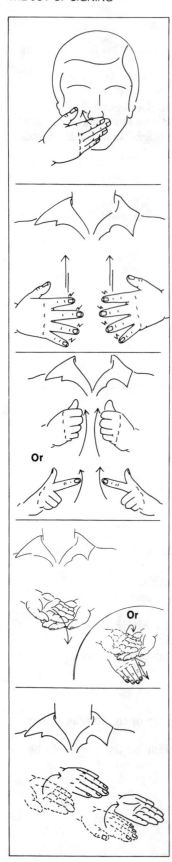

SMELL, FRAGRANCE

Place the palm in front of the nose and move it upward slightly several times.
Origin: smelling something on the hand
Usage: the *smell* of bread in the oven
      the *fragrance* of roses

LIFE

Place the "FIVE" hands, palms facing the body, near the waist and draw the hands up, wiggling the fingers slightly. Or use the "L" hands.
Origin: life surging through the body
Usage: full of *life*
      Life is short.

LIVE, ADDRESS, ALIVE

Both "A" hands, with thumbs pointing up, pass up the sides of the chest beginning at the waist. (This sign may also be made with "L" hands.)
Usage: Where do you *live?*
      What is your new *address?*
      He's *alive!*

BORN, BIRTH, BIRTHDAY

Place the back of the right open hand on the left palm; bring the hands up and forward. For "BIRTHDAY" add the "DAY" sign. Alternate sign: Place the back of the right open hand on the left palm and slide the right hand toward the body, down, and forward; right palm is now facing down.
Usage: *born* in 1958; date of *birth;* happy *birthday* to you

DIE, DEATH, PERISH

Place the right hand palm up and the left hand palm down in front of the right; turn both hands over. Note: For "DYING" make the sign for "DIE" slowly and do not turn the hands completely over.
Origin: to turn over and die
Usage: "It matters not how a man *dies,* but how he lives" (Samuel Johnson).
      dying of starvation
      Many people *perished.*

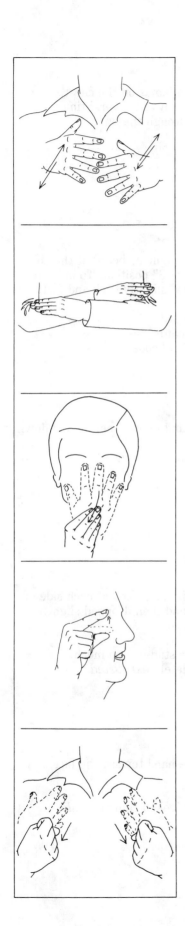

BREATHE

Place both palms on the chest, palms in, and move them in and out to indicate breathing.
Origin: movement of the chest in breathing
Usage: *"Breathes* there a man with soul so dead, who never to himself has said, 'This is my own my native land' " (Sir Walter Scott).
She ran until she was out of *breath.*

REST

Fold the arms in front of the chest, one on top of the other.
Origin: hands in a position of rest
Usage: feel tired and need *rest*

SLEEP

Draw the open fingers down over the face into an "AND" position near the chin, bowing the head slightly. (Repeat this twice for "SLEEPY.")
Origin: hand draws down to represent eyes closing
Usage: hard to get 8 hours of *sleep*
The baby looks *sleepy.*

AWAKEN, WAKE UP

Place both "Q" hands at the sides of the eyes, forefinger and thumb touching; then separate the thumb and index.
Origin: eyes opening
Usage: We couldn't seem to *awaken* her.
Wake up, it's time to go to work.

HEALTHY, WELL, HEAL, WHOLE

The "FIVE" hands are placed on the chest near the shoulders and brought forward into "S" positions.
Origin: The body is strong.
Usage: *healthy* body
in sickness and in *health*
He looks and feels *well.*
The broken bone *healed* quickly.
Archaic use: He was *whole* (well) again.

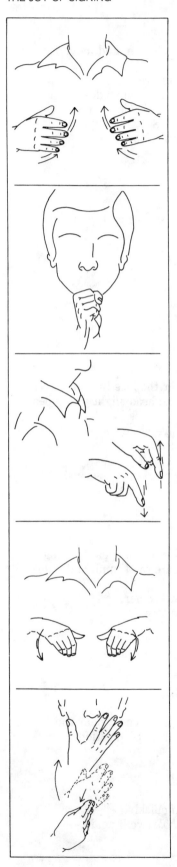

YOUNG, YOUTHFUL

Place the fingertips of both open hands on the chest, several inches apart, and brush upward several times.
Origin: blood flowing quickly through the body
Usage: feel *young* again
　　　That teacher seems *youthful*.

OLD, AGE

The right "C" hand grasps an imaginary beard at the chin and moves slightly down into an "S" position. To indicate great age, the "S" hand is moved slightly back and forth as it moves downward.
Origin: Age is signified by a beard.
Usage: How *old* is that gentleman?
　　　We have a collection of *old* books.
　　　Age before beauty!

CRIPPLED, LAME

Point both index fingers down and move them up and down alternately.
Origin: represents two legs hobbling along
Usage: a *lame* boy
　　　The accident left him *crippled*.

TIRED, WEARY, EXHAUSTED

The fingertips of the bent hands are placed at each side of the body just above the waist and then dropped slightly.
Origin: The body is bent forward.
Usage: *tired* after working all day
　　　My brain is *weary* after studying so much.
　　　The man seemed completely *exhausted*.

PALE

Sign "WHITE"; then direct the hand toward the face and open it.
Origin: having a white face
Usage: After a long illness she looked thin and *pale*.

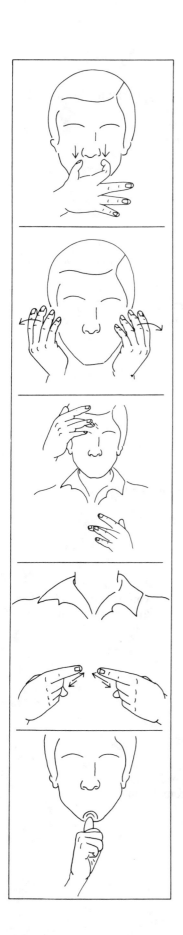

THIN, LEAN, GAUNT

Touch the right cheek with the right thumb and the left cheek with the right index finger; draw the hand in this position down the cheek.
Origin: showing the hollow cheeks
Usage: a *thin* face
       a *lean* and strong young man
       gaunt and starved

FAT, OBESE, CHUBBY, PLUMP

The curved "FIVE" hands face the cheeks and are then drawn slightly away from the face to indicate puffy cheeks.
Origin: the face is fleshy
Usage: a *fat* cat
       a strong woman but not *obese*
       a *chubby* baby
       cheeks rosy and *plump*

SICK, ILL, DISEASE

Touch the forehead with the middle finger of the right hand and the stomach with the middle finger of the left hand.
Origin: Both head and stomach are not well.
Usage: became *sick* after eating; *ill* and in the hospital;
       childhood *disease; sick* of studying (in this idiomatic
       usage both hands are given a twist)

PAIN, ACHE, HURT

The index fingers are jabbed toward each other several times.
Note: This sign is generally made in front of the body but may be placed at the location of the pain, for example: headache, toothache, heartache, etc.
Usage: suffered *pain* after the accident; *aching* all over; my
       knee *hurts;* have an *earache*

SORENESS

Place the tip of the thumb of the "A" hand at the chin and twist it back and forth.
Usage: After exercising I felt *sore* all over.

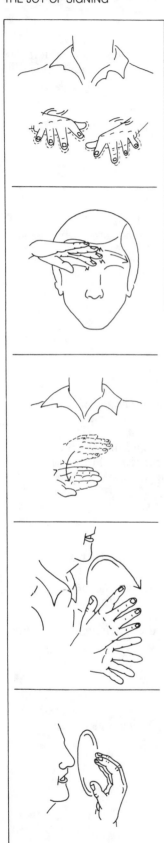

NERVOUS

Place the "FIVE" hands in front of you (palms down) and shake them slightly from the wrist.
Origin: shaking with nervousness
Usage: The new driver is *nervous.*

SWEAT, PERSPIRE

Pass the open, wiggling fingers across the forehead to the left (palm down).
Origin: indicating perspiration at the forehead
Usage: "Blood, *sweat,* and tears . . ." (Churchill).
    "Genius is 1% inspiration and 99% *perspiration*" (Thomas A. Edison).

UPSET

Place the palm of the hand on the stomach and then flip it forward, palm up.
Origin: The stomach turns over.
Usage: She felt *upset* and needed help.
    After eating she had an *upset* stomach.

VOMIT

Place the "FIVE" hands in front of you, one in front of the other (one palm left and one palm right); move them away from the mouth and downward.
Origin: proceeding from the mouth
Usage: a reason for *vomiting*

DIZZY

Place the bent "FIVE" hand in front of the face, palm facing in, and circle slowly several times.
Origin: Everything is going around you.
Usage: felt weak and *dizzy*

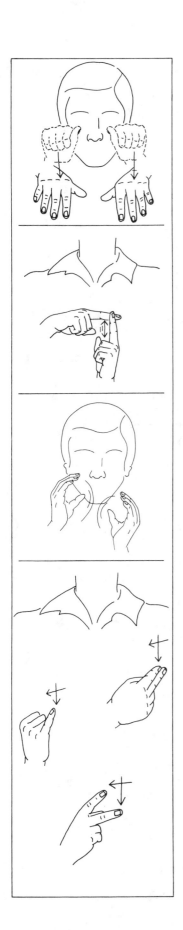

FAINT

Place the "A" hands in front of the face and drop them to "FIVE" positions.
Usage: became ill and *fainted*

TEMPERATURE, THERMOMETER

Hold up the left index, palm facing right. Move the right index (palm down) up and down between the first and second joints of the left index finger.
Origin: indicating the degrees on the thermometer
Usage: What is the *temperature* today?
The *thermometer* shows you have a fever.

EXAMINATION (Physical), CHECKUP

Place both "C" hands in front of the face and move them alternately toward the center in circular motions. Or use the sign for "INVESTIGATE" (right index in left palm).
Usage: an annual physical *examination*
My doctor advises a yearly *checkup*.

HOSPITAL

Make a small cross on the left upper arm with the right index and middle fingers.
Origin: a cross on the sleeve
Usage: a large 300-bed *hospital*

INFIRMARY

Make the sign for "HOSPITAL" using an "I."
Usage: Our school *infirmary* was moved to a new building.

PATIENT

Make the sign for "HOSPITAL" using a "P."
Usage: The deaf *patient* needed an interpreter.

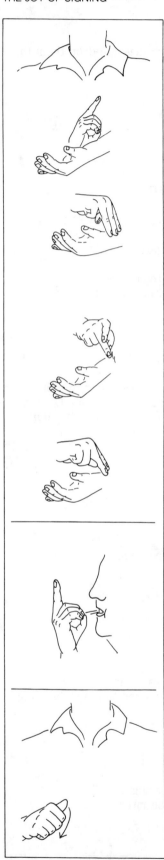

DOCTOR, PHYSICIAN

Place the right "D" on the inside of the left wrist.
Origin: the medical doctor taking a pulse
Usage: See your *doctor* once a year.

MEDICAL

Place the right "M" on the left wrist.
Usage: a well-known *medical* center

PSYCHIATRY, PSYCHIATRIST

Place the right "P" on the inside of the left wrist. For
"PSYCHIATRIST" add the "PERSON" ending.
Usage: *Psychiatry* studies and treats mental illness.
His *psychiatrist* lives on Fifth Avenue.

NURSE

Place the right "N" on the left wrist.
Usage: The night *nurse* works from 11:00 to 7:00.

DENTIST

Place the right "D" at the teeth.
Origin: the initial sign at the teeth
Usage: Let the *dentist* check your teeth.

OPERATION, CUT, INCISION, SURGERY

Make a short stroke along the side of the body (or into the
left palm) with the tip of the right "A." This sign is
sometimes made at the location of the surgery.
Origin: showing the incision
Usage: a short *operation*
a deep *cut*
a long *incision*
Immediate *surgery* was needed.

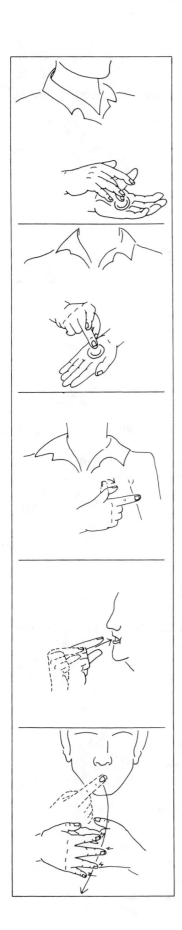

MEDICINE

Rub the tip of the middle finger in the left palm.
Origin: mixing the medicine in the palm
Usage: Take the *medicine* at mealtime.

POISON

Rub the tip of the right middle finger of the "P" in the left palm.
Usage: What is the antidote for that kind of *poison?*

INJECTION, SHOT, HYPODERMIC

With the right hand in the "L" position, place the tip of the index finger against the left upper arm and crook the right thumb.
Origin: the action of injecting the needle
Usage: *injection* for allergy
a typhoid *shot*
The doctor gave him a *hypodermic.*

PILLS, TAKING A PILL

Place the thumb against the index finger and open them as you move the hand quickly toward the mouth.
Origin: as if popping a pill into the mouth
Usage: Time for your *pills.*
Have you *taken your pills?*

BLOOD, BLEED, HEMORRHAGE

Touch the lips with the right index finger; then let the wiggling fingertips move downward across the back of the left hand (or across the palm).
Origin: red and flowing
Usage: lost a lot of *blood*
the *bleeding* stopped
hemorrhaging from the nose

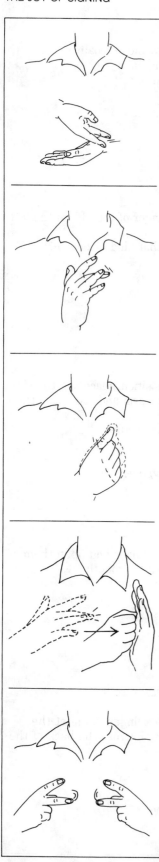

VEIN

Place the middle fingertip of the right "V" (palm up) on the inside of the left wrist.
Origin: indicating the vein of the wrist
Usage: suffering with enlarged *veins*

HEART

Touch the area of the heart with the right middle finger.
Usage: She is physically weak but her *heart* is strong.

HEARTBEAT

Strike the inside of the right "A" against the chest several times.
Origin: indicating the beating heart
Usage: The doctor listens to your *heartbeat*.

HEART ATTACK

Point to the heart with the middle finger; strike the left open palm with the right fist.
Origin: indicates the heart and then the action of an attack
Usage: How can you prevent having a *heart attack*?

PNEUMONIA

Place the middle fingertips of the "P" hands against the chest and rock the hands back and forth with the tips still resting on the chest.
Origin: initial finger and breathing motion of the lungs
Usage: *Pneumonia* can be serious.

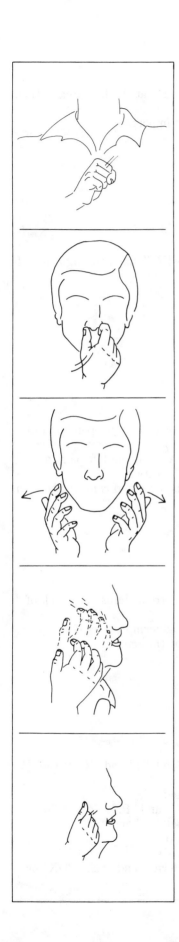

COUGH

Strike the right "S" against the chest several times (palm left).
Origin: action of coughing
Usage: How long have you had that *cough?*

A COLD, HANDKERCHIEF, KLEENEX

Place the bent index finger and thumb at the nose and draw down.
Origin: using the handkerchief
Usage: A bad *cold* kept me home several days.
His pocket *handkerchief* matched his tie.
Do you have any *Kleenex?*

MUMPS

Place the curved "FIVE" hands at the sides of the neck and move them away slightly.
Origin: indicating the swollen glands just below the ear
Usage: a severe case of *mumps*

MEASLES

Place the tips of the curved "FIVE" hand against the face at several places.
Origin: representing the spots on the skin
Usage: *Measles* can cause deafness.

MENSTRUATION, PERIOD

Place the right "A" hand against the cheek and strike the cheek twice.
Usage: *Menstruation* started at the age of 12.
Are your *periods* regular?

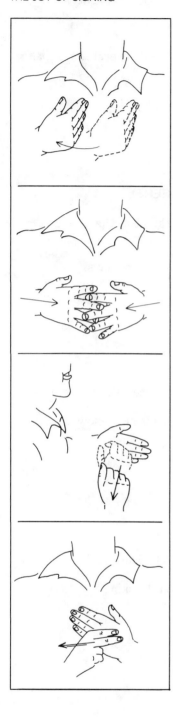

BREAST

Place the tips of the bent hand first at the left breast, then at the right.
Usage: A *breast* examination is important.

PREGNANT

Place the fingers of the right "FIVE" hand through the left "FIVE."
Usage: 3 months *pregnant*

ABORTION

Use the sign for "REMOVE"—hold the left open hand in front of you, palm facing right; place the fingertips of the right curved hand (palm down) against the left palm and move it down, ending in an "A" position.
Usage: People are discussing the pros and cons of *abortion*.

BAND-AID

Use the tips of the right "H" to stroke across the back of the left open hand.
Origin: indicating the bandage adhering to the skin
Usage: You need a *Band-Aid* for that cut.

NOTES

MENTALLY RETARDED—Spell "M" and "R" at the forehead.
HANDICAPPED—Spell "H" and "C."
CEREBRAL PALSY—Spell "C" and "P."
MULTIPLE SCLEROSIS—Spell "M" and "S."
CANCER—Fingerspell the word.
X RAY—Fingerspell the word.
CHICKEN POX—Sign "CHICKEN" and spell "POX" or add the sign for "MEASLES."

19

Home, Furniture, and Clothing

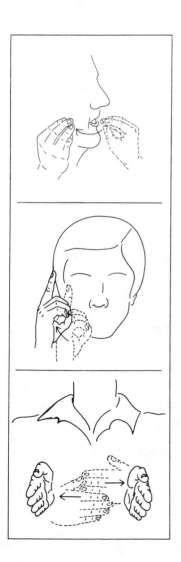

HOME

Place the tips of the "AND" hand against the mouth and then on the cheek. (Or place the flat hand on the cheek.)
Origin: Home is the place where you eat and sleep.
Usage: "The land of the free and the *home* of the brave" (Francis Scott Key).

DORMITORY

Place the right "D" on the chin and then low on the cheek.
Origin: the sign for "home" made with a "D"
Usage: Living in a *dormitory* was a new experience.

ROOM, OFFICE

Place the open hands in front of you with both palms toward you, left hand closest to the body and the right hand behind it (several inches apart); move the hands so they face each other, tips pointing forward. "ROOM" may also be made with the "R" hands. "OFFICE" is signed with the "O" hands.
Origin: indicates the four sides of a room
Usage: How many *rooms* do you have?
Ed goes to his *office* early every day.

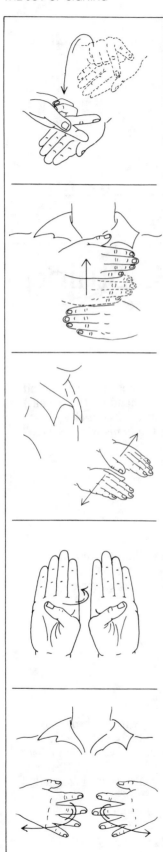

KITCHEN

Place the palm side of the right "K" into the left open palm; then turn over the "K" and place the back on the palm.
Origin: the sign for "cook" made with a "K"
Usage: Our *kitchen* is very small.

WINDOW

Place the left open hand in front of you, pointing right, and place the right hand on the edge of it, pointing left. Move the right hand up a few inches.
Origin: indicates a window being opened
Usage: The living room has four *windows.*

FLOOR

Place both open hands palms down in front of you and pointing forward with index-finger sides touching; move them apart.
Origin: indicates the flat surface of the floor
Usage: The new *floor* is shiny.

DOOR

Place the index-finger edges of the "B" hands together, palms facing forward; swing the index side of the right hand back and forth.
Origin: a door swinging open
Usage: The *door* was painted red.

GATE

Point the tips of the "FIVE" hands toward each other, palms facing you, and swing the "FIVE" hands in and out.
Origin: the swinging of the gates
Usage: We entered the garden through a large *gate.*

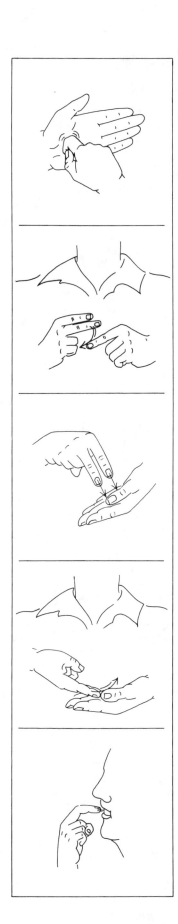

KEY

Place the knuckle of the crooked right index finger into the left palm and turn.
Origin: turning the key in the lock
Usage: Jim lost his car *key*.
What is the *key* to success?

KNIFE

Place the middle finger of the right "H" on the left index and slide it off the edge several times.
Usage: a sharp *knife*

FORK

Place the tips of the right "V" against the left palm.
Origin: as if piercing food with the prongs of a fork
Usage: The child couldn't use a *fork* yet.

SPOON

Place the tips of the right "H" against the left palm and lift; repeat several times.
Origin: as if placing a spoon in a dish and taking food
Usage: We bought a special *spoon* for the baby.

PORCELAIN, CHINA, GLASS, DISHES

Strike the front teeth with the fingernail of the right curved index finger.
Origin: hard as the teeth
Usage: *porcelain* from Germany
English *china*
glass door
set of *dishes*

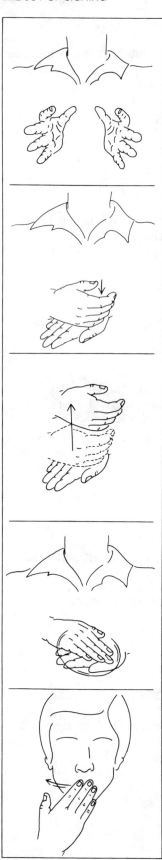

PLATE

Using the index or middle finger and thumb to form a "C" (other fingers extended), indicate the size of a plate.
Usage: We will need eight *plates.*

CUP

Place the little-finger edge of the right "C" on the left palm.
Origin: indicates the shape of a cup
Usage: a large collection of *cups*

GLASS

Place the little-finger edge of the right "C" on the left palm; raise the right "C" to indicate a tall glass.
Origin: indicates the shape and height of a glass
Usage: a *glass* of water

WASH DISHES

The open right hand rubs the open left in a circular motion.
Origin: natural motion of washing dishes
Usage: Have you finished *washing dishes?*

NAPKIN

Using the fingertips as a napkin, wipe the lips.
Origin: the natural motion of using a napkin
Usage: special wedding *napkins*

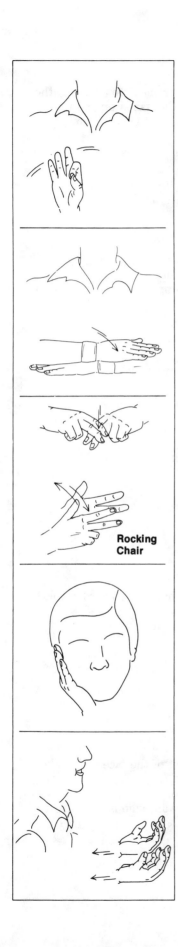

FURNITURE

Shake the "F" hand. (This sign may not be understood unless used in context.)
Usage: We moved all our *furniture* into the new house.

TABLE

Place the right forearm on the left forearm in front of you.
Origin: indicates the top of the table
Usage: The kitchen *table* is too small for us.

CHAIR, SWING, ROCKING CHAIR

Sign "SIT" with a repeated motion (the right curved and middle fingers are placed crosswise on the left curved index and middle fingers, both palms facing down). "SWING"—Rock the sign back and forth. "ROCKING CHAIR"—Use the "THREE" handshapes facing each other and rock them.
Usage: a comfortable *chair*
　　　　Our children really enjoy the *swings*.
　　　　Mom's favorite *rocker*

BED

Place the right open hand on the right cheek, bending the head slightly to the right.
Origin: head on a pillow
Usage: a king-size *bed*

DRAWER

Hold the right "C" in front of you, palm up; draw it toward you.
Origin: pulling out a drawer
Usage: I use all three *drawers*.

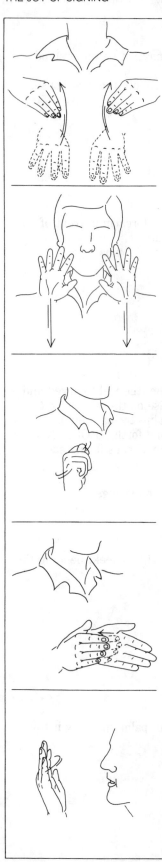

BLANKET

Place the open "AND" hands in front of you close to the body, tips pointing down; draw the hands up and to the neck, closing them as in the final "AND" position.
Usage: blue wool *blanket*

DRAPES

Draw both "FIVE" hands down slowly, palms forward.
Origin: indicating the drape panels
Usage: We ordered lined gold *drapes* for the dining room.

TOILET, BATHROOM

Shake the right "T" (or sign "BATH" and "ROOM.")
Usage: The *toilet* needs repair.
  new rug in the *bathroom*

SOAP

Draw the end of the right open hand downward several times in the palm of the left.
Origin: as if lathering soap in the hand
Usage: a mild *soap*

MIRROR

Hold the right open hand in front of the face and shake it slightly.
Origin: as if looking into a mirror
Usage: *"Mirror, mirror,* on the wall, who is the fairest of them all?"

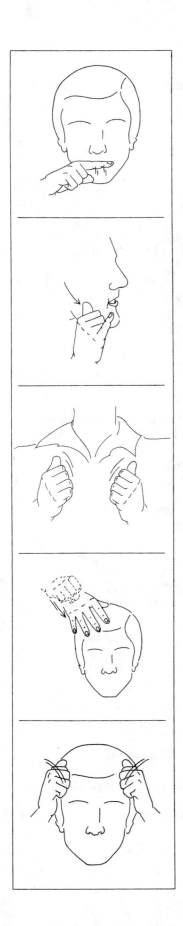

TOOTHBRUSH, BRUSHING TEETH

Using the index finger as a brush, imitate the motion of brushing the teeth. The noun has a short, quick motion; the verb form looks more like the actual motion involved in brushing the teeth.
Origin: natural motion
Usage: Where's my *toothbrush?*
　　　brushing teeth twice a day

SHAVE

Draw the outside edge of the thumb of the right "Y" hand down the cheek as if shaving.
Origin: using a razor
Usage: *Shave* every morning.

BATHE, BATH

Rub the "A" hands on the chest near the shoulder.
Origin: as if washing the body
Usage: *Bathe* every day.
　　　Do you prefer a *bath* or a shower?

SHOWER

Snap open the "S" hand over the head several times, palm side down.
Origin: coming down over the head
Usage: A morning *shower* feels good.

SHAMPOO

Use the "A" hands and rub against the head (or use the slightly curved "FIVE" hands.
Origin: natural motion of shampooing hair
Usage: I'm going for a *shampoo* and cut.

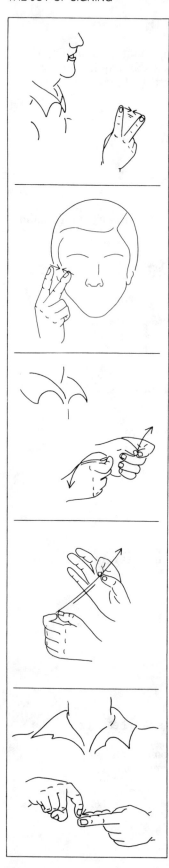

SCISSORS, CUT

Using the index and middle fingers of the right hand, imitate the cutting motion of scissors.
Origin: as if using scissors
Usage: These *scissors* are sharp.
      The mayor *cut* the ribbon.

HAIRCUT

Use the index and middle fingers of both hands in a scissorlike motion at the hair.
Origin: natural motion
Usage: I need a *haircut* today.

TEAR, RIP

Use the modified "A" hands to grasp an imaginary piece of paper and then tear it, one hand moving toward you and the other away.
Origin: natural motion of tearing
Usage: She was upset and *tore up* the letter.
      The sleeve was *ripped.*

SEW

With the right "F" holding an imaginary needle and the left "O" holding the cloth, go through the motion of sewing.
Origin: a natural sign
Usage: *Sew* a button on the coat.

SEWING MACHINE

Pass the fingertips of the right "X" along the left index finger.
Origin: the sewing machine needle stitching rapidly across the fabric
Usage: The *sewing machine* saves time.

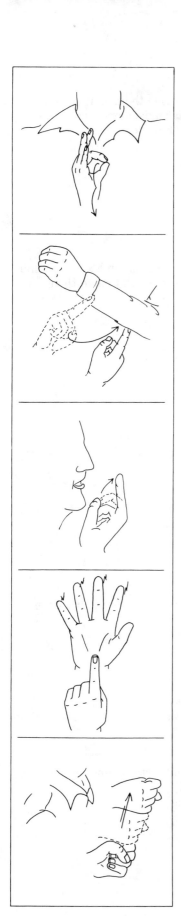

BUTTON

Place the "O" hand (with the other fingers open) against the chest, palm facing left; repeat several times, lower each time.
Origin: indicating buttons on the shirt
Usage: fancy new *buttons*

BASKET

Place the right index finger under the wrist of the left arm; make a semicircle and place it near the elbow.
Origin: carrying a basket with the handle over your arm
Usage: a green and yellow Easter *basket*

LIGHT BULB, A SMALL LIGHT

Snap the index finger in front of the mouth (as in "ELEVEN"), palm side turned toward the face.
Usage: a 100-watt *light bulb*

CANDLE

Place the tip of the left index finger, which is pointing up, against the heel of the right open hand, which is facing left, fingers wiggling.
Origin: representing the candle and flame
Usage: dinner by *candlelight*

UMBRELLA

Place the right "S" above the left "S," as if both hands are holding an umbrella; raise the right "S."
Origin: holding and raising the umbrella
Usage: No one had an *umbrella.*

TIE (A knot)

Using both modified "A" hands move them as if tying a knot (make small forward circular movements, then pull hands away from each other toward the sides).
Origin: natural movement
Usage: *Tie* your shoes.

DYE

Hold an imaginary piece of cloth with the index and thumb of both hands (other fingers extended) and move them up and down as if dipping them in dye.
Usage: We *dyed* the curtains green.

WASH

Rub the "A" hands together palm to palm.
Origin: natural motion of washing by hand
Usage: Clothes need *washing*.

HANG UP CLOTHES (On a rod)

Using the right "X" position, move the arm up and down slightly and toward the right.
Origin: placing hangers on a rod
Usage: *Hang up* your clothes.

IRONING

Slide the right "A" hand back and forth, palm down, across the left palm.
Origin: natural motion of ironing
Usage: *Ironing* is hard work.

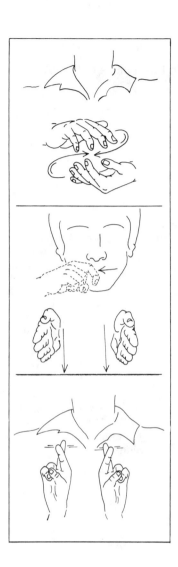

WASHING MACHINE

Move both curved hands (facing each other) in a twisting motion.
Origin: indicates the motion of the agitator
Usage: The *washing machine* broke down.

DRYER

Sign "DRY"; then place both hands in front of you and away from the body (palms facing each other) and move them down a short distance. Note: This ending for objects is to be distinguished from the "PERSON" ending which is made closer to the body and which moves farther down.
Usage: We bought a new washer and *dryer*.

REFRIGERATOR

Shake both "R" hands.
Origin: The sign for "COLD" is initialed.
Usage: a new *refrigerator* in our kitchen

ADDITIONAL HOME SIGNS

FREEZER—"FREEZE" + ending shown above for "dryer"
LIVING ROOM—"LIVE" + "ROOM"
DINING ROOM—"EAT" + "ROOM"
BEDROOM—"BED" + "ROOM"
RECREATION ROOM—"PLAY" + "ROOM"
   Or "R," "E," "C" + "ROOM"
LAUNDRY—"WASH" + "ROOM"
FIREPLACE—"FIRE" + "PLACE"
APARTMENT— Fingerspell "APT"
CONDOMINIUM—Fingerspell "CONDO"
AIR CONDITIONING—Fingerspell "A," "C"
PATIO—Fingerspell

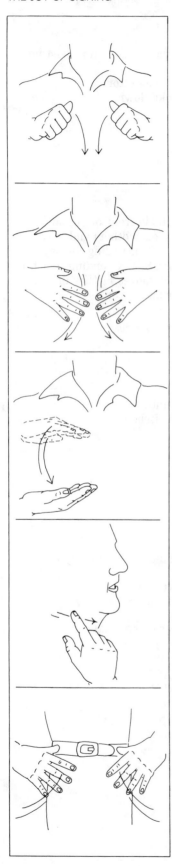

COAT

Trace the form of the lapels with the thumbs of the "A" hands.
Usage: Long *coats* are in style.

CLOTHING, CLOTHES, DRESS

Brush down the chest with the fingertips several times.
Usage: warm *clothing*
　　　　 many new *clothes*
　　　　 a fancy *dress*

BLOUSE, JACKET

Place the slightly curved open hands, palms down, in front of the chest; move them slightly away from the body, down and then in, ending with the little-finger side at the waist.
Origin: indicating the fullness of the blouse
Usage: a yellow *blouse*
　　　　 a heavy *jacket*

COLLAR

Using the right index and thumb slightly separated, trace the collar from the side of the neck forward to the center.
Origin: indicating the collar
Usage: a blue-*collar* worker

SKIRT

Brush the fingertips of both hands downward and slightly outward from the waist.
Origin: indicating the skirt
Usage: a short *skirt*

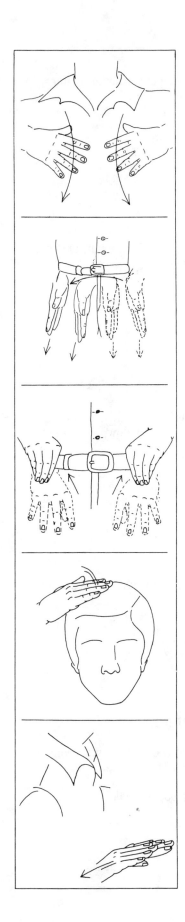

GOWN

Move the fingertips of the open hands down the body beginning at the chest.
Origin: indicating the long gown
Usage: white wedding *gown*

SLACKS, TROUSERS

Place the open hands just below the left side of the waist, palms facing each other and tips downward; give the hands a short upward movement from the wrist. Repeat at the right side.
Origin: indicates both pant legs
Usage: His *slacks* and shirt match.
       new blue *trousers*

PANTS

Draw the palms of the flat hands up against the body to the waist.
Origin: pulling on the pants
Usage: my old brown *pants.*

HAT

Pat the top of the head.
Origin: the hat is placed on the head
Usage: He wears many *hats.*

GLOVES

Stroke down the back of the left "FIVE" hand slowly.
Origin: pulling the gloves on the hand
Usage: long white *gloves*

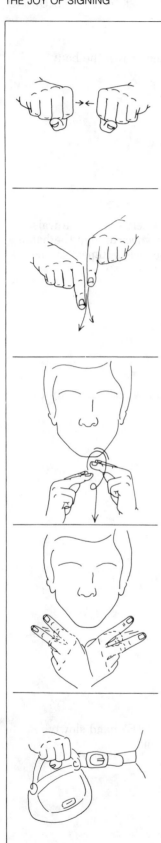

SHOES

Strike the sides of the "S" hands together several times.
Usage: Children like to go without *shoes*.

SOCKS, STOCKINGS, HOSE

Place the index fingers side by side, palms down, and rub them back and forth several times.
Origin: as if knitting socks
Usage: plaid *socks*
      black *stockings*
      expensive *hose*

NECKTIE

Using the "H" hands, tie an imaginary necktie and end with the right "H" being drawn straight down the chest.
Origin: tying the necktie
Usage: a Father's Day *necktie*

BOW TIE

Crossing the hands, palms in, sign "TWELVE" with both hands at the throat.
Usage: He prefers *bow ties*.

POCKETBOOK, HANDBAG, PURSE

Using the "S" hand at the side of the body, away from the chest, hold an imaginary purse by the handle.
Origin: holding the purse
Usage: I went to look for a new *pocketbook*.
      The *handbag* was large.
      A man snatched her *purse*.

20

Food and Related Words

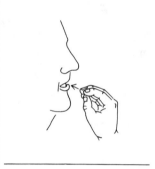

EAT, FOOD

The "AND" hand is thrown lightly toward the mouth several times.
Origin: Food is put to the mouth.
Usage: May I *eat* with you today?
⠀⠀⠀⠀⠀The *food* is cold.
Note: Usually the verb "eat" will have one motion while the noun "food" will have two.

DRINK

Place the "C" hand in front of the mouth, palm facing left, and make a motion as if pouring a drink into the mouth.
Origin: natural motion of drinking
Usage: What would you like to *drink?*

HUNGRY, CRAVE, STARVED

Place the "C" hand just below the throat, palm facing in, and draw it down.
Origin: the passageway to the stomach
Usage: *hungry* for a ham sandwich
⠀⠀⠀⠀⠀She had a *craving* for pickles.
⠀⠀⠀⠀⠀*starved* for food and for attention

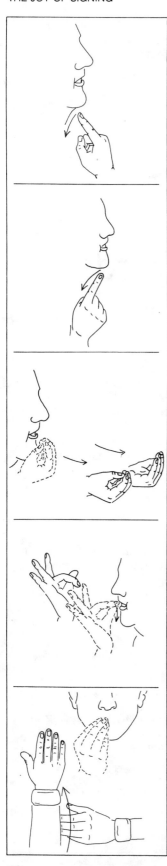

THIRSTY

Draw the tip of the index finger down the throat.
Origin: The throat is dry.
Usage: *thirsty* for cold water

SWALLOW

Draw the index finger down the throat, palm facing left.
Origin: indicating movement down the throat
Usage: couldn't *swallow* solid food

FEED

Place the tips of the right "AND" hand at the mouth; then
move both "AND" hands away from the mouth, palms up,
one behind the other.
Origin: Food is given.
Usage: We'll need lots of hamburgers to *feed* this crowd.

DELICIOUS

Snap the middle finger and thumb (other fingers extended)
in front of the mouth.
Usage: Ellis prepares *delicious* food.

BREAKFAST

Sign "EAT" and "MORNING." Some prefer to initial the
sign by placing the "B" (palm slightly in) in front of the
mouth and moving it slightly upward.
Usage: What time is *breakfast?*

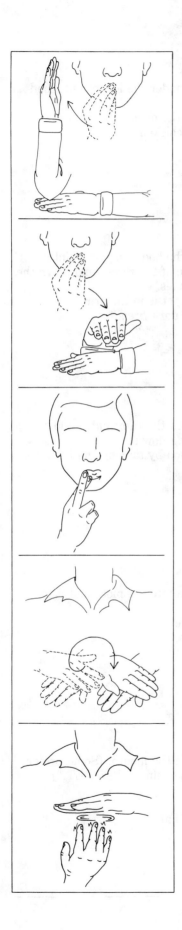

LUNCH

Sign "EAT" and "NOON." Some prefer to initial the sign by placing the "L" in front of the mouth, palm left.
Usage: Mrs. Kahl invited several people for *lunch*.

DINNER

Sign "EAT" and "NIGHT." Some prefer to initial the sign by placing the "D" in front of the mouth, palm in.
Usage: It will be a formal *dinner* at 8:00.

RESTAURANT

Place the right "R" at the mouth, once at each side.
Origin: the sign for "food" made with an "R"
Usage: a fancy *restaurant* in town

FRY, COOK

Place the hands palm to palm; then turn the right hand over, ending with the right upturned hand in the left palm.
Origin: a pancake being turned over
Usage: Would you like your eggs *fried?*
      Cooking can be fun.

BOIL, COOK

Place the right curved hand, palm up and fingers wiggling, under the left palm.
Origin: fire under the kettle
Usage: The water is *boiling*.
      The sauce should be *cooked* for 3 hours.

BAKE, OVEN

Slide the right upturned palm under the left downturned palm.
Origin: as if sliding a pan into the oven
Usage: *baked,* boiled, or fried chicken
     The pie is in the *oven.*

BREAD

Place the left hand in front of the body, fingers pointing right; draw the little-finger side of the right hand down the back of the left hand several times.
Origin: slicing a loaf of bread that is in the arm
Usage: Do you prefer white or dark *bread?*

SALT

Tap the back of the left "N" with the right index and middle fingers (both palms facing down).
Origin: the motion of salting food by tapping the knife on which it has been placed
Usage: Pass the *salt,* please.

PEPPER

Using the right "O" position, imitate the motion of using the pepper shaker.
Origin: shaking pepper over the food
Usage: I'd like some *pepper* too.

SUGAR, SWEET

Draw the fingertips down across the mouth. (Some prefer to draw the fingertips across the chin for "SWEET.")
Origin: as if licking candy
Usage: *Sugar* provides energy.
     Sweet potatoes go with ham.

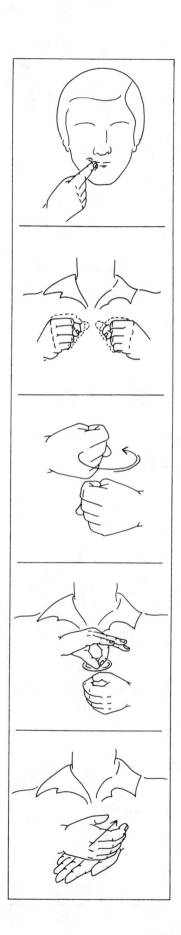

SOUR, BITTER

Place the right index fingertip in the corner of the mouth and twist it slightly, giving the appropriate facial expression.
Origin: Slight puckering of the corner of the mouth and the facial expression indicate bitterness.
Usage: *sour* as a lemon
bitter medicine

MILK

Squeeze the "S" hands.
Origin: milking a cow
Usage: lots of Vitamin D in *milk*

COFFEE

Place the right "S" on the left "S" and make a circular motion with the right "S."
Origin: the motion of grinding a coffee mill
Usage: The *coffee* is ready.

TEA

Place the thumb and index tips of the right "F" into the left "O" and stir.
Origin: stirring the tea
Usage: Would you like some lemon for your *tea?*

CREAM

Draw the little-finger side of the right "C" hand across the left palm from the tips to the heel of the hand.
Origin: skimming the cream off the milk
Usage: Do you like *cream* in your coffee?

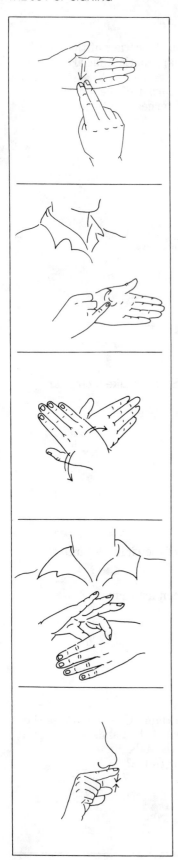

BUTTER

Draw the tips of the right "H" hand downward across the palm of the left hand.
Origin: buttering a slice of bread
Usage: Dip the lobster in hot melted *butter*.

JELLY, JAM

Scratch the tip of the right "J" against the left upturned palm.
Origin: spreading jelly on bread with the initial letter
Usage: peanut butter and *jelly*
Strawberry *jam* is really delicious.

CHEESE

Rub and twist the heel of the right open hand against the heel of the left open hand.
Origin: pressing the cheese into shape
Usage: serve crackers and *cheese*

MEAT

Grasp the fleshy part of the left hand (between the index and thumb) with the right index and thumb.
Origin: The fleshy part of the hand represents the meat.
Usage: *Meat* and cheese provide protein.

CHICKEN

Place the index finger and thumb in front of the mouth, opening and closing the fingers.
Origin: representing the beak
Usage: Southern-fried *chicken* is famous.

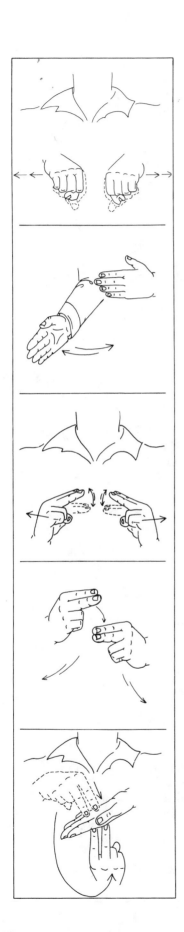

SAUSAGE, BOLOGNA

Move the "S" hands (palms down) apart while squeezing them several times.
Origin: indicating a string of sausages
Usage: *sausage* for breakfast
      bologna-and-cheese sandwich

FISH

Point the right open hand forward, palm facing left (left fingertips touching the right arm near the elbow); move the right hand back and forth.
Origin: the movement of the fish's tail in the water
Usage: The restaurant served all the *fish* we could eat.

BACON

Touch the tips of the "U" fingers of both hands, palms down; move the "U"s up and down while drawing the hands apart.
Origin: indicating the crisp bacon
Usage: a pound of *bacon*

EGG

Strike the index finger of the left "H" with the middle finger of the right "H"; drop them and let them fall apart.
Origin: breaking the shell of the egg
Usage: How do you like your *eggs?*

TOAST

Place the tips of the right "V" first against the palm and then against the back of the left hand.
Origin: the old-fashioned method of toasting bread by using a fork to hold it over the fire, first one side, then the other
Usage: *toast* and coffee every morning

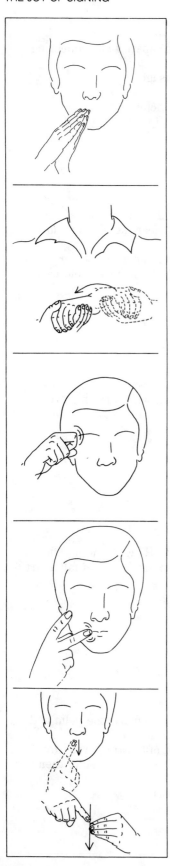

SANDWICH

Place the open hands together.
Origin: represents two slices of bread
Usage: a tuna-salad *sandwich* for lunch

HAMBURGER

Cup the hands as if making a hamburger patty; reverse the position of the hands (right hand on top, then left hand on top).
Origin: making the hamburger patty
Usage: a *hamburger* and a Coke

ONION

Twist the knuckle of the index finger of the right "S" hand at the corner of the eye.
Origin: Onions cause the eyes to tear.
Usage: liver and *onions*

PICKLE

Place the middle fingertip of the right "P" hand in the corner of the mouth.
Origin: initializing the sign for "sour"
Usage: homemade *pickles*

TOMATO

Sign "RED"; then draw the right index down and past the fingertips of the left "AND" hand.
Origin: represents the color and the slicing movement
Usage: a vine full of ripe *tomatoes*

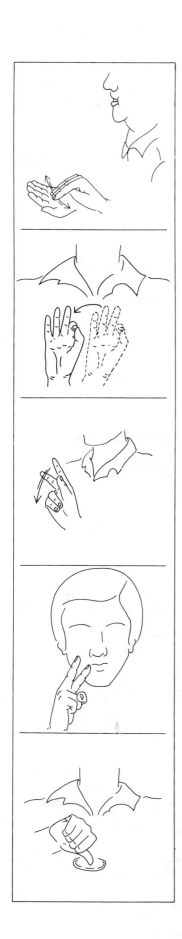

MAYONNAISE

Draw the tips of the right "M" hand across the palm of the left hand.
Origin: the sign for "butter" initialed
Usage: *mayonnaise* on your sandwich

FRENCH FRIES

Make an "F" in front of you twice.
Usage: *French fries* are a favorite American food.

KETCHUP

Point the tips of the "K" hand forward and shake it up and down.
Origin: using the initial letter and shaking ketchup out of a bottle
Usage: He likes *ketchup* on everything!

VINEGAR

Place the index finger of the right "V" against the corner of the mouth.
Usage: apple-cider *vinegar*

SAUCE, DRESSING

Using the thumbtip of the right "A" to represent the spout, make the motion of pouring sauce on food.
Usage: hot fudge *sauce*
          salad *dressing*

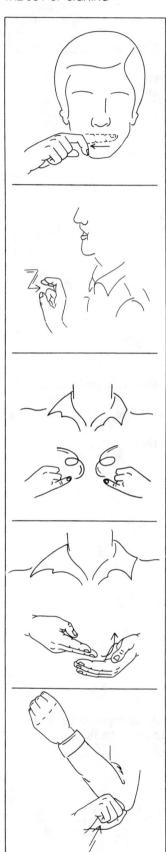

SYRUP

Draw the right index finger across the lips from left to right.
Origin: wiping the syrup from the mouth
Usage: Vermont maple *syrup* is my favorite.

PIZZA

Curve the index and middle fingers, drawing a "Z" with them.
Usage: We ordered a large cheese *pizza*.

SPAGHETTI

Place the tips of the "I" fingers together and draw them apart several times.
Origin: showing the long thin spaghetti
Usage: Italian *spaghetti*

SOUP

Using the right "H" hand as a spoon, dip it in the left palm and up.
Origin: bringing the spoon to the mouth
Usage: Hot *soup* tastes good on a cold day.

CRACKER

Strike the index-finger side of the right "S" against the left arm near the elbow.
Origin: striking the large old-fashioned cracker to break it in pieces
Usage: many varieties of *crackers*

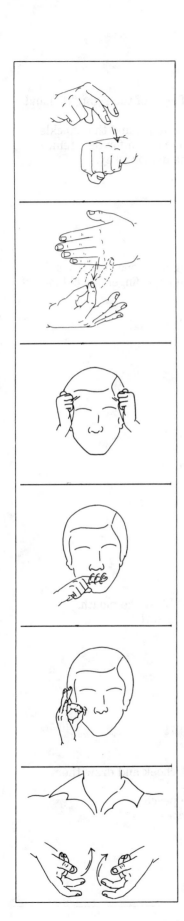

POTATO

Tap the back of the left "S" hand with the tips of the slightly curved right "V."
Origin: placing the fork in the potato
Usage: I like hash-brown *potatoes.*

GRAVY, GREASY, OIL

Hold up the left hand, fingers pointing right; grasp the lower edge of the hand with the right index finger and thumb and draw down several times.
Origin: gravy dripping from the meat
Usage: potatoes and *gravy*
      greasy food
      vinegar and *oil*

CABBAGE

Strike the sides of the head with the wrists of the "A" hands.
Origin: showing the cabbage head
Usage: You can have either white or red *cabbage.*

CORN

Place the right index in front of the mouth and twist it in and out.
Origin: eating corn on the cob
Usage: Do you prefer white or yellow *corn?*

FRUIT

Place the tips of the "F" hand into the right cheek and twist.
Origin: The sign for "apple" is used as a basis for this initial sign.
Usage: She ordered a *fruit* plate.

SALAD

Use the curved "V" hands, palms up, in repeated upward motions.
Origin: tossing a salad
Usage: We enjoyed the *salad* bar.

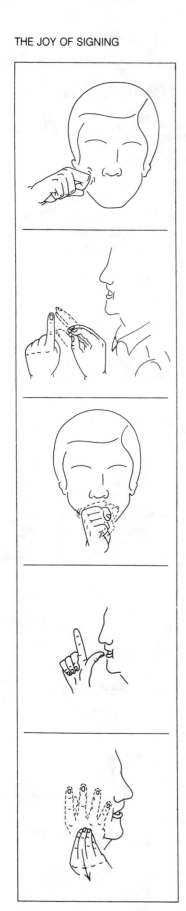

APPLE

Press the knuckle of the index finger of the right "S" hand into the right cheek and twist.
Origin: The cheek represents the apple and the knuckle pressing against it shows the indentation for the stem.
Usage: An *apple* a day keeps the doctor away.

BANANA

Go through the motion of peeling a banana, the left index representing the banana and the right fingertips pulling off the skin.
Origin: peeling the banana
Usage: *Banana* splits are very fattening!

ORANGE

Squeeze the right "S" at the mouth.
Origin: squeezing the juice
Usage: Drink *orange* juice often.

LEMON

Place the thumbtip of the right "L" at the mouth.
Usage: *lemon* meringue pie for dessert

PEACH

Place the fingertips on the right cheek and draw them down into an "AND" position.
Origin: showing the fuzz on the peach
Usage: a bushel of Georgia *peaches*

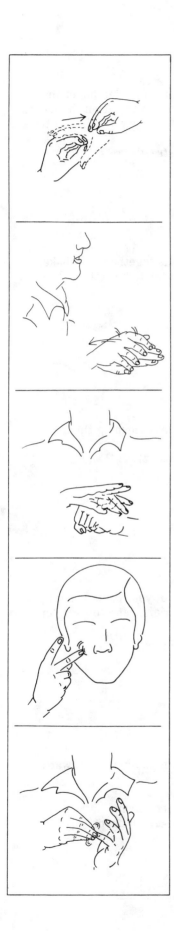

PEAR

Hold the left "AND" hand in front of you, fingertips pointing up; place the five fingers of the right hand over the left and draw up until the tips of both "AND" hands are touching.
Origin: representing the shape of the pear
Usage: *pear*-and-cottage-cheese salad.

GRAPES

Place the slightly curved right fingertips on the back of the left hand; repeat the motion several times, each time a little farther down on the left hand.
Origin: representing a bunch of grapes
Usage: purple or green *grapes*
RAISINS—The right "R" touches the back of the left hand several times.

MELON, WATERMELON, PUMPKIN

Flip the middle finger off the thumb, which is resting on the back of the left "S" hand.
Origin: thumping a melon to test whether it is ripe
Usage: a green *melon; pumpkin* pie with the Thanksgiving dinner; a large, heavy *watermelon*
Note: "WATERMELON" is often preceded by the sign for "WATER."

PINEAPPLE

Place the middle finger of the right "P" into the cheek and twist.
Origin: the sign for "apple" initialed
Usage: *Pineapple* and cheese make a good combination.

BERRIES

Grasp the tip of the left little finger with the right fingertips and twist the right several times.
Usage: picking *berries*
Note: BLUEBERRIES—sign "BLUE" + "BERRY"
BLACKBERRIES—sign "BLACK" + "BERRY"
CHERRY—sign "RED" + "BERRY"

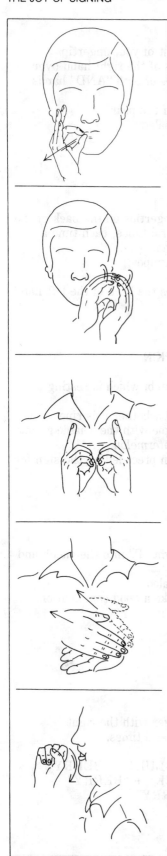

STRAWBERRY

Place the closed tips of the thumb and index finger in front of the mouth and give a sudden pull away from the mouth.
Origin: pulling the stem out of the berry which is in the mouth
Usage: I really enjoy a bowl of *strawberries.*

COCONUT

Touch the tips of the curved hands together and shake.
Origin: shaking a coconut at the ear to hear the milk splashing inside
Usage: a tall *coconut* tree

DESSERT

Place the "D" hands in front of you, touching them together several times.
Usage: What is your favorite *dessert?*

PIE

Place the open left hand in front of you, palm facing up; draw the little-finger side of the right hand toward you twice as if cutting a piece of pie.
Origin: cutting the pie for serving
Usage: Who ate all the *pie?*

ICE CREAM

Place an "S" in front of the mouth and move it toward the mouth and down several times.
Origin: licking an ice-cream cone
Usage: Do you like soft or hard *ice cream?*
What is your favorite *ice-cream* flavor?

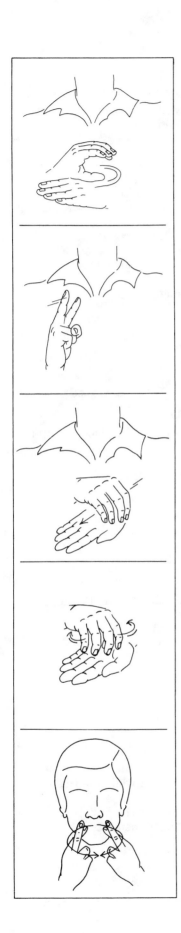

CHOCOLATE

Place the right "C" on the back of the left hand and circle it.
Usage: *chocolate* icing on the cake

VANILLA

Shake the "V" in front of you. (Note: This will only be understood in context.)
Usage: *Vanilla* ice cream is America's favorite dessert.

CAKE

Place the tips of the right "C" on the left palm and move the "C" across the palm to the right.
Origin: showing a slice of cake
Usage: German chocolate *cake*

COOKIE, BISCUIT

Place the tips of the right slightly curved fingers in the left palm, twist and repeat. (The sign for "BISCUIT" is not twisted.)
Origin: using a cookie cutter
Usage: chocolate-chip *cookies*
　　　　homemade *biscuits*

DOUGHNUT

Place both "R" hands at the mouth and circle forward, touching the tips together.
Origin: represents the twisted doughnut
Usage: coffee and *doughnuts*

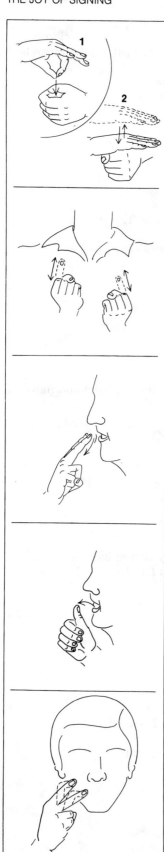

SODA, POP

Place the tips of the right "NINE" into the left "O" (palm right); lift the right out and immediately bring the right palm down on the left and bounce it off.
Origin: pushing the bottle cap on
Usage: a case of orange *soda*
Who will bring the *pop?*

POPCORN

Snap the index fingers up alternately, palms up.
Origin: showing corn popping
Usage: We ate *popcorn* all evening.

CANDY

Rub the tips of the "U" across the lips. Or place the tip of the index into the cheek and turn it.
Origin: licking candy
Usage: Don brought Beth a box of *candy.*

NUTS

Place the thumb of the right "A" hand behind the upper teeth and draw it forward quickly.
Origin: cracking the nut between the teeth
Usage: *Nuts* and mints are on the table.

CHEWING GUM

Place the tips of the curved "V" at the side of the right cheek and move the hand up and down while the tips stay on the cheek.
Origin: showing the chewing motion of the jaw
Usage: We found *chewing gum* under the seats.

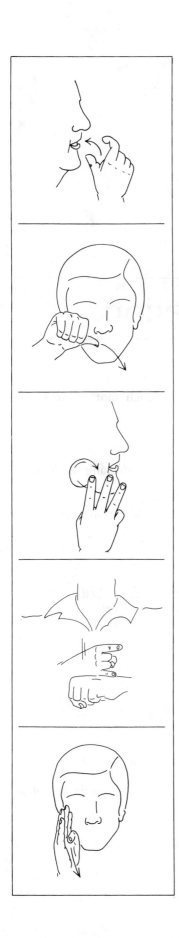

DRINK (Liquor)

Make a small "C" with the thumb and index finger, other fingers closed, and make a motion as if pouring a drink into the mouth.
Origin: drinking from a small glass
Usage: a choice of *drinks* at the bar

DRUNK

Place the "A" hand at the mouth and make a motion as if pouring past the mouth and down.
Origin: pouring motion at the lips
Usage: *drunk* every weekend

WINE

Rub the right "W" in a circular motion against the cheek.
Usage: *wine* and cheese

WHISKEY, LIQUOR

Extend the index and little fingers of the right hand; place the right hand on the back of the left fist; move the right hand up and down once or twice.
Origin: indicating a drink so many fingers high
Usage: He drank *whiskey* at the bar.
opened a new *liquor* store

BEER

Place the right "B" at the side of the mouth and draw down.
Usage: *beer* and pretzels

21

Sports and Recreation

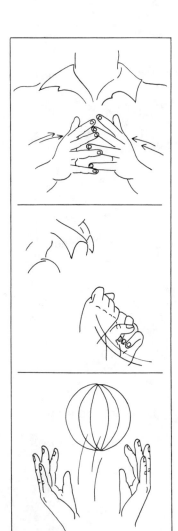

Generally speaking, the sign for each sport pictures an action that identifies it.

FOOTBALL

Bring the "FIVE" hands together, interlocking the fingers; repeat this motion several times.
Origin: represents the teams clashing
Usage: One of our seniors won a *football* scholarship.

BASEBALL, SOFTBALL

Hold an imaginary bat as if ready to hit the ball.
Usage: *Baseball* is a favorite American sport.
　　　　Our *softball* team is practicing today.

BASKETBALL

Hold an imaginary basketball with both hands and toss the ball.
Usage: The tall boy will be a real asset to the *basketball* team.

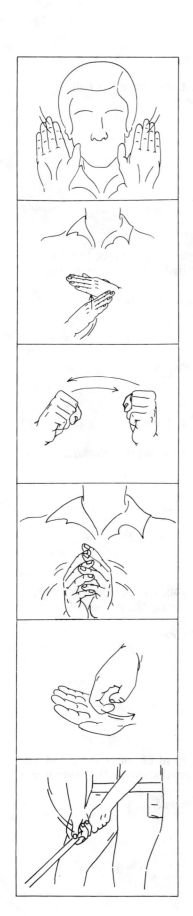

VOLLEYBALL

Hit an imaginary ball over the net with both hands.
Usage: Who wants to play *volleyball* today?

SOCCER

Strike the edge of the left open hand with the index-finger side of the right open hand.
Usage: The German *soccer* team won.

BOXING, FIGHTING

Using the "S" hands, go through the motions of boxing or fighting.
Usage: Joe Louis was a famous *boxer.*
Boys were *fighting* in the street.

WRESTLING

Clasp the hands, locking the fingers, and shake the hands back and forth from the wrist.
Usage: The *wrestlers* had powerful muscles. (Add the "PERSON" ending.)

HOCKEY

Place the right crooked index finger against the left palm; move the crooked right index several times toward you in short scraping motions on the palm.
Usage: Canadians made ice *hockey* famous.

GOLF

Hold an imaginary golf club with both hands as if ready to strike the ball.
Usage: It's a good day for *golfing.*

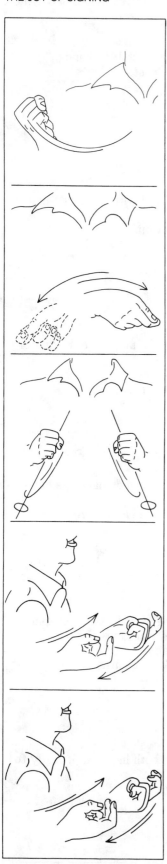

TENNIS

Hold an imaginary tennis racket and serve the ball.
Usage: *Tennis* is played at Forest Hills.

PING-PONG

Hold an imaginary Ping-Pong paddle and move the hand
back and forth as if hitting the ball. Or make the motion
using the "P" handshape.
Usage: The Chinese *Ping-Pong* team won.

SKIING

Hold imaginary poles in both hands and push down and
back as skiers do.
Usage: *Skiing* is a popular winter sport in Colorado.

ICE SKATING

Hold the "X" hands in front of you, one behind the other,
palms up, and move forward showing the motion of
skating.
Usage: Dorothy is a smooth *skater*.

ROLLER SKATING

Hold the curved "V" fingers in front of you, one behind the
other, palms up, and move forward showing the motion of
skating.
Usage: We enjoyed *skating* to music.

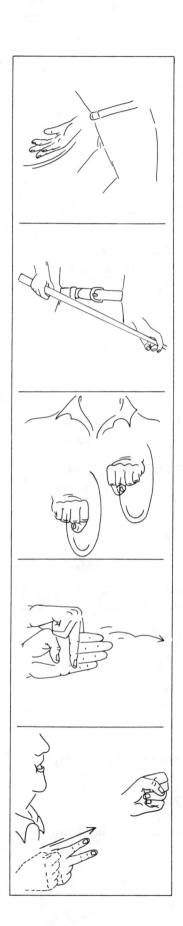

BOWLING

Hold an imaginary bowling ball with the right hand and roll it forward.
Usage: Our group *bowls* twice a week.

POOL, BILLIARDS

Hold an imaginary cue stick with the modified "A" hands and move the right hand ahead as if striking the ball.
Usage: Let's play *pool* after a while.

BICYCLE

Using both "S" hands, palms down, circle them forward alternately as if pedaling.
Usage: *Biking* is good exercise.
Have you seen my new 10-speed *bike?*

HORSEBACK RIDING

Straddle the index side of the left open hand with the index and middle fingers of the right hand, and move the hands up and down in this position.
Usage: *Horseback riding* is great fun.

ARCHERY

Imitate the motion of pulling back the string of the bow and snap out the index and middle fingers as in the number "TWELVE."
Usage: Our *archery* team is the best in the country.

SWIMMING

Use the arms to represent the natural motion of swimming.
Usage: Our *swimming* team went to the Olympics.

ROWING

Hold imaginary oars and make the motion of rowing.
Usage: *"Row, row, row* your boat, gently down the stream . . . ."

CANOEING

With the right hand below the left as if holding a paddle, make the natural motion of paddling a canoe on your right side.
Usage: *Canoeing* in rough water can be dangerous.

FISHING

Place the right modified "A" hand behind the left modified "A" hand and make a quick upward turn from both wrists.
Origin: pulling up on the line
Usage: Let's leave early for our *fishing* trip.

HUNTING, SHOOT, GUN, RIFLE

Point both "L" hands forward, one behind the other, and move the thumbs up and down.
Usage: They go deer *hunting* every fall.
        A man was *shot* by accident.
        All *guns* must be registered.
Note: Only one hand is used to represent a handgun.

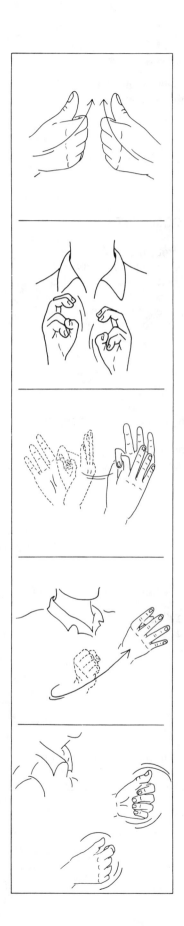

GAME, CHALLENGE

Bring the "A" hands toward each other (palms toward the body) in a slightly upward motion.
Origin: two sides facing each other in competition
Usage: The *game* starts at 2 o'clock.
Who wants to *challenge* our team?

TOURNAMENT

The bent "V" hands, facing each other, are moved up and down alternately.
Usage: The *tournament* lasted all day.

OLYMPICS

Lock the index and thumbs of both hands (other fingers extended) several times, facing in and out alternately.
Usage: Julie won a gold medal in the *Olympics*.

THROW

Throw the right "S" hand toward the left as the hand is opened.
Note: The hand position may change depending on the kind of object being thrown.
Usage: *Throw* the ball to me.

JOGGING

Both arms bent at the elbows move as if in the action of jogging.
Usage: Daily *jogging* keeps him well.

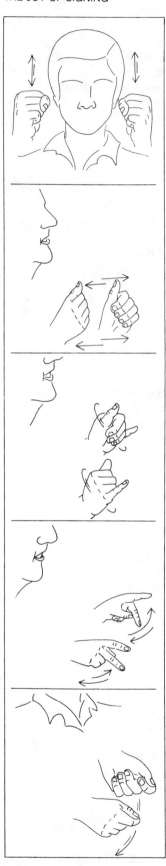

EXERCISE

Move the "S" hands in an exerciselike motion.
Usage: Doctors recommend regular *exercise*.

RACE, CONTEST, RIVALRY, COMPETITION

Place the "A" hands in front of you, palms facing each other, and move them back and forth alternately.
Origin: First one gets ahead, then the other.
Usage: The *race* begins promptly at 9 A.M.
Have you ever seen a pie-eating *contest?*
There was *rivalry* between teams before *competition* began.

PLAY (Recreation)

Place the "Y" hands in front of you and shake them in and out from the wrist several times.
Origin: activity indicated by the hands
Usage: All work and no *play* makes Jack a dull boy.

PARTY

Place the "P" hands in front of you and swing them from side to side.
Origin: The above sign for "play" is initialed.
Usage: People enjoy a good *party*.

PLAYING CARDS

With the left hand holding an imaginary pack, use the right hand as if dealing out cards.
Usage: They sat around *playing cards* every Saturday night.

22

Countries, Cities, and States

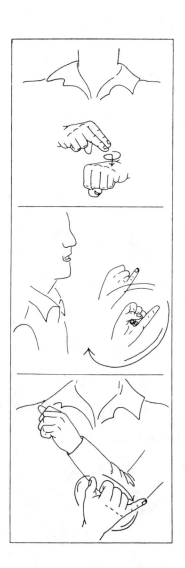

NATION, NATIONAL

Circle the right "N" over the left hand in a clockwise direction and then place it on the back of the left hand.
Usage: A *nation* is no stronger than its people.
Unemployment is a *national* problem.

INTERNATIONAL

Revolve the right "I" hand around the left "I."
Origin: circling the globe
Usage: an *international* conference on deafness

COUNTRY

Rub the inside of the right "Y" hand in a circular motion on the left arm, near the elbow.
Usage: This is my *country*.

FOREIGN

Rub the side of the right "F" hand in a circular motion on the outside of the left arm, near the elbow.
Origin: the sign for "country" made with an "F"
Usage: Do you know any *foreign* languages?

AMERICA

Interlock the fingers of both "FIVE" hands, palms facing the body and tips pointing out, and move them in a semicircle from right to left.
Origin: the old American rail fence
Usage: "God bless *America,* land that I love . . . ."

INDIAN (American)

Place the tips of the thumb and forefinger of the right "F" on the nose and then on the lobe of the ear.
Origin: ring in the nose and ear, or warpaint
Usage: *Indians* have a sign language of their own.

CANADA

Grasp the lapel with the right "A" hand.
Usage: Ottawa is the capital of *Canada.*

MEXICO

Rub the fingertips of the right "M" down the lower edge of the right cheek.
Usage: *Mexico* is our neighbor to the south.

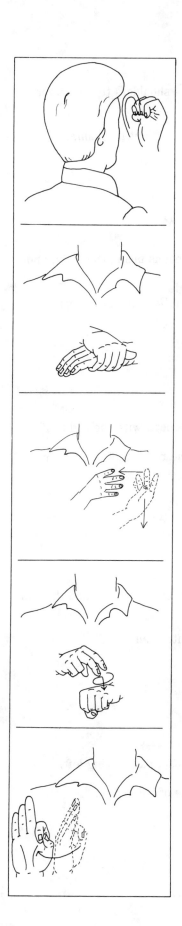

EUROPE

Make a small circle in front of you with the right "E."
Usage: Tourism is big business in *Europe.*

ENGLAND

Place the left hand in front of you, palm down; grasp the
outside edge of the left hand with the right "A," palm
down.
Origin: The English were known to be great handshakers.
Usage: The queen of *England* visited Canada.

SCOTLAND

Draw the back of the right "FOUR" hand down the left
upper arm; then draw the fingertips across the arm toward
you.
Origin: Scottish plaid
Usage: *Scotland* is famous for plaids, kilts, and bagpipes.

IRELAND

Circle the right curved "V," with the fingertips pointing
down, over the back of the left hand in a clockwise
direction and place the fingertips on the back of the left
hand.
Origin: similar to the sign for "potato," referring to the
Irish potato
Usage: *Ireland* has had many problems because of religious
differences.

FRANCE

Place the "F" hand in front of you, palm facing in; turn it
so the palm faces forward, moving it slightly to the right
and up.
Origin: using the initial letter
Usage: The Eiffel Tower is one of the attractions of
France.

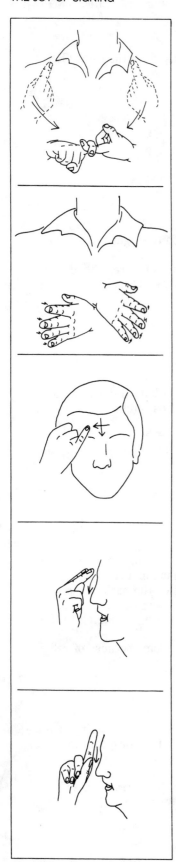

SPAIN

Draw the index fingers from the shoulders to the center, hooking one over the other.
Origin: the large scarf tied in front
Usage: Would you like to see a bullfight in *Spain?*

GERMANY

Cross the hands at the wrists, palms facing the body, and wiggle the fingers.
Origin: showing the double eagle
Usage: East *Germany* and West *Germany* have separate governments.

ITALY

Draw a cross in front of the forehead with the right "I" hand, palm facing in.
Origin: The cross represents the religion of the country.
Usage: The Vatican is in *Italy.*

ROMAN

Place the tips of the "N" fingers on the bridge and then on the tip of the nose.
Origin: the Roman nose
Usage: "Friends, *Romans,* countrymen . . . ."

GREECE

Draw the right "G" down the nose, palm facing left.
Origin: the Grecian nose
Usage: a vacation on the islands of *Greece*

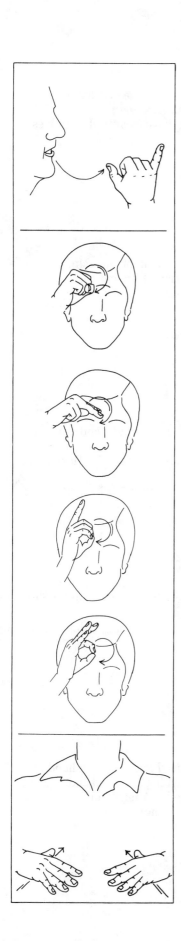

HOLLAND, DUTCH

Place the thumb of the right "Y" on the lips; then draw the hand down and out.
Origin: indicating the pipe used by the Dutch
Usage: *Holland* exports tulip bulbs.
　　　The *Dutch* are known for their wooden shoes.

SWEDEN

Make a circle in front of the forehead with the "S" hand.
Usage: *Sweden* is called the land of the midnight sun.

NORWAY

Make a circle in front of the forehead with the "N" hand.
Usage: Oslo is the capital of *Norway*.

DENMARK

Make a circle in front of the forehead with the "D" hand.
Usage: Copenhagen is the capital of *Denmark*.

FINLAND

Make a circle in front of the forehead with the "F" hand.
Usage: *Finland* is in northern Europe.

RUSSIA

Place the thumbs of the "FIVE" hands on and off the waist several times.
Origin: hands in position for the Russian dance
Usage: Schools for the deaf in *Russia* support
　　　fingerspelling.
COMMUNIST—Place the thumbtips of the "C" hands at the waist.

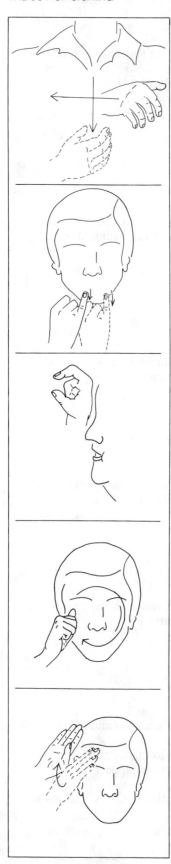

SWITZERLAND

Make a large cross on the chest using the "C" hand.
Origin: the white cross of the Swiss flag
Usage: *Switzerland* is one of the most beautiful countries in the world.

ISRAEL

Draw the tip of the "I" down each side of the chin.
Origin: a combination of the initial letter and the beard
Usage: The Gallaudet dancers performed for the international conference in *Israel.*

EGYPT

Make a "C" with the thumb and index finger and place it on the forehead, palm forward.
Origin: represents the crescent on the flag of a Moslem country
Usage: Tourists enjoy seeing the pyramids of *Egypt.*

AFRICA

Make a circle in front of the face with the "A" hand, using a counterclockwise motion.
Usage: Many *African* countries are becoming independent.

AUSTRALIA

Place the fingertips at the forehead and turn the hand so the palm faces forward, tips touching the forehead.
Origin: represents the hat worn by Australians
Usage: Travel fare to *Australia* is high.

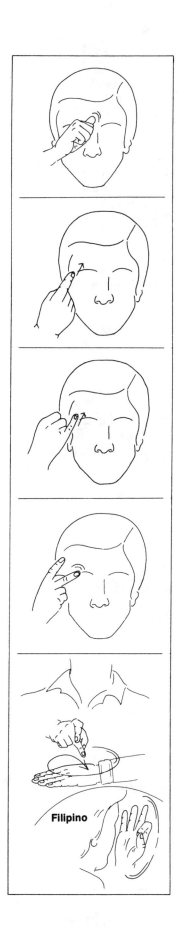

INDIA

Place the tip of the thumb of the "A" hand against the center of the forehead and twist slightly.
Origin: the red dot on the forehead of some Indian women
Usage: *India* has a problem of overpopulation.

CHINA

Place the tip of the index finger at the corner of the right eye and push upward.
Origin: representing the eye of the Oriental person
Usage: Peking is the capital of *China*.

JAPAN

Place the tip of the little finger at the corner of the right eye and push upward.
Origin: an initialed sign representing the eye of the Oriental
Usage: *Japanese* cherry trees were brought to America.

KOREA

Place the tip of the middle finger of the "K" hand at the side of the eye.
Origin: an initialed sign representing the eye of the Oriental
Usage: Seoul is the capital of *Korea*.

PHILIPPINE ISLANDS

Circle the right "P" clockwise above the left downturned palm and then touch the left with the middle fingertips of the right "P."
Usage: Did you hear about the earthquake in the *Philippines?*

FILIPINO

Circle the right "F" in front of the face, palm in.
Usage: a *Filipino* lady in our class

CITIES AND STATES

Many of the larger cities as well as some states have signs that are known and recognized throughout the country. However, signs used for some of the smaller cities are known only locally. States and cities having compound names are usually signed by describing small circles with the initial letters. This is the case with Los Angeles, St. Louis, San Francisco, New Hampshire, etc. States that have long names are usually abbreviated, for example: Mass. for Massachusetts and Pa. for Pennsylvania. Pictured below are signs generally known and used.

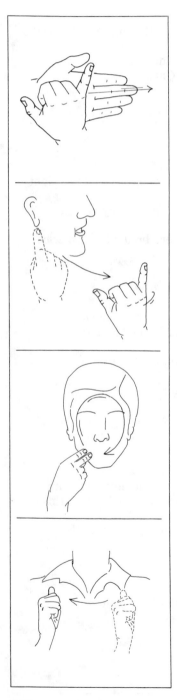

NEW YORK

Slide the right "Y" back and forth across the left palm.
Usage: *New York* City is an island.

CALIFORNIA

Touch the ear with the index finger and bring the "Y" hand forward, giving it a quick twist (as in "GOLD").
Origin: California is associated with the gold rush.
Usage: *California* is approximately 750 miles from north to south.

HAWAII

Circle the right "H" in front of the face, fingers pointing toward the face.
Usage: *Hawaii* is a favorite vacation area.

ATLANTA

Place the right "A" on the body just below the left shoulder, then at the right shoulder.
Usage: We always change planes in *Atlanta*.

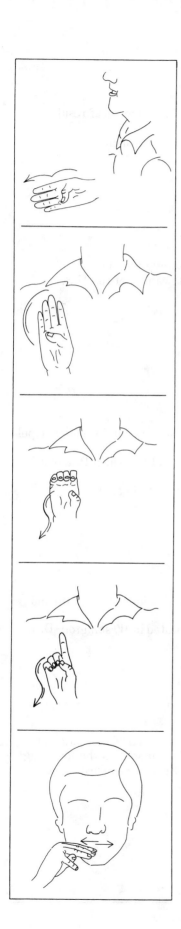

BALTIMORE

Move the right "B" hand forward twice (palm facing left and tips pointing forward).
Usage: *Baltimore* is known for its white steps and blue blinds.

BOSTON

Move the "B" in a slightly circular motion in front of you.
Usage: the famous *Boston* Tea Party

CHICAGO

Draw the "C" hand down with a wavy motion.
Usage: *Chicago* is in northern Illinois

DETROIT

Draw the "D" hand down with a wavy motion.
Usage: *Detroit* is the home of the automobile makers.

MILWAUKEE

Draw the right "M" back and forth just below the lips.
Origin: Beer is wiped from the lips.
Usage: *Milwaukee* has been famous for beer.

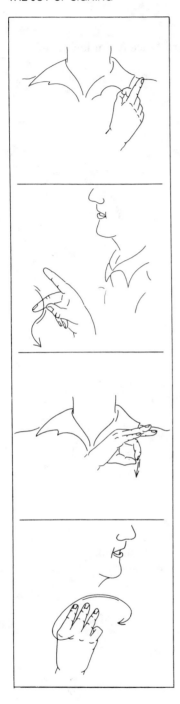

MINNEAPOLIS

Place a "D" at the left shoulder.
Origin: The "D" refers to David, a former deaf resident of Minneapolis.
Usage: *Minneapolis* and St. Paul are twin cities.

PHILADELPHIA

Draw the "P" downward with a wavy motion.
Usage: *Philadelphia* was the first capital of the U.S.

PITTSBURGH

The right "F" hand places an imaginary pin in the left lapel with a downward movement.
Origin: The pin represents the steel for which Pittsburgh is famous.
Usage: The *Pittsburgh* Pirates won the game.

WASHINGTON

Place the right "W" at the right shoulder; draw it up and forward.
Usage: Gallaudet University is located in *Washington,* D. C.

Note: The sign for a person from a particular location is made by adding the "PERSON" ending as in the following examples: America—American; Spain—Spaniard; New York—New Yorker.

23

Animals

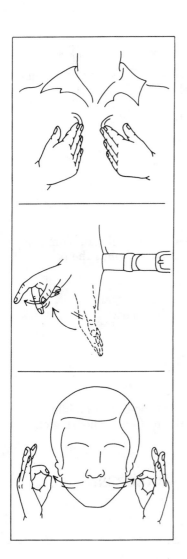

ANIMAL

Place the fingertips on the chest and rock the hands back and forth with the tips still resting on the chest.
Origin: represents the breathing motion of an animal
Usage: The children enjoyed the *animals* in the zoo.

DOG

Pat the leg and snap the fingers.
Origin: imitating the natural motion of calling a dog
Usage: a boy and his *dog*

CAT

Place the "F" hands at the sides of the mouth and draw out to the sides.
Origin: represents the cat's whiskers
Usage: Siamese *cat*

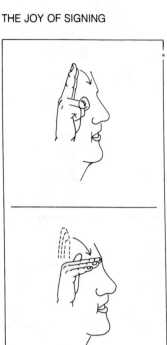

HORSE

Place the "H" hands at the sides of the head, palms facing
forward, and move the "H" fingers up and
down. (Or use only the right hand.)
Origin: represents the ears of the horse
Usage: betting on the *horse* races

MULE, DONKEY

Place the open hands at the sides of the head, palms facing
forward, and bend them forward and backward several
times. (Or use only the right hand.)
Origin: representing large ears
Usage: an old *mule* on the farm

COW

Place the thumbs of the "Y" hands at the sides of the head
and twist hands up. (Or use only the right hand.)
Origin: representing the horns
Usage: "The *cow* jumped over the moon."

BUFFALO, BISON

Place the "S" hands at the sides of the forehead, palm side
forward; move them forward and around until the palm
side faces to the back.
Origin: the horns of the buffalo
Usage: Have you ever eaten a *buffalo* burger?
   The *bison* is found in North America.

SHEEP, SHEPHERD

Hold out the left arm; use the right index and middle
fingers as scissors and imitate the motion of shearing on
the back of the left arm.
Origin: shearing the sheep
Usage: one black *sheep*
SHEPHERD—Sign "SHEEP" + "KEEPER."

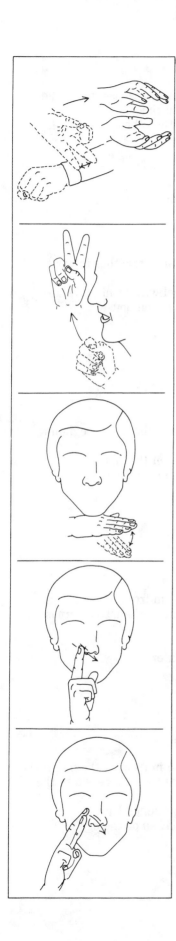

LAMB

Make the sign for "SHEEP"; then bring the open palms toward each other several times to indicate the sheep is small.
Origin: Lambs are small sheep.
Usage: It was interesting to see the new *lambs*.

GOAT

Place the "S" hand at the chin, changing it to a "V" hand as it is placed at the forehead.
Origin: showing the beard and the horns
Usage: Here come Heidi and her *goat!*

PIG

Place the back of the right open hand under the chin and bend and unbend the hand several times.
Origin: represents being full and having eaten to the chin; also, wallowing in mud up to the chin
Usage: the story of the three little *pigs*

MOUSE

Brush the tip of the nose several times with the tip of the right index finger.
Origin: the pointed nose of the mouse
Usage: She was afraid of *mice*.

RAT

Brush the tip of the nose several times with the tips of the right "R."
Origin: the sign for "mouse" made with an "R"
Usage: *Rats* were used for testing.

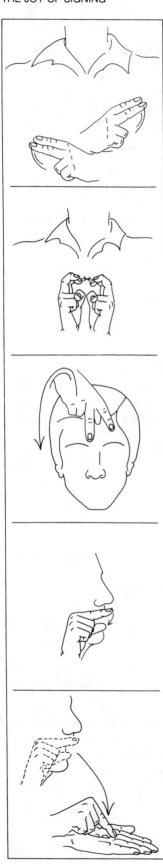

RABBIT

Place the right "H" on the left "H" crosswise; move the "H" fingers back and forth several times.
Origin: representing the ears of the rabbit
Usage: a white *rabbit* with pink eyes

SQUIRREL

Strike the tips of the bent "V" hands together in front of you several times.
Origin: indicates a sitting squirrel with front paws up
Usage: *Squirrels* can do damage in the house.

SKUNK

Draw the right "K" hand back over the head, beginning at the forehead.
Origin: indicates the white stripe of the skunk
Usage: *Skunks* know how to keep people away.

BIRD

Place the index finger and thumb in front of the mouth, representing the bill; flap the arms. (The latter part is often omitted.)
Origin: the bird's bill and wings
Usage: *Birds* fly south in the winter.

CHICKEN

Place the index finger and thumb in front of the mouth, representing the beak, then place these fingers into the palm.
Origin: represents the chicken pecking at grain
Usage: Which came first, the *chicken* or the egg?

DUCK

Make a bill in front of the mouth using two fingers and the thumb.
Origin: the wide bill of the duck
Usage: Kim and Kay loved to play with the *ducks.*

ROOSTER

Place the thumb of the "THREE" hand at the forehead.
Origin: the rooster's comb
Usage: Can you hear *roosters* crowing in the morning?

TURKEY

Place the right "Q" hand under the nose and shake it back and forth.
Origin: represents the wattle of the turkey
Usage: a *turkey* dinner with all the trimmings

EAGLE

Hook the right "X" over the nose; flap the arms to represent wings.
Origin: the hooked beak and wings of an eagle
Usage: The *eagle* flew above the mountains.

OWL

Place the "O" hands in front of the eyes so that the eyes see through the circle of the "O"; twist them toward the center several times.
Origin: the large eyes of the owl
Usage: a wise old *owl*

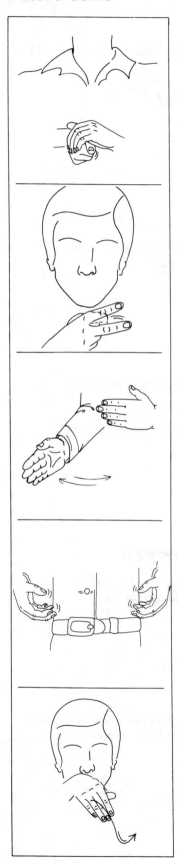

TURTLE

Place the left hand on the right "A," which has the palm facing left, and wiggle the right thumb.
Origin: represents the head of the turtle protruding from under the shell
Usage: Have you read the story of the *turtle* and the hare?

FROG

Place the "S" hand at the throat and then snap out the index and middle fingers, ending in a "V" position that is pointing left.
Origin: showing both the croaking and the leaping of the frog
Usage: The little green *frog* sat there looking at me.

FISH

Point the right open hand forward, palm facing left (left fingertips touching the right arm near the elbow); move the right hand back and forth from the wrist.
Origin: the movement of the fish's tail in the water
Usage: many gold*fish* in the pond

MONKEY

Scratch the sides of the body just above the waist.
Origin: typical action of a monkey scratching
Usage: playful *monkeys* in the cage

ELEPHANT

Place the back of the right hand in front of the mouth; push up-forward-down.
Origin: the trunk of the elephant
Usage: *Elephants* never forget.

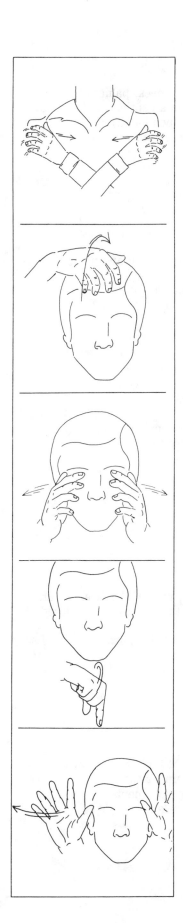

BEAR

Cross the arms, placing the right hand on the left upper arm and the left hand on the right upper arm; pull the hands across the arms towards the center.
Origin: showing a bear hug
Usage: a huge white polar *bear*

LION

Place the slightly curved "FIVE" hand over the head, fingers slightly separated and pointing down; move the hand back over the head in a shaking motion.
Origin: representing the lion's mane
Usage: The *lion's* roar frightened everyone.

TIGER

Place the slightly curved "FIVE" hands in front of the face, palms in; draw hands apart several times and claw the hands.
Origin: represents both the stripes and the clawing action
Usage: a big yellow *tiger*

GIRAFFE

Move the "G" hand upward at the neck.
Origin: indicating the long neck of the giraffe
Usage: a tall *giraffe* looking over the fence

DEER, ANTLERS, REINDEER, MOOSE

Place the thumbs of the "FIVE" hands at the sides of the forehead and draw the hands away from the head.
Origin: representing the antlers
Usage: *deer* crossing
　　　　large *antlers*
　　　　Santa and his *reindeer*
　　　　Canadian *moose*

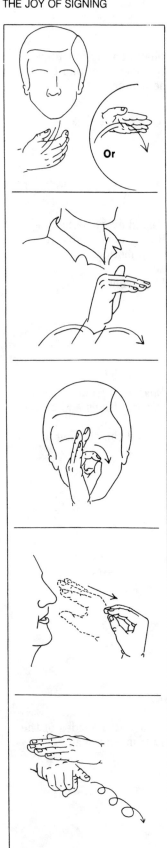

CAMEL

Place the "C" hand in front of the neck, palm facing up; move the hand up and forward in a gentle swaying motion. (Or indicate the hump with the open hand.)
Origin: showing both the long neck and the swaying motion
Usage: traveled by *camel*

KANGAROO

Place the right bent hand in front of you and move it forward in a hopping motion.
Origin: natural movement of the kangaroo
Usage: a *kangaroo* from Australia

FOX

Place the right "F" over the nose and twist slightly.
Origin: the pointed muzzle of the fox
Usage: a sly *fox*

WOLF

Place the open "AND" hand in front of the face, fingers pointing to the face, and draw them away into a closed "AND" position.
Origin: representing the shape of the muzzle
Usage: a *wolf* in sheep's clothing

SNAKE

Pointing forward, move the right "G" hand forward in a circular motion, passing it under the left arm.
Origin: indicating the crawling movement
Usage: bitten by a poisonous *snake*

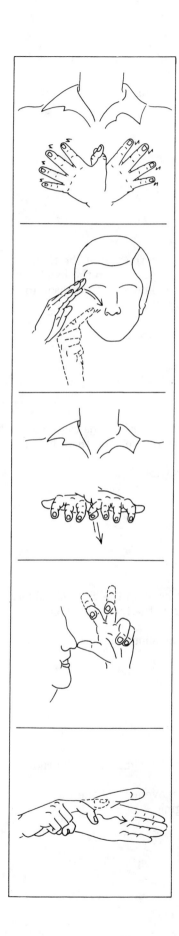

BUTTERFLY

Cross the "FIVE" hands in front of you, palms facing the body, and lock the thumbs; wiggle the fingers.
Origin: the fluttering wings of the butterfly
Usage: a colorful *butterfly* among the flowers

BEE

Place the tip of the right index finger against the cheek; then brush the open hand forward as if brushing off a bee.
Origin: brushing a bee from the face
Usage: a honey *bee*

SPIDER

Cross the curved "FIVE" hands, palms facing down, and interlock the little fingers; wiggle the fingers to represent the legs of a spider.
Origin: represents the spider legs crawling along
Usage: "Along came a *spider* and sat down beside her."

BUGS, ANTS

Place the thumb of the "THREE" hand on the nose and crook the index and middle fingers.
Usage: afraid of *bugs*
      millions of busy *ants*

WORM

Place the right index finger on the left palm and wiggle it as it moves forward.
Origin: represents the worm crawling
Usage: a can of *worms*

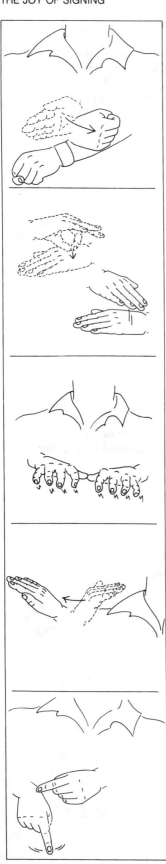

FLY

Use the right hand to catch an imaginary fly on the left forearm.
Usage: that awful *fly*

MOSQUITO

Touch the back of the left hand with the tips of the thumb and index (in the "NINE" position); then slap the hand.
Origin: indicating the bite and the killing of the mosquito
Usage: many *mosquitoes* near the water

INSECT

Touch the thumbtips of the bent "FIVE" hands together, palms down; wiggle the bent fingers, working them like a crawling insect.
Origin: the movement of the crawling insect
Usage: afraid of all *insects*

WINGS

Place the fingertips of the right hand on the right shoulder; draw the hand away and turn it so the fingertips point away from the body.
Origin: wings extending from the shoulder
Usage: large *wings* of an eagle

TAIL

Place the tip of the left index at the right wrist; the right index swings below.
Origin: showing the shape and movement of the tail
Usage: The dog's *tail* was wagging.

24

Religion

Signs used in the religious context often vary in different churches. This is perfectly acceptable but it is important for the signer to know and to use those signs that are known to the congregation and accepted and understood by them. It should be noted that certain religious signs have theological implications associated with particular churches. An example is the word *baptize,* in which the choice of sign itself indicates whether immersion or sprinkling is meant. While Catholics and Protestants sign *Bible* as "JESUS" + "BOOK," Jews either spell the word or sign "GOD'S" + "BOOK" or "HOLY" + "BOOK."

CATHOLIC

Using the "N" hand, palm toward the face, describe a cross in front of the face.
Origin: the cross made in front of the face, almost as if crossing oneself
Usage: The *Catholic* Church has many priests who can sign.

JEWISH

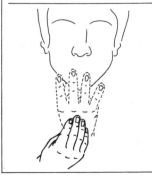

Place all the fingers on the chin, palm facing you, and draw down, ending with all the fingertips together.
Origin: representing the chin whiskers
Usage: The *Jewish* family celebrated Passover.

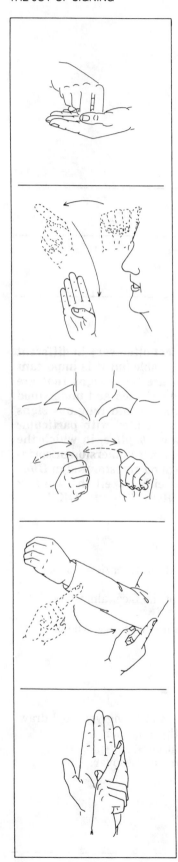

PROTESTANT

Make the sign for "KNEEL."
Origin: representing the Protestant in the act of kneeling
Usage: He attends one of the *Protestant* churches in our
city.

ASSEMBLIES OF GOD

Place the right "A" hand on the forehead, palm facing left;
then sign "GOD."
Usage: an *Assemblies of God* publication

BAPTIST

Turn both "A" hands to the right and down (thumbtips
pointing to the right), then bring them back up.
Origin: baptism by immersion
Usage: a good *Baptist* preacher

EPISCOPAL

Using the right index finger, describe a semicircle under
the left arm from the wrist to the elbow.
Origin: represents the flowing sleeve of the minister's robe
Usage: Rev. Berg is an *Episcopal* priest.

LUTHERAN

Place the thumbtip of the right "L" against the left palm.
(Or place the thumbtip against the chest.)
Usage: *Lutheran* services are at 10 a.m.

METHODIST

Rub the palms together, as in the sign for
"ENTHUSIASM."
Origin: represents the fervor of the early Methodists
Usage: an old *Methodist* hymnal

PRESBYTERIAN

Place the middle fingertip of the right "P" in the left palm.
Usage: a *Presbyterian* Sunday school class

QUAKER

Clasp the hands, interlacing the fingers, and let the
thumbs revolve around each other.
Origin: reputedly from the fact that the Quakers twiddle
their thumbs while waiting for the moving of the Spirit
Usage: the gentle, friendly *Quaker* people

RELIGION

Place the right "R" at the heart and draw it forward, palm
facing out.
Origin: pointing to the heart where religious feelings
originate
Usage: People sing about the old-time *religion*.

OTHER RELIGIOUS GROUPS

Some of the other religious groups use their initial letters,
such as S.D.A. for Seventh Day Adventists and L.D.S. for
Latter Day Saints. Other names of religious groups may be
signed literally, using the standard sign for each word. For
example, Church of Christ, Church of God.

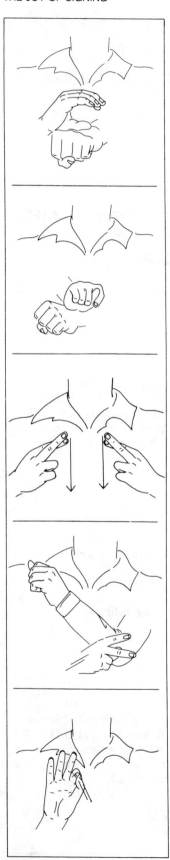

CHURCH

Place the right "C" on the back of the left "S" hand.
Origin: the church shown as being on a rock
Usage: Europe has many old *churches.*

TEMPLE

Place the right "T" on the back of the left "S" hand.
Usage: The *temple* was in Jerusalem.

RABBI

Place the tips of the "R" hands just below the shoulder and draw them down the chest.
Origin: indicating the ecclesiastical stole
Usage: A *rabbi* teaches the Jewish law.

PASSOVER

Strike the right "P" against the left arm near the elbow.
Origin: the sign for "cracker" made with the initial "P"
Usage: *Passover* is an annual feast of the Jews.

PREACH, PREACHER, MINISTER, PASTOR

Hold the "F" hand in front of you and move it forward and backward several times. For "PREACHER," "MINISTER," and "PASTOR," add the "PERSON" ending.
Origin: "F" for "friars" combined with the sign for "lecturing"
Usage: practice what you *preach;* a famous *preacher;* the *minister* of our church; our good *pastor*

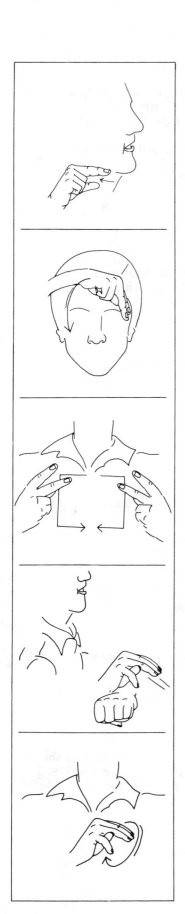

PRIEST, CLERGY, CHAPLAIN, MINISTER

Trace a collar from the center of the neck to the sides, using the right thumb and index fingers spread about an inch apart.
Origin: priestly collar
Usage: The *priest* will perform the wedding.
member of the *clergy*
our hospital *chaplain*
Episcopalian *minister*

NUN

Use the right "N" to trace the outline of the face (up the left side, across the forehead, and down the right side).
Origin: indicating the veil
Usage: a *nun* in the Catholic school

PRIEST (Old Testament)

Using the "P" fingers, trace the form of the breastplate worn by the priests of the Old Testament.
Usage: Melchizedek was called a *priest* of the Most High God.
Old Testament *priests* offered sacrifices.

MINISTRY

Strike the wrist of the right "M" on the wrist of the left hand.
Origin: the sign for "work" made with an "M"
Usage: One of the *ministries* of the church is to the elderly.

MISSION, MISSIONARY

Make a circle over the heart with the right "M" hand, fingers pointing left. For "MISSIONARY" add the "PERSON" ending.
Usage: Is your church interested in overseas *missions*?
The apostle Paul became a *missionary*.

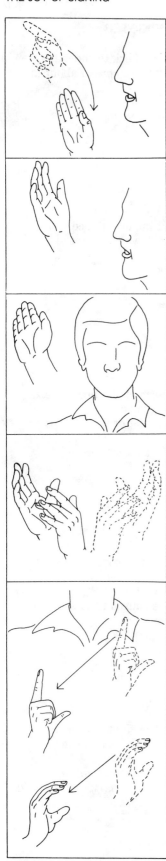

GOD

Point the "G" forward in front of you, draw it up and back down, opening the palm, which is facing left.
Origin: hand raised heavenward and then down in a reverent motion
Usage: "In *God* We Trust" is inscribed on our coins.

THEE, THOU

Lift the open hand upward, palm in.
Usage: We give *Thee* the glory.
          Thou, God, hearest us.
Note: When referring to people, point forward with the index finger as in the commandment: *"Thou* [you] shalt not steal."

THINE (Deity)

Direct the open palm outward and upward.
Usage: *"Thine* is the kingdom."

JESUS

Place the tip of the middle finger of the right open hand into the left palm and reverse.
Origin: indicating the nailprints
Usage: *Jesus* was born in Bethlehem.

LORD

Place the right "L" at the left shoulder, then on the right waist.
Origin: indicating the stole worn by royalty
Usage: Sunday is often called the *Lord's* Day.

CHRIST

Place the right "C" at the left shoulder and then at the right waist. (Some prefer to use the sign for "JESUS.")
Origin: indicating the stole worn by royalty
Usage: Jesus *Christ,* the Son of God.

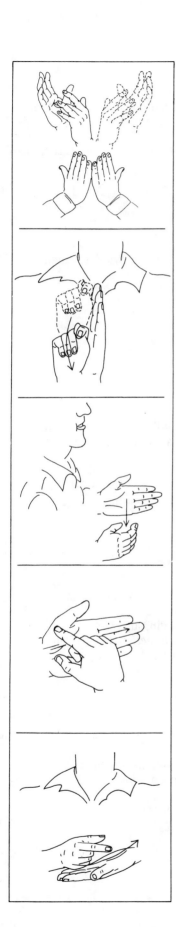

BIBLE

Sign "JESUS" + "BOOK." Alternatives are to fingerspell the word or to sign "GOD'S" + "BOOK" or "HOLY" + "BOOK."
Usage: The *Bible* contains words of wisdom.

TESTAMENT

Hold up the left open hand, palm facing right; place the side of the right "T" against the left palm twice, the second time slightly lower than the first.
Origin: the sign for "commandment" formed with a "T"
Usage: the Old and the New *Testaments*

CHAPTER

Place the left hand in front of you, tips pointing forward; draw the right "C" down across the left palm.
Origin: showing a lengthy passage
Usage: He read several *chapters* in the Bible every day.

VERSE

With the thumb and index fingers about an inch apart (other fingers closed) draw them across the left open palm from left to right.
Origin: a short portion, as indicated by the space between the two fingers
Usage: chapter 3, *verse* 16

GOSPEL

Brush the little-finger side of the "G" hand across the heel of the left hand from right to left.
Origin: The gospel means good news and this sign represents the sign for "news" made with a "G."
Usage: He preached the *gospel*.

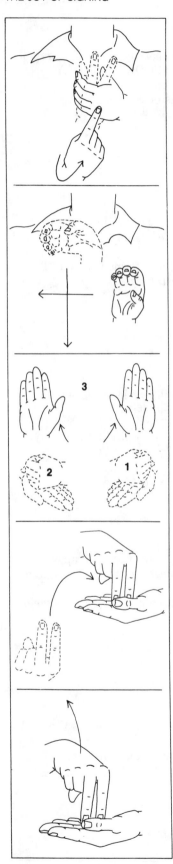

TRINITY

Draw the right "THREE" hand down through the left "C," changing it into a "ONE" after it has passed through the left hand; bring the "ONE" forward and up.
Origin: three in one
Usage: The doctrine of the *Trinity* refers to God in three Persons.

CROSS

Draw a cross with the right "C" hand (down first, then across).
Usage: The *cross* is the symbol of Christianity.

CRUCIFY

Strike the left palm with the little-finger side of the right "S"; repeat in the right hand; raise both open hands to the sides.
Origin: hammering the nails into the palms with the hands raised on a cross
Usage: *Crucifixion* is a cruel form of death.

RESURRECTION

Raise the right "V" from a palm-up position to a standing position and place it on the left palm.
Origin: lying down and then standing up
Usage: Jesus said, "I am the *resurrection* and the life." Jesus *rose* from the dead on the third day.

ASCENSION

Place the tips of the right "V" hand on the left palm and raise the right "V," tips still pointing down.
Origin: rising into the heavens
Usage: The church celebrated the *ascension* of Christ. He *ascended* to heaven.

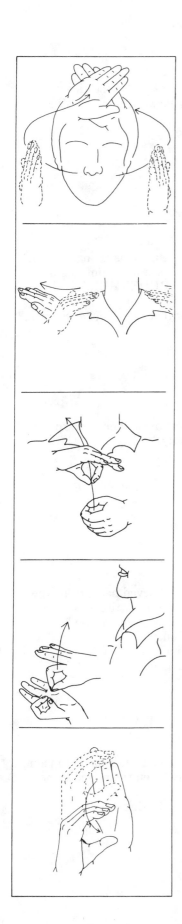

HEAVEN, CELESTIAL

Using both open hands, palms facing in, bring them around in a circle toward you and then pass the right open hand under the left and up. Or circle the downturned palms around each other and then draw them out to the sides. Both versions are made slightly above eye level.
Usage: "Our Father, who art in *heaven* . . . ."
The choir sang about the *celestial* city.

ANGEL, CHERUBIM, SERAPHIM

Place the fingertips on the shoulders and draw the hands away so the fingertips point away from the body.
Origin: indicating angel wings
Usage: Isaiah saw a vision of *angels.*

SOUL

Place the thumb and index fingers of the right "F" hand into the left "O," which is close to the body, and draw the right hand upward. Note: Some show no difference between the signs for "SOUL" and "SPIRIT."
Usage: Bless the Lord, O my *soul.*

SPIRIT, GHOST

The right palm is above and facing the left palm with fingers spread; as the right hand moves up, the index and thumbtips of both hands close.
Usage: "The *spirit* shall return unto God who gave it" (Ecclesiastes 12:7).
He believes in the Father, Son, and Holy *Ghost.*

COMMANDMENTS

Hold up the left open hand, palm facing right; place the side of the right "C" against the left palm twice, the second time slightly lower than the first.
Origin: The left hand represents the tablet on which the commandments were written.
Usage: The Ten *Commandments* are also called the Decalogue.

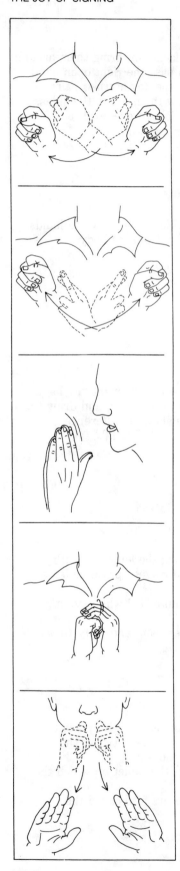

SALVATION, SAVE, SAVIOR

Cross the wrists with the "S" hands out to the sides, turning them so they are facing forward. For "SAVIOR" add the "PERSON" ending.
Origin: bound and then set free
Usage: the *salvation* of the soul
　　　Jesus, the *Savior*

REDEEM

Cross the "R" hands in front of you, palms facing in; then draw them to the sides in an "S" position, palm side out. Add the "PERSON" ending for "REDEEMER."
Origin: the sign for "save" is initialed
Usage: Our choir sang, "I know that my *Redeemer* liveth."

PRAY, AMEN

Place the hands palm to palm and draw them toward the body as the head is bowed slightly.
Origin: hands in a position of prayer
Usage: Let us *pray.*
　　　May the God of peace be with you all. *Amen.*

WORSHIP, ADORE, AMEN

Place the right "A" inside the left curved hand; draw the hands up and toward you in a reverent attitude.
Note: This sign is sometimes also used for "amen."
Usage: The people *worshiped* God.
　　　"O come let us *adore* Him . . . ."
　　　In Thy name we pray, *Amen.*

BLESS

Place both "A" hands in front of the mouth, palm to palm; bring the hands forward slightly, open them, and bring them down.
Origin: hands move in an act of blessing
Usage: God *bless* you.

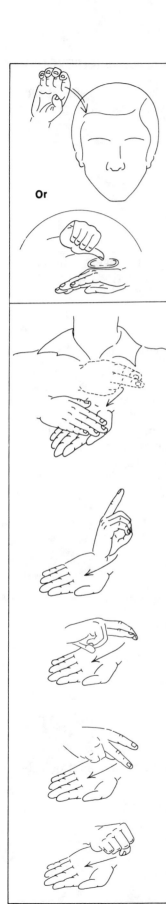

ANOINT

Using the right "C" hand, make a pouring motion over the head. Or use the thumb of the right "A" hand, pointing downward, to make a counterclockwise circle above the back of the left to show a pouring motion.

Usage: "Thou *anointest* my head with oil . . ." (Psalm 23:5).

HOLY, HALLOWED

Make an "H" and pass the right palm across the left palm.

Origin: "H" + "CLEAN"

Usage: We visited the *Holy* Land.

". . . *hallowed* be thy name" (Matthew 6:9).

Note: With this group of words, some prefer to continue the initial letter across the palm instead of changing to the sign for "clean."

DIVINE

Sign "D" + "CLEAN."

Usage: "To err is human, to forgive *divine*" (Alexander Pope).

RIGHTEOUS

Sign "R" + "CLEAN."

Usage: a truly *righteous* man

PURE

Sign "P" + "CLEAN."

Usage: "Blessed are the *pure* in heart" (Matthew 5:8).

SANCTIFY

Sign "S" + "CLEAN."

Usage: "The very God of peace *sanctify* you" (1 Thessalonians 5:23).

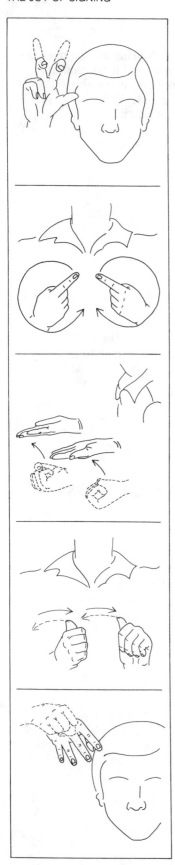

DEVIL, SATAN, DEMON (Used also for MISCHIEVOUS)

Place the thumb of the "THREE" hand on the side of the temple; bend and unbend the index and middle fingers several times.
Origin: the horns of the devil
Usage: a real *devil*
       dreamed about green *demons*
       a boy full of *mischief*

SIN, EVIL, WICKED

Using the index position on both hands, fingers pointing toward each other, make simultaneous circles, the right hand clockwise and the left counterclockwise.
Usage: forgive our *sins*
       deliver us from *evil*
       a *wicked* man
Note: "Evil" and "wicked" are sometimes signed "BAD."

SACRIFICE

Place both "S" hands in front of you, palm side up; lift both hands up and forward, opening the hands with palms up.
Origin: the sign for "offer" preceded by an "S"
Usage: The people brought an animal to the altar for a *sacrifice.*

BAPTISM, IMMERSION

Turn both "A" hands to the right and down (thumbtips pointing to the right), then bring them back up.
Origin: demonstrating the act of immersion
Usage: He was *baptized* in the river.
       This church believes in *immersion.*

BAPTIZE, CHRISTEN

Hold the "S" hand over the head and then open it quickly as if sprinkling water on the head.
Origin: the act of sprinkling water over the head
Usage: The priest *christened* the baby.

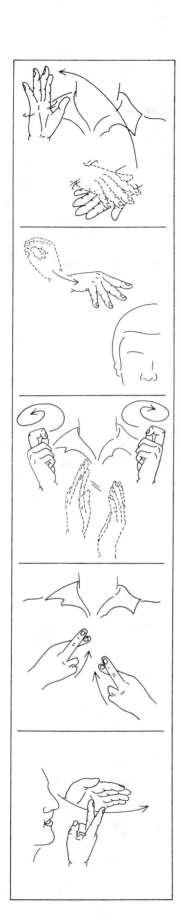

GLORY

Clap the right hand against the left; lift the right and make a large arc in front of you with the right hand, shaking the hand as it moves.
Origin: indicates shining splendor
Usage: *"Glory* to God in the highest . . ."* (Luke 2:14).

GRACE

Hold the "AND" hand over the head; bring it down and open it over the head, palm facing down (or over the heart, palm facing in). Another version has the "G" coming from the left "O" (which is near the heart), as in "SOUL."
Origin: coming from above down to man
Usage: May the *grace* of God be with you.

HALLELUJAH

Clap the hands once and then sign "CELEBRATION."
Usage: Our choir sang the *"Hallelujah* Chorus" from Handel's *Messiah.*

REVIVAL

Move the tips of the "R" hands alternately up the chest.
Origin: feelings are stirred, as in "excite"
Usage: We are planning for some *revival* meetings.
Note: "Revive" may be signed "INSPIRE," as in the song: *"Revive* us again, fill each heart with thy love . . . ."

VISION

Make the sign for "SEE" and let it pass forward under the left hand, which is in a palm-down position.
Origin: seeing something not actually present; therefore, the sign is made under the left hand
Usage: a *vision* of heaven

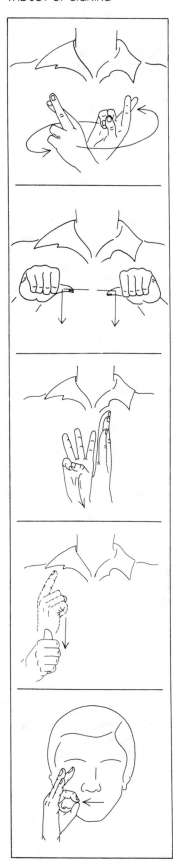

REPENT

Place the "R" hands in front of you, the inside of the wrists touching and the right hand on top; twist them around until the left hand is on top.
Origin: the sign for "change" made with an "R"
Usage: The man *repented* and started a new life.

ALTAR

Place the "A" hands in front of you; move them apart and down.
Origin: indicates the shape of the altar
Usage: the *altar* of the church

WILL (God's)

Hold up the left open hand, palm facing right; place the side of the right "W" against the left palm.
Note: Some prefer to substitute "desire," "decision," or "law" for "will" in this context.
Usage: "Thy *will* be done."

TITHE

Sign "ONE"; lower the hand and sign "TEN."
Origin: A tithe is one-tenth.
Usage: The people in this church believe in giving a *tithe* of their earnings every week.

FAST (To refrain from eating)

Draw the right "F" across the lips.
Origin: The lips are sealed and prevented from eating.
Usage: a 3-day *fast*

NAMES OF BIBLICAL CHARACTERS

For the most part, names of people in the Bible are fingerspelled. However, some of the more commonly known characters have been given sign names such as those listed below. If the name of a particular person is used repeatedly in a sermon and no standard sign has been assigned, it is suggested that a sign name be created and used for that occasion. An example would be Nebuchadnezzar. This would be spelled out the first time it is used and after that the "KING" sign could be initialed with an "N," since he was a king and "N" is the first letter of his name. This principle is also followed for David.

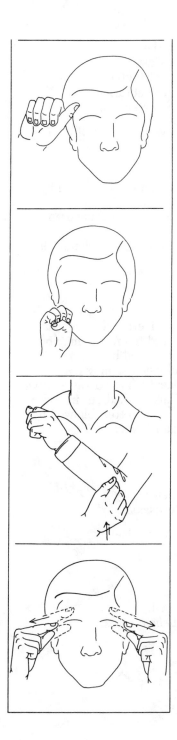

ADAM

Place the "A" hand at the side of the forehead.
Origin: an initial sign at the location of the "male" sign
Usage: *Adam* was the first man.

EVE

Place the "E" hand at the side of the chin.
Origin: an initial sign at the chin indicating the female
Usage: *Eve* was the first woman.

ABRAHAM

Hold the left arm up with the hand near the right shoulder; strike the arm near the elbow with the right "A" hand.
Usage: *Abraham* is called the father of the Jewish people.

MOSES

Place the thumb and index finger (slightly separated) at the sides of the temple; draw them away and close them.
Usage: *Moses* was the author of the first five Books of the Bible.

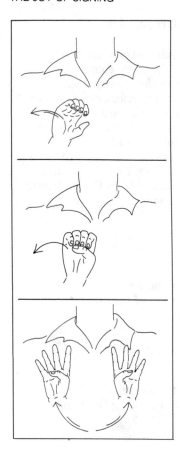

CHRISTMAS

Make an arc in front of you, using the right "C" hand. Or place the "C" at the chin (palm in) and move it out-down-in to show the beard of Santa Claus. (This sign is also used for "SANTA CLAUS.")
Usage: Everyone wished for a white *Christmas*.

EASTER

Make an arc in front of you, using the right "E" hand. Other signs are used to represent Easter, such as "RABBIT," "EGG," and "RESURRECTION."
Usage: *Easter* is an annual church celebration commemorating Christ's resurrection.

HANUKKAH

Hands in "FOUR" positions, palms forward and side by side, are moved outward and upward.
Origin: representing the eight candles of the menorah (candelabra)
Usage: *Hanukkah* commemorates the rededication of the Temple of Jerusalem.

NAMES OF PLACES

Names of places (cities, countries, rivers, etc.) are usually fingerspelled, but if a city is referred to often it may be signed by using the initial letter followed by the sign for "CITY." This is especially helpful when signing music, where fingerspelling is to be avoided (as in "O Little Town of Bethlehem"). Names of rivers are spelled but in music they may be represented by the initial letter followed by the sign for "RIVER" (e.g., Jordan River).

JERUSALEM

Sign "J" + "CITY." (Or fingerspell.)
Usage: The Wailing Wall is in *Jerusalem*.

BETHLEHEM

Sign "B" + "CITY." (Or fingerspell.)
Usage: Many tourists visit *Bethlehem*.

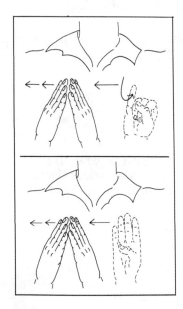

ADDITIONAL WORDS USED IN THE RELIGIOUS SETTING

The following words used in religious settings do not have specific signs but suggestions are made here for substitutions or combinations of standard signs.

Atonement. Use the "A" as in "ANOINT" (pouring over the left hand).

Calvary.
"MOUNTAIN"
+
"CROSS"

Christian.
"JESUS" or "CHRIST"
+
"PERSON" ending

Collection.
"MONEY"
+
"COLLECTION"

Communion (Lord's Supper).
"WINE"
+
"BREAD"

Condemn. Fingerspell or sign "JUDGE."

Consecrate. The sign most appropriate for the intended meaning should be used: (1) make holy, (2) presented, or (3) offered to God.

Conviction. "CONSCIENCE"

Covenant. "AGREEMENT" or "PROMISE"

Create. "MAKE," or use the "C" hands to sign "MAKE."

Deacon. Sign "MEMBER" using the "D" hands.

Dedicate. Sign "OFFER" or precede it with a "D."

Denomination. "CHURCH" or "RELIGION"

Disciple or Apostle. "FOLLOWER"; "TWELVE" + "FOLLOWERS"; or "FOLLOW" made with the "D" hands

Doctrine. "TEACH"

Father. The sign for "Heavenly Father" is made with two hands.

Flesh. "BODY"

Hail. "HONOR" or "CELEBRATE"

Hell. Fingerspell or point downward and sign "FIRE."

Hymnal.
"SONG"
+
"BOOK"

Master.
"M"
+
"OVER"
+
"PERSON" ending

Messiah. Fingerspell or use the "M" as in "KING."

Miracle.
"WONDERFUL"
+
"WORK"

Nature (of a person). "N" over the heart

Omnipotent.
"ALL"
+
"POWER"

Omnipresent.
"EVERY"
+
"WHERE"

Omniscient.
"ALL"
+
"KNOWLEDGE"
or
"KNOW"
+
"EVERYTHING"

Parable. "STORY"

Service (a church service). "MEETING" or "SERVE"

Supplication. Lift the sign for "BEG."

Thanksgiving.
"TURKEY" or "THANKS"
+
"GIVING"

Trespass.
"BREAK"
+
"LAW"

Verily. "TRULY" (sign "TRUE")

25

Numbers

 ONE

Hold up the index
finger.

 FOUR

Hold up the four
fingers (separated).

 TWO

Hold up the index and
middle fingers.

 **FIVE**

Hold up the five
fingers (separated).

 THREE

Hold up the index
finger, middle finger,
and thumb.

 SIX

Touch the tip of the
thumb with the tip of
the little finger (other
fingers spread).

SEVEN

Touch the tip of the thumb with the tip of the fourth finger (other fingers spread).

TEN

Shake the right "A" hand, thumb pointing up.

EIGHT

Touch the tip of the thumb with the tip of the middle finger (other fingers spread).

ELEVEN

Hold the "S" in front of you (palm in) and snap the index finger up.

NINE

Touch the tip of the thumb with the tip of the index finger (other fingers spread).

TWELVE

Hold the "S" in front of you (palm in) and snap the index and middle fingers up.

THIRTEEN—Sign "TEN" (palm in) and "THREE" (palm out).
Note: Follow this pattern for numbers 13 through 19.

FOURTEEN   **FIFTEEN**   **SIXTEEN**

| **SEVENTEEN** | **EIGHTEEN** | **NINETEEN** |

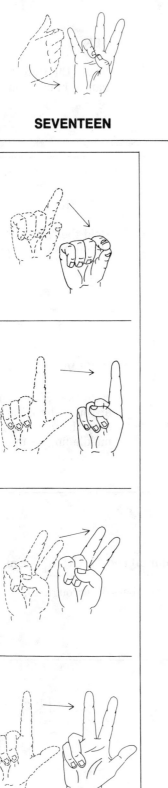

TWENTY—Bring the thumb and index finger together (other fingers closed).

TWENTY-ONE—Extend the thumb and index; close the thumb, leaving the index up.

TWENTY-TWO—sign "TWO" and swing it in an arc to the right.

TWENTY-THREE—Extend the thumb and index; lift the middle finger to make a "THREE."

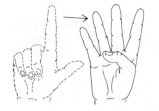

TWENTY-FOUR

TWENTY-FIVE

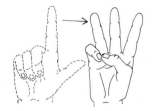

TWENTY-SIX

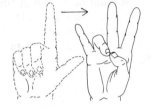

TWENTY-SEVEN

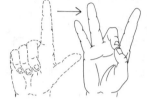

TWENTY-EIGHT

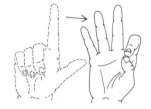

TWENTY-NINE

THIRTY

Sign "THREE"; then form an "O" with the three fingers.

THIRTY-THREE

Sign "THREE" and swing it in an arc to the right.

THIRTY-ONE

Sign "THREE"; move slightly to the right and sign "ONE."

THIRTY-FOUR

Sign "THREE"; move slightly to the right and sign "FOUR."

THIRTY-TWO

Sign "THREE"; move slightly to the right and sign "TWO."

THIRTY-FIVE

Sign "THREE"; move slightly to the right and sign "FIVE."

THIRTY-SIX TO NINETY-NINE

Follow the pattern shown for the thirties. Care should be taken to sign the number as it is written. The number 31, for example, should be signed "THREE" "ONE" and not "THIRTY" "ONE," (see picture). Repeated digits should be made as pictured for 22 and 33, swinging the hand from left to right and pointing the fingertips slightly forward instead of straight up. For the numbers 66, 77, 88, and 99 the thumb separates slightly from the finger before making the second digit.

Special care should be taken with double digits that combine any two numbers between six and nine. When the smaller digit is first, the hand moves in a small arc to the left; when the larger digit is first, the hand moves in a small arc to the right. The following numbers move from right to left: 67, 68, 69, 78, 79, 89. Moving from left to right are 76, 87, 96, 97, 98.

ONE HUNDRED

Sign "ONE" and "C." (Represents the Roman numeral.) Combine this with any of the preceding numbers to form any combination in the hundreds.
Try these numbers: 416; 897; 852; 639; 225; 712; 150; 365; 367; 296; 828; 911; 705; 113; 125.

THOUSAND

Place the "M" tips in the left palm. (Represents the Roman numeral.)
Try the following combinations: 1,723; 8,116; 3,578; 9,693; 5,500; 6,892; 2,319; 4,225; 7,309; 6,111; 17,300; 60,789.

MILLION

Strike the "M" tips into the left palm twice. (Represents 1,000 thousand.)
Try the following combinations: 1,500,000; 8,231,000; 2,670,000; 7,486,105; 50,625,000; 500,000,000.

MONEY

DOLLARS—The number may be followed by the sign for "DOLLAR," as described in a previous chapter. However, there is a shortcut that is commonly used from $1 to $9. Hold up the number, palm forward, and turn it from the wrist, swinging downward and up to a palm-in position. Examples of this shortcut are pictured here:

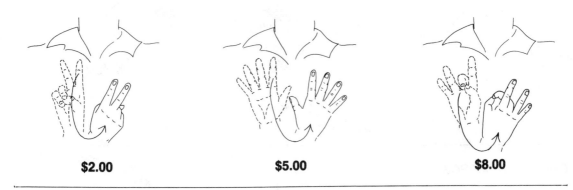

$2.00   **$5.00**   **$8.00**

CENTS—Touch the forehead with the index finger and follow with the number.

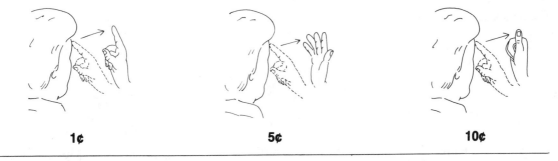

1¢   **5¢**   **10¢**

ADDRESSES

Addresses are signed as they are spoken:
145 Blair Road is signed "1-4-5 B-l-a-i-r R-o-a-d."
1600 Pennsylvania Ave. is signed " '16' 'C' P-a. A-v-e."

TELEPHONE NUMBERS

Phone numbers are signed as they are spoken, with seven separate digits.
Try a few: 447-0837; 524-8162; 352-9719; 624-9176; 621-8969.

YEARS

Years are signed as they are spoken. For instance, 1865 is signed "18" "65."
Try a few: 1800 ("18" "C"); 1492; 1776; 1963; 1980.

FRACTIONS

Sign the numerator, then lower the hand slightly and sign the denominator.

See the following examples:

½

¾

⅔

ORDINAL NUMBERS

Signs for "FIRST" to "NINTH" are made by forming the cardinal number with the palm forward and then giving the hand a quick twist inward.

Examples are shown here.

First

Third

Seventh

In the case of "TENTH" and other higher numbers having a "TH" ending, the cardinal number is made first and the letters "T" and "H" are added.

Usage: *first* child; *second* row; *third* seat; 25*th* anniversary

Appendix

MASTERING THE ART OF SIGNING NATURALLY

Thomas Hopkins Gallaudet spoke of "the great importance of being masters of the natural language of signs, of excelling in this language, doing it with spirit, grace and fluency and for the love of doing it."[1] Although written in the 19th century, these words apply today and this natural language of signs is becoming ever more popular. The following pages are intended to help the signer communicate expressively, clearly, and in a natural way with deaf adults.

The mode of communication described is simply the use of signs taken from the American Sign Language vocabulary, using English word order, permitting certain omissions, and emphasizing the visual nature of this form of communication. Referred to also as the Simultaneous Method of Communication, it assumes you will be signing while speaking English or using lip movements to represent the English language. This is considered the generally accepted and most natural form to use when hearing people converse with deaf people.

In using the language of signs along with the spoken word it is important to remember that only the visual portion of your communication is understood by the deaf person. Facial expression is to sign language what vocal intonation is to spoken language. Therefore, all vocal cues should have a visual counterpart through facial expression, body language, or the strength or force of the sign. The more visual clues included the clearer the communication becomes and the less likelihood of misunderstanding. Developing a feel for signs and how to use them comes primarily through contact with deaf persons as well as through observation of native or near-native signers and will result in appropriate and skilled usage.

You will find in these pages a brief introduction to some of the elements of the American Sign Language which you may wish to include in your signing (apart from the basic form of signs as pictured in the dictionary). Information is presented on which words are spoken without requiring the addition of a sign; the use of space and directionality in providing a visual picture; pluralization; tense; incorporating numbers; regularity and continuity; showing the difference between nouns and verbs when the actual sign formation is identical; indicating the difference between a statement, a command, and a question when identical signs are used; and more. When full use is made of the principles included here, spoken English will seem rather cluttered, for a sign accompanied by other visual information can portray the equivalent of a number of spoken words.

How much of the information contained in these pages is used by the signer will be his own decision. Some signers may wish to use more English-oriented language and sign or fingerspell almost every word, while others may find it more comfortable to use some or all of the components suggested here. Usage will be governed not only by the signer's skill but also by the signing preference of the deaf person with whom one is communicating as well as by the situation and setting in which the communication takes place.

Claire Safran in an editorial review[2] spoke of

---

[1]Thomas Hopkins Gallaudet, "The Natural Language of Signs and Its Value and Uses in the Instruction of the Deaf and Dumb," *American Annals of the Deaf*, I (1847), 55-59; 79-93.

[2]Claire Safran, "How To Raise a Superstar," *Reader's Digest*, January 1985, pp. 111-114.

the three stages usually seen in reaching a talent peak (and no one in the reported research study on talented persons reached that peak in less than 10 years of hard work). First is a time of falling in love with a chosen pursuit; second is the stage of precision, when techniques are worked on for their own sake, for the challenge and sense of competence; and finally, the stage of making it on your own, when a personal style is developed. In developing skill and fluency in sign communication, it is important to remember that first the act of communication itself is pleasurable, then comes the hard work involved in attaining skill, and finally a distinctive personal style that is developed by each communicator. Watch for the styles of the deaf persons around you and become a master of the natural language of signs in your own right!

WORDS FOR WHICH SIGNS ARE NOT ALWAYS REQUIRED

When signing in English word order, one has a natural tendency to want to include a sign for every word spoken. However, this is not necessary, particularly when communicating with adults. In this section we will look at those words for which a sign is not required, although these words will be spoken (or formed on the lips). Reasons for not requiring a sign would include the following: the sign does not add to, take away from, or change the meaning of the sentence; context provides the information without using the sign; facial expression and body language convey the meaning of the English word not being signed.

A, An, The

The articles are spoken but not signed. An exception is made when the signer wishes to emphasize something that is the best known or the most important of its kind. An example would be, "Arty's is THE place to eat in this town!"

To

When a verb is used in its infinitive form, the sign for "to" is not necessary.

Example: Sam likes *to* read. (Omit "to.")
When the verb is used to indicate direction, it is a matter of choice whether "to" is signed or not.

Examples: going *to* Chicago; speak *to* me; bring it *to* her
In these examples, some prefer to fingerspell "to," but others omit it completely, relying on

the signer's lip movement to indicate that "to" is being used.

When showing action toward someone or something, "to" can be signed or fingerspelled.

Examples: *to* my way of thinking; *to* my surprise; wet *to* the skin; rotten *to* the core
In these examples "to" is needed since its omission would change the sense of the phrase and would make it appear, for instance, that you were saying "wet skin" instead of "wet to the skin."

That

The sign for "that" is overused by many people learning sign language. It is properly used as a demonstrative pronoun or adjective.

Examples: *That* is not right.
        That book is Jennifer's.
When "that" is used as a conjunctive, no sign is necessary.

Example: He said *that* he was going.
This sentence would be equally correct in the English language if "that" were omitted: He said he was going.

How

When "how" is used in combination with "much" or "many," it is not necessary to sign "how."

Examples: *How* many children do you have?
        How much money do you want to spend?
In both cases, the sign for "how" can be omitted and the words "how many" or "how much" are spoken while only the second word is signed along with a questioning look on the face.

Contractions Used To Form the Negative

When contractions are used to form a negative in the English language, the signer simply signs "not" instead of signing the two words that form the contraction.

Examples: haven't, hasn't, hadn't, isn't, aren't, wouldn't, won't, don't, didn't
In these instances the signer simply says any of the above words, with a questioning look on his face, while signing "not" or "not yet" as the case may be.

Omitting the Auxiliary in Questions

In asking questions the auxiliary is spoken but is not always signed (although some prefer to either fingerspell or sign the word). If the question word is not signed but the face shows a questioning expression (raising the eyebrows and tilting the head slightly forward), it is clear that a question is being asked. Try the following examples, omitting the sign for the italicized word but forming the word on the lips:

Examples: *Have* you seen the morning paper?
Has Tom left?
Had they already left when I called?
Do you enjoy traveling?
Did you see my glasses anywhere?
Does Julie jog every morning?
Is Jonathan coming soon?
Am I included?
Are you finished?
Shall I wait for you?
Would you make a call for me?
Will you take me with you?

As has been mentioned previously, the signer has choices about how much English should be included in his signing. Mastering the art of signing certainly allows room for choices, that is, whether to omit, to fingerspell, or to sign the question word.

STATEMENTS, COMMANDS, QUESTIONS

In spoken language, the hearer depends heavily on tone of voice, modulation, pitch, inflection, and force. Hearers have learned to derive specific meanings from the way messages are spoken. The printed word depends on descriptive phrases to provide clues, as in the following example: "I'm leaving!" he said with anger in his voice and a scowl on his face. In manual communication the signs for "I'm leaving!" would be made along with a scowl on the face and very strong emphasis on each of the signs.

Researchers are exploring ways deaf signers commonly use facial expression and body posture to specifically identify sentence types. One must remember, however, that people vary greatly in the amount of facial expression and body language they use. The suggestions contained in this section are not to be followed so stringently that individual personality ceases to play a part. They are merely suggestions, providing some guidelines for clearer communication. Without doubt less miscommunication occurs when appropriate nonmanual behaviors accompany signing.

Statements can become questions, not by any change in signs but by change in facial expression. As a simple example, the following statement, question, and command consist of exactly the same two signs but require different facial expressions:

Statement: You're going.
Question: You're going? (Add an eyebrow lift and tilt the head up a bit.)
Command: You're going! (Lower the eyebrows.)

TYPES OF QUESTIONS

Facial expression changes according to the type of question being asked. A rhetorical question (one that does not require an answer and is asked only for effect) is accompanied by uplifted eyebrows and frequently by raised shoulders.

Example: Who knows whether there is life on Mars?

A question that requires an answer is better understood when the eyebrows are squeezed together.

Example: Why are you moving to Texas?

Questions that require a yes or no answer are accompanied by raised eyebrows.

Example: Are you coming with us tomorrow?

A question that is puzzling in nature is accompanied by a squint and often a tilt of the head.

Example: (After hearing someone say the cat was seen at the top of the telephone pole) *Where* did you say you saw the cat?

THE CONDITIONAL SENTENCE

The conditional sentence takes raised eyebrows but only during the condition.

Example: (Raise eyebrows) If you have the time (pause, lower eyebrows), you are welcome to go with us.

COMMANDS

When commands are given, strong emphasis is placed on the verb, usually with a quick, sharp movement.

Examples: *Hurry*, the train is coming!
Come, I need help!

PLURALIZATION AND FREQUENCY

In the English language, plurals are usually formed by adding an "s" or by changing the form of the word, as in "mouse" and "mice." Signs do not require the addition of an "s" to indicate the plural form. (Manually coded English systems, however, frequently add the "s" or fingerspell the pluralized form in order to provide the deaf child with a complete visual model of the English language.) Following are examples of pluralization in sign language as used with deaf adults.

Repetition

Simply repeating the sign with short, quick movements can be an indication of the plural.
Examples: books, cups, hats, tables, trees, girls
Two-part signs require repetition of only the last part.
Examples: brothers, women, pictures, mountains, workshops
When a statement contains either a definite or an indefinite number, the noun may or may not need repetition, depending on the signer's preference.
Examples: We have five *men* on the committee.
It rained for several *days.*
We saw a beautiful variety of *flowers.*

Pluralizing Pronouns

Pronouns are pluralized by making either sweeping motions or short, repeated motions. Repeated motions are made when referring to individual members in a group.
Example: Children, *your* mothers are waiting for you.
Since each child has a different mother, it would be more appropriate to use the sign in repetition, that is, the open palm directed toward the children in short forward movements, while moving the arm from either left to right or right to left.

Sweeping motions are made when referring to a group as a whole rather than to individual members.
Example: The 12 singing signers performed beautifully and *their* rhythm was perfect.
Either sweeping or short, repeated motions can be made for the following plural forms, depending on context: they, these, those, them, their, your, yours.

Pluralizing Action

When an action is performed several times, the sign is repeated several times.

Examples: She *collects* until her closets are full.
He *reads* all the time.
We *met* people all day long at the convention.

Frequency

Frequency, as in the case of time signs, is clearly illustrated in chapter 3. To indicate frequency, the sign is simply repeated.
Examples: hourly, weekly, monthly, yearly

NOUN/VERB PAIRS

When related nouns and verbs have the same sign, a change in movement shows the difference. The sign for the noun is made with a short or abrupt, repeated movement; the verb usually has a longer and smoother movement. (See description and illustrations for "sit/chair," p. 96, and "airplane/airport/fly," p. 104."

Noun Short repeated movement	Verb Longer, smoother movement
telephone	to phone
chair	sit
plane	go by plane, fly
gas	put in the gas
paint	to paint
violin	play the violin
door	open (or close) the door

The signer has a choice of making the longer, smoother movement to represent the verb form while speaking three or four words, as in "went by plane," or of staying closer to English and simply signing and saying each individual word. English has no rule that forces us to choose between saying "We went by plane" and "We flew"; neither does sign language.

INTENSITY AND DEGREE

Instead of using a separate sign to indicate intensity of color, feeling, or action, the sign itself is made with various amounts of intensity.

Color

In spoken language we differentiate intensity of color by the addition of words, for example:

deep blue, bright red, a strong yellow. When signing, those colors that are initialized simply require a more intense twist from the wrist when a strong color is intended. The signs for bright red and deep pink are simply given added emphasis when drawn down over the mouth. Facial expression also becomes more intense with eyes opening wide for bright colors and squinting for dark colors.

Feeling

Both facial expression and the intensity and size of the sign reveal the depth of feeling. Examples of feelings that can be shown in this way include the following: love, hate, anger, fear, like, happy, excited, lonely, pain.

Descriptive Signs

These are usually exaggerated in order to show degree. Examples of such signs are the following: beautiful (the same sign is used for pretty, lovely, fair, gorgeous), thin, fat, old, young, good, bad, long, short, cold, hot.

Action

The way in which a sign is produced can show intensity of action. The sign for "walk," for instance, may be made to show a fast walk, a slow walk, or a determined walk. Again, facial expression adds an important dimension. Other examples of action words are the following: search/desperately searching, study/studying very hard, work/working very hard, rain/raining hard.

LOCATION OF SIGNS IN A STORY

Signs are placed in specific locations if a story is to be told effectively.

Example: A tree is placed on your right. A child walks toward the tree coming from the left, then climbs the tree. Birds that have been perched on a branch fly away. A cat is sitting below looking up. The sun is shining down on the scene.

It is important to remember where you have put the tree or you might have the child climbing a tree on the left that you had originally placed on the right. Keep the visual image alive in your mind.

USE OF EYES AND INDEX FINGER IN POINTING

Your eyes play an important part in using space. This is particularly true when you cannot place a sign in a certain location simply because its proper location is against the body. This occurs with signs like soldier, father (and other family signs), policeman, etc. In these cases the sign is made first, then the index finger points to the location of the person and the eyes look in that direction. For practice in the use of the eyes and index finger try the following paragraph:

As Jim sat there (pointing and looking in a specific direction), his lawyer stood before the judge (point to the location of the judge). The courtroom was full of people (follow this by the sign for "audience," p. 80), all looking toward the judge. The jury was on the right, all 12 members also looking at the judge—waiting for his announcement.

THE SIGNER BECOMING THE CHARACTER IN THE STORY

Frequently the signer becomes each person in the story and moves to the location representing that person. He then turns to face the character to whom he is speaking in the story. The signer may look up if he is taking the part of a child looking up at an adult, or downward if he is an adult speaking to a child. Try this paragraph:

The little boy looked up at the farmer and said, "What are you doing?" The farmer, looking down at the boy, replied, "I'm planting corn." "Can I help you?" asked the boy. "Sure, why not!" replied the farmer.

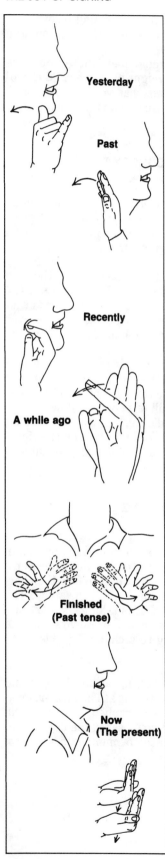

Yesterday

Past

Recently

A while ago

Finished
(Past tense)

Now
(The present)

TENSE

A sign does not change to show tense as is the case in the English language where words frequently show tense by a change in spelling (run, ran; walk, walked; keep, kept). However, there are ways of clearly indicating tense and these are described in this section. It should also be remembered that there is a visual time line that the signer should keep in mind. The future is before you and the past is behind you as pictured here.

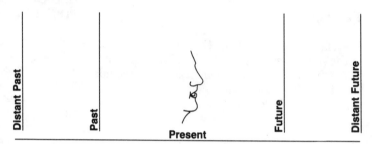

The larger, more slowly, more to the back the sign for "past" is made, the greater the distance in the past is meant.

Past Tense

The following sentences show past tense by context without the need for any type of indicator.

Examples: Yesterday I *went* to the dentist. He *filled* three teeth and I *left*. It *didn't* hurt.

The italicized words when signed will be recognized as being past tense because "yesterday" preceded them.
When context does not supply the necessary information the "finish" sign can be added either before or after the verb or even at the end of the sentence.

Present Tense

To establish that an event is occurring or is to occur at the present time, the sign for "now" may be added. In fact, it is a very common sign and is used in combination with "day" and "night" to represent "today" and "tonight."

Examples: Do it *now*. *Now* is the time. *This* morning. The *present* world crisis.

Note that signs indicating the present are made immediately in front of you.

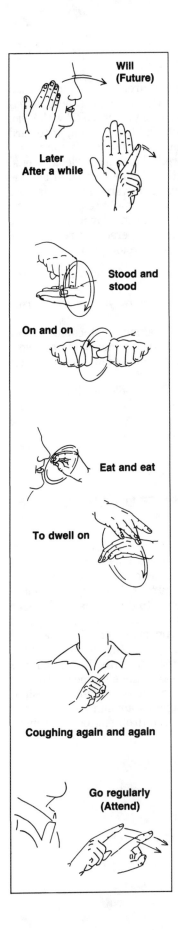

Will (Future)

Later After a while

Stood and stood

On and on

Eat and eat

To dwell on

Coughing again and again

Go regularly (Attend)

Future Tense

Future tense is usually established in context, using specific signs that can be easily matched to the spoken word.

Examples: *Tomorrow* I leave for Hawaii.

The mailman *will* be here *later*.

Travel *will* change *in the future*.

I'll see you *after a while*.

Note that all signs indicating the future have a forward movement. The farther to the front the sign for "future" is made, the farther in the future is intended.

CONTINUITY, CONTINUOUS ACTION, DURATION

To add the dimension of continuity, the basic sign is made with a circular movement. The movement is not made too quickly and the emphasis is on the downward part of the circle.

Examples:

Same	I've heard that speech before and he always says the *same old thing*.
On and on	I thought she'd never stop talking, she went *on and on*.
Eat	It's not surprising she has a weight problem—she *eats and eats and eats*.
Dwell on	He can't seem to forget the problem but *dwells on it all the time*.
Sick	He used to be a healthy person but now is *sick all the time*.
Stand	We *stood there and stood there* and thought the doors would never open.

In the above sentences the signer may prefer to make signs for all the words that are spoken instead of using the circular movement to cover the complete phrase.

REGULARITY

Regularity differs from continuity in that the action takes place again and again rather than continuously. For action that starts, stops, then starts again, the sign is simply repeated with short movements.

Examples:

Cough	I heard John *cough and cough* last night.
Sick	She misses work a lot—she's *sick frequently*.
Go	Julie *attends* our meetings regularly.

Try the principle of regularity and make up your own sentences. Here are a few words to get you started: work, give, think, preach, drink, complain, laugh.

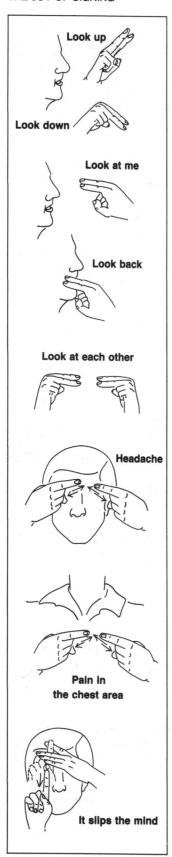

Look up

Look down

Look at me

Look back

Look at each other

Headache

Pain in
the chest area

It slips the mind

DIRECTIONALITY OF SIGNS

A single sign made in an intended direction says more than a sign produced in just its basic form. This can best be explained by using as an example the sign for "look," which can be made pointing toward the left, right, up, down, or toward one's self, depending on what one intends to say. While speaking the words, "Look over there," the sign for "look" would simply be pointed in that direction. While saying, "Look me over," the sign would face inward, toward the signer, and move up and down. "Look him over" would require that the sign be turned outward and moved up and down and that the eyes be directed toward the intended person. If referring to an aerial view (from above) the sign would point downward.

Examples: borrow/lend—toward the body or away from the body (p. 93)

my fault/your fault—toward you or away from you (p. 140)

copy—downward if making photocopies; away from you if you are asking someone to copy you; toward you if saying you copied something (p. 190)

advise—toward you if you are receiving advice; away from you if you are advising another (p. 57)

give—away from you if you are giving; toward you if someone is giving to you (p. 132)

SIGNS PLACED AT APPROPRIATE LOCATIONS ON THE BODY

Some signs may be moved to specific locations on the body for clarity. The sign for "pain," for instance, may be made at the forehead if speaking of a headache, at the stomach if the pain is there, etc. The sign for "surgery/operation" may also be placed appropriately or simply into the left hand. The sign for "pop up/appear suddenly" can be made in front of you if referring to a person suddenly appearing, or at the forehead if speaking of a thought suddenly popping up in the mind. When made in the opposite direction (with the right index dropping instead of moving upward) the sign means to drop out or disappear. It can be placed at the forehead to show that a thought has suddenly slipped your mind or in front of you if you are referring to a person dropping out (of school, society, etc.)

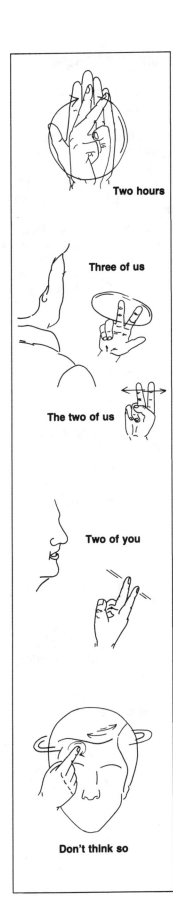

Two hours

Three of us

The two of us

Two of you

Don't think so

INCORPORATING NUMBERS

Certain time signs are frequently made to include a number. Examples of such signs are hour, day, week, and month (illustrated on pages 40-41). Using this type of incorporation results in making one sign for two or more words.

Examples: two hours; three days; four months; in two years; every year; a year ago

NUMBERS USED WITH PERSONAL PRONOUNS

When numbers are joined with personal pronouns, the number itself is moved in the appropriate direction while speaking the desired words.

Examples: three of us; we two, or both of us; the four of them; etc.

NEGATION

To show the negative, signers have the option of either signing "don't" or "not" or of omitting the negative sign and simply shaking the head while signing.

Examples: I believe. (Two signs are made.)
I don't believe (The same two signs are made while shaking the head.)

Try the following short sentences in both the positive and negative forms without using the "not" sign:
I _____; I don't _____(understand, think, feel, expect, see)
I'm _____; I'm not _____(sure, sick, going)

Several signs have a built-in negative; with these the negative head shake is an additional indicator of negation.

Examples: Want/don't want (p. 74). The sign for "want" is simply turned down.
Know/don't know (p. 47). The sign for "know" is turned outward.
Like/don't like (p. 66). Simply turn the palm outward (still in the "like" position) with a twist.

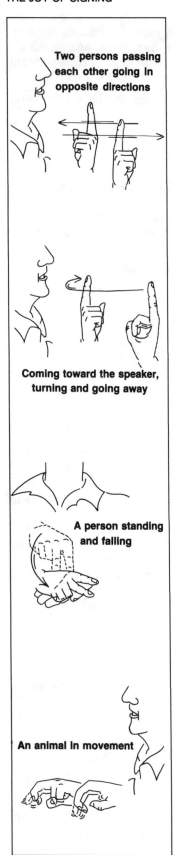

Two persons passing each other going in opposite directions

Coming toward the speaker, turning and going away

A person standing and falling

An animal in movement

CLASSIFIERS AND SIZE AND SHAPE SPECIFIERS

Classifiers are handshapes used to indicate location and movement. They usually do not stand alone and generally represent objects that have already been identified. Size and shape specifiers are handshapes used to show size, shape, amount, height, surface texture, and also location. These handshapes serve in many instances as pronouns but may also function as verbs, as is the case with brushing teeth: the index finger, which represents the toothbrush, becomes a verb when the action of brushing the teeth is shown.

In some cases it is difficult to say whether a particular handshape should be identified as a classifier or as a size and shape specifier. Sometimes a handshape does the work of both, indicating size and shape as well as location, as is the case with the "O" handshape used for "button." Just as it is important in the English language to identify the noun before using the pronoun, so with signs it is necessary to name or identify the noun before using the classifier.

The index finger pointing upward represents a person

The index finger pointing upward represents a person (1) in a specific location, (2) facing a certain direction, (3) in relationship to another person (by using both the right and the left index fingers), or (4) moving in the intended direction. This classifier can be pluralized by forming the desired number.

Examples: The man *turned around and went away.*
The woman *came toward me.*
The boy and girl *passed each other going in opposite directions.*

The "V" handshape pointing downward represents a person, an animal, or an object having legs

The "V" handshape pointing downward can represent a person, an object having legs (such as a tripod), or an animal in motion (using two hands to show a four-legged creature). (See pages 94-95 for examples and actions represented by this handshape.)

Examples: It was icy and she *slipped and fell.*
The horse *galloped away.*
The tripod *fell over.*

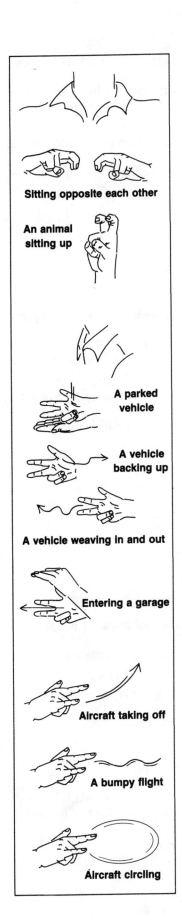

Sitting opposite each other

An animal sitting up

A parked vehicle

A vehicle backing up

A vehicle weaving in and out

Entering a garage

Aircraft taking off

A bumpy flight

Aircraft circling

The curved "V" represents a person or an animal in a sitting or crouched position

After the person or small animal has been identified, the curved "V" may be used to show action or location.

Examples: We all *sat in a circle* talking.
Helen and Jan *sat facing each other.*
The dog *sat up* and begged for food.

The "3" handshape represents vehicles

The "3" handshape, thumb pointing up, represents the location or movement of a vehicle, such as a car, bus, truck, bicycle, or tractor (see p. 102). Frequently both "3" hands are used to show the location of vehicles in relationship to each other.

Examples: I bought the car, drove home, and *pulled into the garage.*
Several cars were *parked behind each other* waiting for the wedding party.
The car *wove in and out of the lanes.*
We saw the tractor *flip over and land on its side.*
We looked and looked for a place to *park* and finally found one and *backed in.*

The "Y" handshape with index finger extended represents winged aircraft

This handshape represents the direction, movement, or location of aircraft.

Examples: The plane *took off.*
Our flight was *bumpy.*
We *circled over* New York for an hour before *landing.*

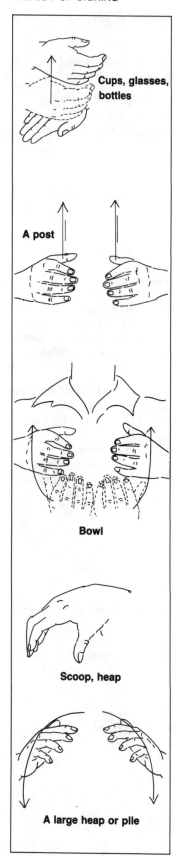

Cups, glasses, bottles

A post

Bowl

Scoop, heap

A large heap or pile

The "C" handshape represents glasses, cups, bottles, cans

The palm side of the "C" faces left, with the little-finger side down, and the hand is raised to the approximate height of the object.

Examples: As wedding gifts, she received several sets of *glasses*.
He enjoyed his *cup* of coffee every morning.
We bought a *bottle* of ginger ale.

Both hands in the "C" position show large round objects

Both hands in the "C" position are used to indicate the shape of items such as bowls, balloons, balls, thick poles, a well, a supporting pillar.

Examples: He couldn't see because he was sitting behind a *post*.
She brought a large *bowl* of potato salad.

The "C" handshape represents small piles, or heaps

The "C" handshape, palm side down, represents scoops of ice cream, a heap of food, etc.

Examples: I'd like some chocolate ice cream—two *scoops*, please.
That's a *heap of* mashed potatoes!

Two curved hands represent large piles

Both curved hands, palms down, are moved slightly apart and down, ending with palms facing each other to indicate a pile, or heap.

Examples: John left *a pile of* dirty clothes.
The truck picked up *a large heap of* trash.

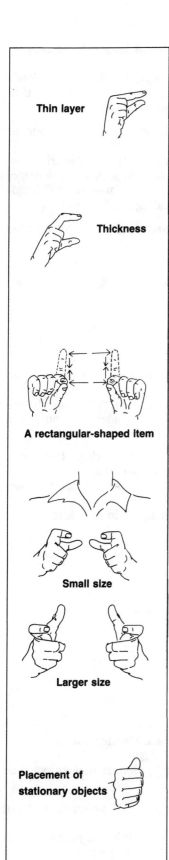

Thin layer

Thickness

A rectangular-shaped item

Small size

Larger size

Placement of stationary objects

The "G" handshape is used to show a thin layer, small width, or small amount

The "G" handshape is used to represent things such as a thin layer of icing on a cake, an edging, a picture frame.

Examples: The picture *frame* was brown.
The cake had a *thin layer of* pink icing.
The lace *edging* was beautiful.
How much milk was left? Oh, about *this much*.
We had only about *an inch* of snow.

The "L" handshape (slightly curved) is used to indicate thickness

The "L" handshape, with the index finger slightly curved, is used to indicate thickness or a depth of several inches. It can represent the thickness of carpets, snow, a sandwich, etc.

Examples: We walked in mud *this deep*.
It was snowing hard and was getting *deep*.
The room had a *thick* red carpet.
His sandwich was *huge*.

The "L" handshapes are used to draw a rectangular shape

The two "L" hands (facing out) separate and the index finger and thumb close, drawing a rectangular shape in the air. This shape can be used to represent a postcard, credit card, check, envelope, photograph, etc.

Examples: I have paper but no *envelope*.
I have no cash but I'll write you a *check*.
Do you have an American Express *card?*

The modified "L" handshapes show sizes of objects

Both "L" handshapes, with index fingers slightly bent (palms facing each other), are used to show the size of objects, such as plates, a piece of meat, a large hole, or the size of an area.

Examples: My steak was *small*, his was *large*.
Let's use the fancy dinner *plates* today.
We noticed a large *hole* in the wall.

The "A" handshape represents stationary objects

The "A" handshape with the thumb pointing up represents stationary objects and their placement. This classifier is used to represent vases, lamps, statues, buildings, etc.

Examples: I saw several beautiful vases (fingerspell) *lined up* for display.
His many trophies (fingerspell) were *sitting on the shelf.*
There were statues *all over the place.*

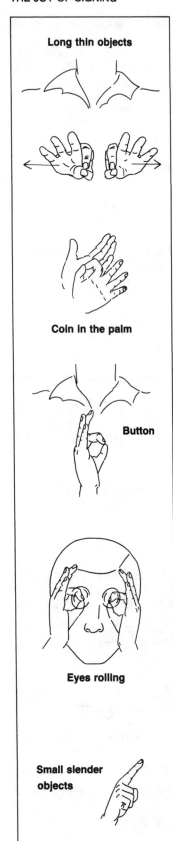

Long thin objects

Coin in the palm

Button

Eyes rolling

Small slender objects

Two open "F" handshapes represent long thin objects

Both hands form the "O" handshapes (other fingers extended) and are pulled apart to indicate the length of a long thin object, such as a pole, stick, degree, telescope.

Examples: He walked across the stage and was proud to receive his *degree.*
The magician used a *long stick* for his trick.
We looked at the moon through our *telescope.*
(To represent the telescope, use the "O" handshapes without extending the fingers.)

The distance between the two hands is adjusted to show the length of the object.

The open "F" handshape represents small objects or areas

The right thumb and index finger form an "O" (other fingers extended) to represent a small object, such as a button, a coin, a small hole, eyes, a watch.

Examples: My red blouse has five *buttons down the front.*
He *rolled his eyes* in amazement.
She showed me several *coins* from South America.
The cigarette burned a *hole* in her skirt.

The index finger represents small, slender objects

The index finger represents small, slender objects, such as a toothbrush, pencil, pole, leg.

Examples: I bought a new toothbrush (fingerspell) and *put it in the holder.*
Pencils (fingerspell) were *lying all over* my desk.
He broke his leg and had to *prop it up.*

"B" handshapes represent height and width

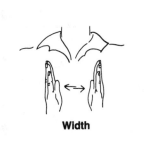

Width

Both hands in an open, flat position, palms facing each other, show the height or width of piles of paper, books, or magazines; the depth of water or of a box; etc.

Examples: We collected *stacks of* newspapers for the Boy Scouts.
The box was *too wide* and the post office would not accept it.

Height, depth, pile

The flat open hand represents flat objects

Books lined up on a shelf

The flat open hand (with fingers together) represents flat objects, such as books, papers, magazines, letters.

Examples: The books were *lined up* on the shelf.
My papers were *all over the floor.*
The new books were *stacked in piles.*
I received a *stack of letters* yesterday.

One or both flat hands indicate surfaces

A flat surface

One or both flat open hands are used to indicate surfaces, as in showing the sides of a building (p. 210), a table (p. 247), a mountain (p. 224), a valley (p. 224), the floor (p. 244).

Examples: The lake was as *smooth* as glass.
We saw a *dip* in the road.

A dip (in the opposite direction, a hump)

The handshapes shown in the Classifier Section and the examples given are intended as only an introduction to their use. Observe expert users of sign language, particularly deaf persons, and watch for these descriptive handshapes.

Notes

Suggested References

Benderly, Beryl L. *Dancing Without Music: Deafness in America.* New York: Doubleday & Co., 1980.
An account of deafness written in a lively, anecdotal style. Discusses manual and oral education.

Gannon, Jack R. *Deaf Heritage: A Narrative History of Deaf America.* Silver Spring, Md.: National Assoc. of the Deaf, 1981.
A comprehensive history of deafness in the United States from 1812 to the present. Includes rare and interesting photographs.

Greenberg, Joanne. *In This Sign.* New York: Holt, Rinehart and Winston, 1970.
The story of a deaf couple's life and their hearing children at the turn of the century.

Guillory, L. M. *Expressive and Receptive Fingerspelling for Hearing Adults.* Baton Rouge, La.: Claitor's Book Store, 1966.
Learning to fingerspell phonetic elements found in the English language instead of learning individual letters.

Jacobs, Leo M. *A Deaf Adult Speaks Out.* Washington, D.C.: Gallaudet College Press, 1980 (Second Edition).
A deaf man's honest account of the world of deaf adults. Discusses educational methods, economic aspects, and the adult deaf community.

Lane, Harlan. *When the Mind Hears.* New York: Random House, 1984.
Presents a wealth of information from the founding of the first school for the deaf in France in the 18th century to the spreading of sign language throughout Europe and across the Atlantic.

Meadow, Kathryn P. *Deafness and Child Development.* Berkeley, Calif.: Univ. of Calif. Press, 1980.
Deals with the social and psychological consequences of lack of communication for deaf children, in the context of total communication programs.

Mindel, Eugene, and Vernon, McCay. *They Grow in Silence: Understanding Deaf Children and Adults, second edition.* Boston, Mass.: College Hill Press for the National Assoc. of the Deaf, 1987.
Knowledgeable authors provide updated comprehensive information about deaf people and deafness.

Moores, Donald F. *Educating the Deaf: Psychology, Principles, and Practices.* Boston: Houghton Mifflin, 1982 (Second Edition).
An excellent introduction to education of the deaf, historical background, communication, language, teacher training. A comprehensive bibliography.

Northern, J. L., and Downs, M. P. *Hearing in Children.* Baltimore, Md: Williams & Wilkins Co., 1974.
A comprehensive text on the audiological problems of children, providing information for the physician, audiologist, and educator.

Schlesinger, H. S., and Meadow, K. P. *Sound and Sign: Childhood Deafness and Mental Health.* Berkeley, Calif.: Univ. of Calif. Press, 1972.
Covers the development of deaf children with excellent information on their communication needs and proposes a combination program.

Spradley, Thomas S., and Spradley, James P. *Deaf Like Me.* New York: Random House, 1978.
A heartwarming, inspiring story of a family trying to reach across the barrier of silence. A "must" for any family with deaf children.

Collections of Favorite Songs, Including Melody Line, Chords, Words, and Illustrated Sign Interpretations

Gadling, D., and Pokorny, D. *You've Got a Song.* Silver Spring, Md.: National Assoc. of the Deaf, 1979.
Eight songs, including, "You Light Up My Life," "Silent Night," "Sunshine on My Shoulder."

Gadling, Donna; Pokorny, D.; and Riekehof, L. *Lift Up Your Hands.* National Grange, 1616 H St., N.W., Washington, D.C. 20006 (1976).
Ten songs including "Amazing Grace," "America the Beautiful," "He's Got the Whole World in His Hands."

Weaks, D. G. *Lift Up Your Hands, Vol. 2.* Washington, D.C.: National Grange, 1980. Ten songs, including "Born Free," "This Is My Country," "There's Just Something About That Name."

Organizations Serving the Deaf

American Society for Deaf Children, 814 Thayer Ave., Silver Spring, MD 20910. Phone: (301) 585-5400. Publication: *The Endeavor* (bimonthly). Membership organization providing information and support to parents and families with children who are deaf or hard-of-hearing.

American Deafness and Rehabilitation Association (ADARA), P.O. Box 55369, Little Rock, Ark. 72225. Phone: (501) 663-4617. Publications: *Journal of Rehabilitation of the Deaf* (quarterly); *ADARA Newsletter* (quarterly). A membership organization and network that promotes, develops, and expands services, research, and legislation to deaf persons.

Conference of Educators Serving the Deaf (CESD) and Convention of American Instructors of the Deaf (CAID). Publication: *American Annals of the Deaf* (bimonthly plus special issues, including a directory issue.) Address: Kendall Demonstration Elementary School, PAS 6, 800 Florida Ave., N.E., Washington, D.C. 20002. Phone: (202) 651-5341.

Gallaudet University, 800 Florida Ave., N.E., Washington, D.C. 20002. Publications: *Gallaudet Today*. National Information Center will send information about deafness. Gallaudet University Press will send their Catalog of Publications. Bookstore will send their catalog. Media Center will provide a listing of sign language videotapes. A 92-acre campus with the college as its primary focus, Gallaudet also serves high school students at the Model Secondary School for the Deaf and preschool through elementary levels at the Kendall Demonstration Elementary School. The university grants degrees through the doctoral level.

National Center for Law and the Deaf, Gallaudet University, 800 Florida Ave., N.E., Washington, D.C. 20002. Develops and provides a variety of legal services and programs to the deaf community.

National Association of the Deaf, 814 Thayer Ave., Silver Spring, MD 20910. Phone: (301) 587-1788. Publications: *The Broadcaster; The Deaf American*. Publication list available. A consumer-oriented membership organization that works on behalf of deaf people. Concerned with communication skills, legislation, employment rights, and other topics of interest.

Junior National Association of the Deaf, 814 Thayer Ave., Silver Spring, MD 20910. Phone: (301) 587-1788. Publication: *Junior Deaf American* (3 to 4 times a year). Develops leadership skills among deaf high school students by creating opportunities where students can get hands-on experience through participation in various activities.

Registry of Interpreters for the Deaf, Inc., 51 Monroe St., #1107, Rockville, Md. 20850. Phone: (301) 279-0555. Publications: *Interpreter Views; RID Interpreting Journal*. Professional organization providing information on interpreting, evaluation, and certification requirements for interpreters for the deaf.

National Congress of Jewish Deaf, 9102 Edmonston Court, Greenbelt, MD 20770. Phone: (301) 345-8612. Publication: *N.C.J.D.* (quarterly). Advocates religious and cultural ideals and fellowship for Jewish deaf persons.

Helen Keller National Center for Deaf-Blind Youths and Adults, 111 Middle Neck Road, Sands Point, NY 11050. Phone: (516) 944-8900. Publication: *The Nat-Cent News*. The only national facility providing comprehensive evaluation and prevocational rehabilitation training. Conducts extensive network of field services through regional offices, affiliated programs, and national training teams; maintains National Register of Deaf/Blind Persons; designs and improves sensory aids.

American Athletic Association of the Deaf, 3916 Lantern Drive, Silver Spring, MD 20902. Phone: (301) 942-4042. Promotes athletic tournaments in the United States and coordinates American involvement in international competitions.

Vocabulary Index

BELMONT UNIVERSITY LIBRARY

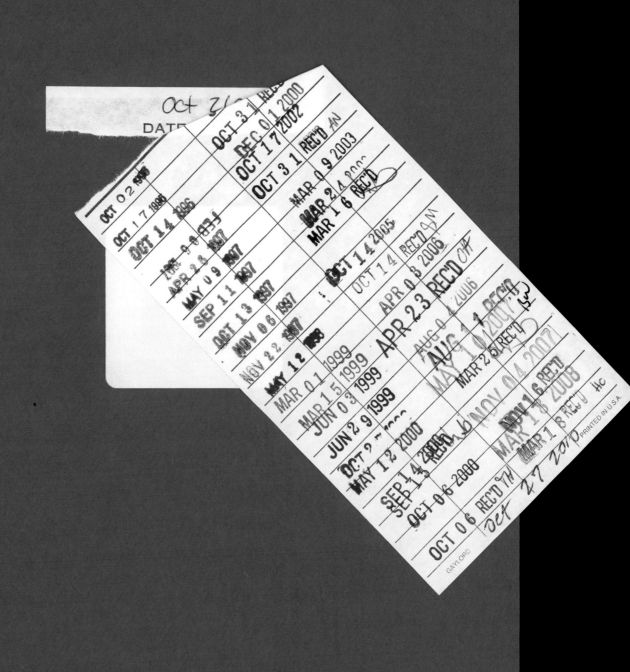